TROPICAL BUTTERFLIES

models	mimics
Bematistes alcinoe, female	a female-limited form
Bematistes epaea, female	a female-limited form
Bematistes vestalis, males and females are alike	a form occurring in both sexes
Bematistes macaria, male	a male-limited form
Bematistes epaea, male	a form occurring in both sexes

1. Mimicry in *Pseudacraea eurytus* (Nymphalidae). On the left are various species and sexes of the models, *Bematistes* (Acraeidae), and on the right the corresponding polymorphic and mimetic forms of *Pseudacraea eurytus*. All the specimens are from a single locality in Sierra Leone. Slightly enlarged.

TROPICAL
BUTTERFLIES

*The ecology and behaviour of
butterflies in the tropics with
special reference to African species*

BY

D. F. OWEN

DEPARTMENT OF ANIMAL ECOLOGY
UNIVERSITY OF LUND
SWEDEN

CLARENDON PRESS · OXFORD

1971

Oxford University Press, Ely House, London W.1

GLASGOW NEW YORK TORONTO MELBOURNE WELLINGTON
CAPE TOWN IBADAN NAIROBI DAR ES SALAAM LUSAKA ADDIS ABABA
DELHI BOMBAY CALCUTTA MADRAS KARACHI LAHORE DACCA
KUALA LUMPUR SINGAPORE HONG KONG TOKYO

PRINTED AND BOUND IN ENGLAND BY
HAZELL WATSON AND VINEY LTD
AYLESBURY, BUCKS

PREFACE

ALTHOUGH the title of this book is *Tropical Butterflies*, it is mainly about African butterflies, because I know more about them than about the butterflies of other tropical regions. However, some experimental work on South American and Asian butterflies is also discussed.

Butterflies have always attracted attention and butterfly collecting is a popular hobby. In addition butterflies provide useful material for certain kinds of ecological and genetic research: the phenomenon of mimicry, for example, is best developed and best studied in butterflies. Most species are relatively large and conspicuous; and because they have been more extensively collected than other groups of insects, much more is known about the systematics and distribution of butterflies. The technique of capturing, marking, releasing and recapturing, which provides essential information on many aspects of the structure of animal populations, can be applied to butterflies with greater ease than to almost any other group of animals. It is therefore not astonishing that butterflies have been much used in population studies and in investigations into the ecological genetics of populations.

One of my aims in this book is to show that important biological information can be obtained without the use of complicated and expensive equipment and without mounting expeditions to remote areas: in the tropics one need go no further than the garden for the study of some of the fascinating problems in the biology of butterflies. I advocate throughout the study of living butterflies in their natural environments, and although I am not against building up a collection, I would rather see collectors devote some of their energy to finding out more about living butterflies. This, I suggest, is increasingly worthwhile in a world that is rapidly becoming over-populated and polluted, and where the environment is being drastically altered in the cause of economic development.

This book is essentially an account of the ecology and aspects of the genetics and behaviour of butterflies in tropical Africa. No attempt is made to provide a means of identifying butterflies, but in Chapter 15 books and papers useful for the identification of the African species are listed and discussed. I have not described the anatomy and physiology of butterflies except where these are important for the understanding of an ecological problem. The book is therefore directed at the field biologist, professional and amateur, who wants to know more about butterflies as living animals.

The scientific names I have used are derived from a variety of sources; in general I have retained the name used in the original source of information, but some changes have been necessary. In making these changes I have been guided by the check-list of African species (Peters 1952), and to some extent by the revisions suggested in *The Butterflies of Liberia* (Fox, Lindsey, Clench, and Miller 1965). Mr. T. G. Howarth of the British Museum of Natural History has also offered useful advice on the names of some species and has provided access to the extensive collections under his care. Unfortunately there is little agreement over the use of common names for most tropical butterflies and so I have used scientific names throughout.

The photographs illustrating this book are not intended as works of art; indeed some of them are of rather poor quality, but these have been included because they show features of special interest, some of them illustrating phenomena that have not been illustrated before. I have tried to reduce the number of technical (especially statistical) concepts to a minimum, but I have given references to sources where the reader can obtain fuller information. Most technical terms are defined when they are first used, but when a term is used without explanation the glossary at the end of the book will provide a definition.

My interest in butterflies started as a schoolboy in south-east London. The growth of vegetation on bombed sites in the late 1940s provided opportunities for studying the insect fauna of areas recently colonized by weeds. Later I was able to travel throughout the British Isles and I formed a collection that was aimed at showing geographical variation rather than simply displaying rare species and unusual varieties. This was followed by visits to various parts of the Mediterranean area, in particular watching and recording butterfly migrations in southern Europe. I then lived for four years in the United States and was able to study and collect butterflies in a rich temperate region quite unlike western Europe with its impoverished fauna. During this period I was introduced to the tropics on a trip to Mexico. Here I first appreciated the complexities of mimetic resemblance and also the remarkable diversity of species in the tropics. I saw for the first time hordes of butterflies feeding at urine and was impressed by the importance of rainfall in determining the seasonal occurrence of different species.

I have spent eight years in African universities, first in Uganda and latterly in Sierra Leone. During this time I have been able to travel over much of tropical Africa, usually on university business, but always armed with a net and a notebook. In Uganda and in Sierra Leone I have been preoccupied with two quite different aspects of butterfly biology: the diversity and seasonal changes in the butterflies of tropical gardens, and the population ecology and population genetics of one species, *Acraea encedon* (which has in recent years been my major research interest). The reader will find repeated references to gardens and *Acraea encedon* throughout this book.

My recent research on *Acraea encedon* has been largely in collaboration with Mr. D. O. Chanter of the Department of Biomathematics in the University of Oxford. We first met in Uganda where he had been posted as a mathematics teacher. He has repeatedly helped with mathematical calculations and with the design of experiments, some of them reported in this book. Dr. Jennifer Owen drew most of the text figures and took many of the photographs. She has also made many improvements to the text by critically reading through it on several occasions. My bird-watching friend, Mr. G. D. Field, has often brought back interesting specimens of butterflies from the forests of Sierra Leone, and has also operated on my behalf a baited trap in his garden at Freetown; I am most grateful for his help. Field work on tropical butterflies requires a knowledge of plants. Miss A. C. Tallantire in Uganda and Professor J. K. Morton in Sierra Leone have answered numerous questions about plants and between them, although they may not admit it, have enabled me to become a fairly competent botanist. I also appreciate the enthusiasm of my laboratory assistant in Sierra Leone, Mr. J. S. Comba, who helped enormously in unfolding some of the mysteries surrounding the biology of *Acraea encedon*.

Various people and organizations have generously granted permission to reproduce figures and plates. These are acknowledged in the appropriate places in the text, but I would especially like to thank Dr. T. Eisner, Professor C. A. Clarke, and Professor H. E. Hinton for photographs.

D.F.O.

Freetown, Sierra Leone
August 1970

CONTENTS

LIST OF PLATES

I

INTRODUCTION

MY first encounter with tropical butterflies was in secondary forest at the foot of El Salto, a spectacular waterfall in central Mexico. The previous day had been spent in driving south through northern Mexico; the countryside was dry and not unlike the country I had passed through in southern Texas. I reached El Salto at dusk and camped near the waterfall. There was rain during the night and the early morning was misty and damp. Eventually the sun broke through and I climbed the steep forested slopes near the waterfall. There were butterflies everywhere and within an hour I had caught my first *Morpho*, an enormous iridescent blue nymphalid that I had difficulty in fitting into the killing jar. Travelling south from El Salto to Chiapas in southern Mexico I found more and more species that I had never seen before, and in common with everyone first experiencing the richness of the butterfly fauna of the tropics, I became bewildered by the superficial similarity of many of the specimens I collected: there were moths that looked almost exactly like heliconiids, and butterflies almost identical in colour and marking that on close inspection obviously belonged to different families.

In North America or Europe if one sees a butterfly of a particular species the probability of the next butterfly seen being the same species is high; in the tropics, especially in forest, the probability is much lower. This simple observation is perhaps the most fundamental difference between the temperate and the tropical butterfly fauna.

I had been in Africa some years when an eminent ecologist, known for his mathematical formulations in population ecology, paid me a visit. He had never visited the tropics before (indeed he had rarely been in the field anywhere) but had some views on species diversity that he badly wanted to describe in mathematical terms. Could he see something of the high diversity of tropical species about which he had heard so much? I sent him to the Budongo Forest in Uganda and urged him to try and form some impressions from the butterflies. The Budongo is one of the richest in species of the East African forests. He returned a few days later and said that although he had seen plenty of butterflies there were very few species. On the basis of his observations he was prepared to reject the notion that the tropics are richer in species than the temperate regions. But upon questioning it was obvious that he had made only a superficial inspection of the butterflies. He was not aware of mimicry between species and not aware that many forest butterflies that look alike are in reality quite different. He admitted that it would take more than a few days to learn enough about forest butterflies to appreciate the intricacies of their similarities and differences.

This episode, like my own experience in Mexico, illustrates another important difference between the butterfly fauna of temperate and tropical regions: in the tropics species that look alike are in reality often quite different, and also, but to a lesser extent, butterflies that look quite different are often of the same genus or even the same species. In the tropics one has to learn anatomical differences, especially in wing venation, in order to identify butterflies whereas in temperate areas one can usually rely upon the superficial impression created by colour and pattern. Thus in the forest around my house in Sierra Leone there are lycaenids that look almost exactly like pierids or acraeids, and papilionids that look very like danaids, acraeids, or nymphalids. A remarkable number of butterflies are boldly marked in black and white, or orange and black, and there are many unrelated species that live near the forest floor that are brown, intricately marked with yellow. Some of the latter are shown in Plate 12. In Europe the observer may sometimes become confused over the different species of fritillary butterflies (Nymphalidae), but at least butterflies that look like fritillaries are related; this is not so in the forests of Africa and elsewhere in the tropics.

In butterflies, as in other groups of animals, it is the forest fauna that is most distinctive in the tropics. Tropical forest has received a variety of descriptive names, but the term rain forest is most often used (Richards 1952). Rain forest develops in areas of the tropics where there is high rainfall and where the dry season is not too prolonged. Its outstanding characteristics are discussed in detail by Richards (1952) and also, with special reference to West Africa, by Hopkins (1965). There are three main rain forest areas of the world: South America, especially the Amazon basin and the area extending northwards to Mexico; West and Central Africa, especially the Congo basin; and south-east Asia, the latter area, extending from western India to New Guinea, Queensland and many of the Pacific islands, being split into many fragments. I shall in this book repeatedly mention the destructive impact of man on the rain forest for, except in inaccessible mountain areas, the forest has been or is being destroyed at an alarming rate.

One of the main features of rain forest is that the majority of the plants are woody. Even the undergrowth is largely woody and often consists mainly of saplings of the taller trees. In undisturbed (primary) forest the floor is relatively clear of vegetation and access is easy; indeed the presence of grass is in most cases indicative of human disturbance. Another striking feature of the forest is the remarkable diversity of species of trees. In a

2. A forest path in Uganda. Such paths provide some of the best places for observing and collecting butterflies in the tropics. (*Photo by C. H. F. Rowell*)

3. Lake Mutanda, Kigezi district, Uganda. The Virunga volcanoes, rising to over 4000 metres, are in the background. They are covered with montane vegetation, but terraced cultivation is rapidly spreading up the slopes of the mountains. (*Photo by Jennifer Owen*)

temperate forest the trees represent several species, usually no more than twenty, and pure stands are common, but in the rain forest there are usually more than a hundred species of trees per square kilometre. Richards (1952), discussing species diversity in rain forest trees, quotes from Alfred Russel Wallace who in 1878 wrote, 'If the traveller notices a particular species and wishes to find more like it, he may often turn his eyes in vain in every direction. Trees of varied forms, dimensions and colours are around him, but he rarely sees any one of them repeated. Time after time he goes towards a tree which looks like the one he seeks, but a closer examination proves it to be distinct. He may at length, perhaps, meet with a second specimen half a mile off, or may fail altogether, till on another occasion he stumbles on one by accident.' The remarkable diversity of rain forest trees is in part responsible for the high diversity of animal, including butterfly, species in the forest. It is true that the traveller in the forest often experiences difficulty in finding a particular species of tree, and it would also seem likely that herbivorous animals, including butterflies, experience the same difficulty in locating their food-plants.

In the forest climbing plants and epiphytes are abundant and the overall impression is of great vegetational complexity. Many of the larger trees have conspicuous buttresses or stilts, possibly as a consequence of the shallow rooting systems that often occur in rain forest trees. In the mature forest the trees are tall, often reaching 45–55 metres, taller than trees in most temperate forests. Most rain forest trees retain their leaves all the year round (hence the commonly used term 'evergreen forest'), but there is in most areas a seasonal cycle of leaf fall and leaf production. Leaf fall is highest at the end of the dry season, and in an exceptional dry season some trees become almost as bare as oaks in winter in a temperate forest. Leaf production occurs all the year round, but in most trees reaches a peak at the onset of the rains.

The interior of the forest is gloomy, but when the sun is overhead the floor and ground vegetation are speckled with extremely bright patches of sunlight. One effect of this is that a fast-flying forest butterfly seems to appear and disappear as it moves in and out of sunlit areas and is soon lost to sight. Most butterfly collectors entering the forest follow man-made tracks; here it is somewhat easier to observe and to collect, but other plants, especially grasses, become established along pathways, and the butterflies observed will also include non-forest species.

In Sierra Leone I have found that one of the best ways of observing forest butterflies is to follow a stream. This procedure has two advantages: one can work in undisturbed forest and yet have a relatively clear view of what is going on, and if the stream is of reasonable size the forest canopy dips towards it so that one can see something of the canopy fauna without actually being in the canopy.

Even in the dry season the rain forest is damp and humid. It is also fairly cool and working in the forest can be most pleasant. In the wet season the rain is often torrential, but a remarkable number of butterflies can be found whenever there is a brief pause in the rainfall. Contrary to popular belief one is not molested by hordes of noxious insects and snakes, but reasonable care must be exercised in placing hands and feet. It is not easy to describe the delights of walking and working in the forest; these have to be experienced. The traveller by car may see some fine trees by the road-side, but it is the walker who will see and feel the real thing. The forest has its own sounds and smells, and the brilliance of the birds, butterflies, and other animals adds colour to a walk. My many visits to the Budongo Forest in Uganda were frequently enlivened by the presence of large troops of chimpanzees whose barking, whooping, and drumming contributed greatly to the pleasure of butterfly hunting.

Much of the area of the world that is shown as rain forest on vegetation maps is now secondary forest, or secondary bush, as it is often called. This habitat, although rich in butterflies, is less easy to penetrate unless it is well grown. Secondary forest results after the big trees have been removed and especially after the land has been cultivated for a few years and then abandoned. In Africa secondary forest differs from undisturbed primary forest in having a dense tangle of undergrowth and in the presence of plants, especially grasses, that quickly colonize disturbed land. Umbrella trees, *Musanga*, are characteristic of secondary forest in Africa, and their presence is a sure indication of human alteration of the original vegetation. Needless to say secondary vegetation is extremely varied, depending partly on how recent and how thorough was the destruction. Secondary forest is easily recognized from the air, appearing almost like a patch-work quilt, as a consequence of small areas being cleared and left to revert at different times. I have frequently noticed this characteristic pattern when flying over the Ivory Coast: undisturbed forest appears as a continuous green area with haphazardly spaced emergent trees, while secondary forest appears as a series of roughly circular patches of uniform vegetation, each patch a slightly different colour due no doubt to varying stages of secondary succession.

The butterflies of the savanna are more reminiscent of temperate species and there are also fewer species than in the forest. The dominant vegeta-tion of savanna is grass, often in pure stands of a single species over limited areas. Nowadays the grass is burnt over in the dry season. Trees are often present and the term wooded savanna is widely used in Africa to describe grassland with a relatively dense stand of trees. In many areas clumps of woody vegetation originate from termite mounds, and this accounts for the characteristic spacing of the clumps of vegetation in the grassland. Many savanna trees and shrubs are fire-resistant. Savanna areas experience one

or two long dry periods each year. During the wet season the rain may be
torrential and there is a marked increase in insect activity. Savanna butterflies are more common in the wet than in the dry season, and in a very dry
season butterflies may become extremely scarce.

FIG. 1.1. Political map of Africa showing the present territorial boundaries and, with one
exception, the modern names of countries mentioned. Abyssinia is now generally known
as Ethiopia, but the older name is retained because of possible confusion with the
Ethiopian region which is Africa, including Madagascar, south of the Sahara.

One problem encountered in the study of African butterflies is that
place names change frequently. It is often difficult to match up the localities
on data labels of museum specimens with place names in current use. For
the reader unfamiliar with the geography and politics of modern Africa
the present political divisions as used in this book are shown in Fig. 1.1.

Fig. 1.2 is a generalized vegetation map of Africa. I say generalized because almost everywhere man has had a destructive and unifying effect on the natural vegetation. In a sense the map shows what Africa would be like if there were no people. A few words of explanation are necessary. Thus montane vegetation as shown in Fig. 1.2 includes forest, moorland, and

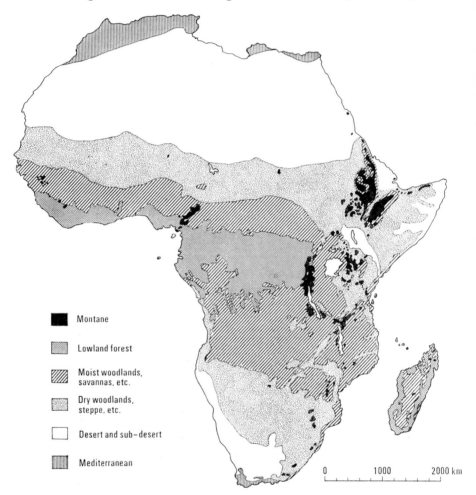

Montane

Lowland forest

Moist woodlands, savannas, etc.

Dry woodlands, steppe, etc.

Desert and sub-desert

Mediterranean

0   1000   2000 km

FIG. 1.2. Vegetation map of Africa.

grassland, depending on altitude. On the tops of high mountains, such as Kilimanjaro and Ruwenzori, there is effectively no vegetation, nothing but snow, ice, and rock, but the scale of the map does not allow this alpine zone to be shown. The lowland forest has suffered most from human intervention and in particular the boundary between lowland forest and savanna is no longer evident in most places. The transition is best seen in gallery forest growing along river banks in what is otherwise savanna country. Near the river the forest may be as well developed as in larger expanses of forest, but there is an abrupt change as one moves away from the river. The moist savanna shown in Fig. 1.2 merges into dry savanna to the north and south of the tropical area of Africa. Grazing by domestic animals has drastically altered much of the savanna, and the drier the landscape the more important become the effects of seasonal fires on the fauna and flora. In North Africa, the vegetation, where it occurs, is typically south European and a similar flora occurs in the extreme south of Africa, as shown in Fig. 1.2.

The study of tropical butterflies began when exploratory expeditions from Europe returned home with examples of spectacular tropical animals and plants. Men who penetrated into the interior of the unexplored tropics were often more than casually interested in tropical animals and were keen to take examples of their discoveries home. In Africa the period of exploration was followed by the period of colonization and the fragmentation of the continent into administrative and political units. Colonial administrators, missionaries, and others often found themselves with time on their hands and frequently turned to natural history for relaxation. As far as butterflies are concerned natural history usually meant forming a collection which eventually found its way into a European museum. Some administrators became interested in life history studies and others, encouraged by professional zoologists at home, developed an interest in such topics as mimicry and polymorphism.

Many rare species were collected, and some of these are still known only from the unique types, never having been collected since. The largest butterfly in Africa, *Papilio antimachus* (Papilionidae), was first collected in Sierra Leone in 1782, but it was not until 1864 that a second specimen was brought to Europe. Butterfly collecting as a form of trophy hunting was extremely popular in Europe a hundred years ago. As a consequence many residents in the tropics sold their collections to dealers. Then collectors came to Africa and took butterflies in enormous numbers for sale. Mr. Robert C. Goodden informs me that one collector, Le Moult, sold many himself, that a further sale from his collection of about a million specimens took place in Paris a few years ago, and that there are still about a million left in the collection.

But although administrators and other visitors to the former colonial territories often collected and frequently sold specimens, others were content simply to observe and admire the richness of the tropical environment, often without even bothering to find out the names of the animals and plants they saw. One such was Mrs. Melville, wife of a judge in the former colony of Freetown in Sierra Leone. In 1841 she wrote, 'I wish it were in my power to send you a description of the splendid butterflies I see every sunny day; but like all of their tribe, they never remain long enough for me to examine them distinctly, merely settling upon a leaf and flower a single moment, or enamelling the grass with their gorgeous hues. A very common one looks as if cut out of black satin, and embroidered with purple silk. Another is black with white dots; and a third broader across the wings than a humming bird, is also of a rich blue-black, with a belt of bright green stretching from the tip of one wing to another. There are also many lesser ones all of one colour, such as pale blue, yellow, or lilac, that look like flower blossoms flitting through the air. I particularly observe a small white butterfly in the bush here that seems as if it were carrying off a few threads of a silk fringe that had got entangled with it. But I found on a narrower examination this appearance to be caused by the hinder wings of the insect being lengthened out into flexible tapering points, which give a still lighter air to its graceful body. Altogether I must candidly confess that the view, the weather, the flowers, birds and the butterflies render me somewhat idle at times.'

Mrs. Melville's observations, published in 1849, were made in the area now partly occupied by the University of Sierra Leone. Happily much of the forest and many of its butterflies still survive; indeed one can see the descendants of Mrs. Melville's butterflies flying around the overgrown ruins of her house.

2

CLASSIFICATION
AND ZOOGEOGRAPHY

Some problems of butterfly classification

MOST insects that an average observer recognizes as butterflies belong to the superfamily Papilionoidea of the order Lepidoptera. Members of another superfamily, the Hesperioidea, or skippers, are also usually regarded as butterflies, partly because, like most butterflies and unlike most moths, they are day-flying, and partly because they share a number of features with the Papilionoidea. All the remaining Lepidoptera are collectively known as moths.

Butterflies occur in all parts of the world, but they are primarily tropical. About 13 000 species are known, of which 2674 occur in Africa south of the Sahara and Madagascar. Undoubtedly there remain some undescribed species, but compared with most groups of insects they are well known and most species have now been discovered and described. Carcasson (1964) estimates that 85 per cent of the African butterflies have been discovered and described. A provisional check-list of 2653 species known from the Ethiopian region is given in Peters (1952), but even since that date species have been added to the list. The number of species of butterflies varies markedly in different parts of Africa, as shown in Fig. 2.1. The largest number of species occur in the forests in and around the Congo basin. There is a decrease in the number of species both to the north and to the south of the equatorial forest and also towards the east coast, which is comparatively dry and not forested, except in isolated areas.

Many older works on African butterflies describe as different species what are now known to be polymorphic forms, seasonal forms, geographical subspecies, and even the two sexes of one species. Errors such as this are not astonishing as most collecting in Africa has been of adults without detailed studies of life histories, and it is only relatively recently that it has been realized that many species are immensely variable. There is however still considerable disagreement as to how butterflies should be classified. The main source of disagreement is over the definition of what constitutes a family or a subfamily. Thus some authors downgrade the families Danaidae, Satyridae, Acraeidae, and Nymphalidae to subfamilies (Danainae, Satyrinae, Acraeinae, and Nymphalinae) and place them all in the Nymphalidae. The huge family Lycaenidae is by some split into three or

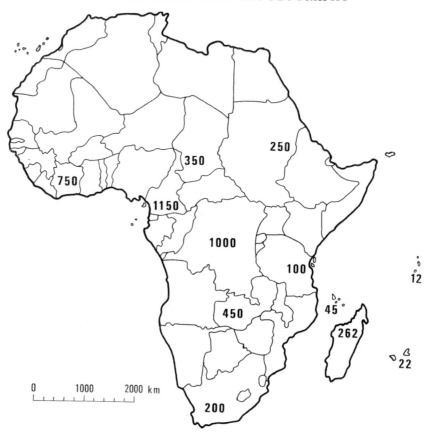

FIG. 2.1. Regional variation in the number of species of butterflies known from different parts of Africa. Adapted from Carcasson (1964).

more families, while others would regard the family Riodinidae as a sub-family of the Lycaenidae. These and many other differences of opinion as to the systematic status of groups of butterflies are of little scientific consequence since the basis of disagreement amounts to judgements made on the relative importance of anatomical features.

Biologists interested in butterfly classification are often concerned with evolutionary (phylogenetic) relationships, but since there is no significant fossil record of butterflies much of what has been written is highly specu-lative. In particular, 'primitive' anatomical features have been identified and these have been used in arranging butterflies in a supposedly phylo-genetic sequence. Needless to say there is no evidence whatsoever as to which anatomical features are primitive and which are derivative. In general, classifications of butterflies are based upon similarities and differences; close similarity may or may not indicate close phylogenetic relationship, and wide differences may not necessarily indicate lack of close relationship. Similarities and differences are the products of evolution, but the actual lines of descent and the degree of evolutionary change in the past are not known.

But apart from these rather technical considerations it is likely that each group of butterflies, whether it is called a family or a subfamily, comprises genera and species that are more closely related to each other than to any other group. Thus the Papilionidae, Pieridae, Danaidae, Satyridae, Acraeidae, Libytheidae, Riodinidae, and Hesperiidae probably represent 'natural' groups of the same evolutionary origin, but the Nymphalidae and Lycaenidae, because of the considerable anatomical diversity within them, may each contain genera of different evolutionary origin; that is, these families may be polyphyletic. In particular, the *Charaxes* butterflies, which are here considered as Nymphalidae, could be of different evolutionary origin from other members of the family, and the three subfamilies of Lycaenidae, Lipteninae, Liphyrinae, and Lycaeninae, are so different from one another that they could have been independently evolved. These questions of evolutionary relationship are unlikely to be finally resolved, and indeed they are of very little scientific importance; all that remains is to decide upon a classification and to be consistent. That is what I shall do in this book.

All the major groups of butterflies are represented in Africa. Table 2.1 shows the estimated number of species in Africa south of the Sahara and

TABLE 2.1

Families of butterflies present in Africa south of the Sahara and Madagascar, and estimated number of species†

Family	Known species	Species of doubtful status‡
Papilionidae	86	—
Pieridae	121	3
Danaidae	25	—
Satyridae	245	7
Nymphalidae	500	28
Acraeidae	168	8
Libytheidae	2	—
Riodinidae	12	—
Lycaenidae	1092	22
Hesperiidae	423	—
Total	2674	68

† From Carcasson (1964).
‡ Species of doubtful status and distribution, including some species described on the basis of one or very few individuals. These figures should probably be substracted from the known species.

Madagascar in the ten families of butterflies here recognized. The figures in Table 2.1 are reasonably accurate and it is probably only in the Lycaenidae that there remain a significant number of undescribed species.

The families of African butterflies

1. Papilionidae

The swallowtails are among the most conspicuous butterflies in the tropics (Plate 10). Not all species have 'swallow-tails' and some are mimetic bearing little resemblance to typical non-mimetic species unless examined closely. There are two conspicuous genera, *Papilio* (49 species) and *Graphium* (36 species). Although most species are associated with forest habitats, there are several typical of savanna, including the widely distributed *Graphium pylades*. The citrus swallowtail, *Papilio demodocus*, is one of the best known butterflies in Africa, being especially common in gardens where the larvae feed on cultivated *Citrus*. The family includes *Papilio antimachus*, the largest butterfly in Africa, and one of the largest butterflies in the world, and *Papilio dardanus*, a mimetic species the genetics of which have been extensively studied. *Atroplaneura antenor*, a large Madagascan swallowtail, belongs to a group of Aristolochiaceae-feeding species well represented in the Asian and American tropics, but absent from the African mainland. Swallowtails attract the attention of even the most casual observer and the fact that many species enter flower gardens makes them well known.

2. Pieridae

The 'whites', subfamily Pierinae, and the 'yellows', subfamily Coliadinae, are conspicuous butterflies that are especially abundant in the savanna. There is one distinctive species placed in another subfamily, the Pseudopontiinae, which is so different in general appearance from most butterflies that it was first described as a moth. This species, *Pseudopontia paradoxa* (Plate 21), which is entirely translucent white, is weak-flying and is confined to the forests of tropical Africa. The Pierinae include some conspicuous, mainly savanna, species some of which enter gardens in the forested areas of Africa. The most important genera are *Belenois* (23 species), *Mylothris* (25 species), and *Colotis* (40 species). The Coliadinae includes *Colias*, a mainly north temperate genus confined to high ground in Africa, and *Eurema*, small yellow butterflies with black borders to the wings, as well as *Catopsilia florella* which is found everywhere in open areas in Africa.

3. Danaidae

These are the monarch butterflies. Probably all species are highly unpalatable or even toxic to potential predators. They are extremely tough and can withstand a remarkable amount of rough handling. In Africa monarchs are abundant butterflies but relative to the Asian tropics there are rather few species. There are three genera, *Danaus* (3 species), *Amauris* (18 species) and *Euploea* (5 species, all confined to the Malagasy area). *Danaus* includes the conspicuous orange, black, and white *Danaus chrysippus*, which is one of the commonest butterflies in Africa. Many of the *Amauris* species are similar and are difficult to identify; most occur in forest, but a few enter gardens and similar habitats. The best known species is *Amauris niavius*, which is boldly marked with black and white, and which, with other species of *Amauris*, is a model for various Papilionidae and Nymphalidae.

4. Satyridae

The 'browns' are relatively inconspicuous, medium-sized or small butterflies. Most are some shade of brown with eye spots near the outer margins of the underside of the wings. A great many African species bear a close resemblance to the European ringlet butterfly, *Aphantopus hyperantus*. The family is not particularly well developed in Africa, but in some areas they are extremely abundant in the wet season. The generic classification of the Satyridae is in a somewhat confused state. A great many species are now grouped together in the genus *Bicyclus*, but this genus has been much divided by some authors in the past. One species, *Elymnias bammakoo*, is strikingly black and white or black and orange (Plate 20), and is a mimic of *Bematistes* (Acraeidae). There has been a tendency among collectors to overlook the Satyridae and this has resulted in relatively few museum specimens and hence confusion over generic classification.

5. Nymphalidae

This family includes the most conspicuous and varied assortment of butterflies in Africa. Many species are brilliantly coloured and many are powerful fliers. Nymphalidae occur in all habitats, but especially in forest; many occur in gardens. The African species can easily be distinguished from butterflies in other families by the open cell on the hindwing. This character is often helpful as some nymphalids are close mimics of Danaidae and Acraeidae. Some of the larger and better known genera are as follows:

Charaxes (86 species) are mainly large and powerful butterflies, often brightly coloured and especially abundant in forest. The front edge of the forewing of many is serrated and they use their wings to drive others away from a localized food source, such as rotten fruit or animal remains. *Charaxes* are difficult to collect with a net because they fly high and fast but they can be collected in large numbers in baited traps.

Cymothoe (63 species) are low-flying butterflies, many of which are brown with white or yellow markings. There are several species in which the males are bright red and the females whitish with dark markings (Plate 21). Most species occur in forest, but a few are confined to more open habitats.

Najas (=*Euphaedra*), *Euriphene*, and *Bebearia* form a group containing about 150 species. They are so similar that there is considerable disagreement as to the limits of each genus; they could probably all be placed in one large genus. All are forest butterflies and typically they fly near the ground. Many have patches of iridescent blue on the wings and a pale subapical bar (Plate 20). A few species appear to be mimics of certain dayflying moths, notably *Aletis*.

Neptis is a genus of 47 species of rather small black and white butterflies with a slow gliding flight, essentially confined to forest. The species are difficult to identify, and there are probably still a few undescribed. *Asterope* (15 species) are small brown butterflies with eye spots on the wings bearing a strong superficial resemblance to Satyridae (Plate 21). The genus is related to a much larger South American group. There are forest as well as savanna species. They are easily overlooked and at least in forest regions rarely collected, but they sometimes appear in very large numbers. *Hypolimnas* (12 species) are large mainly black and white butterflies, mostly found in forest (Plate 20). One species, *Hypolimnas misippus*, occurs in open situations and is extremely common in Africa and in many other parts of the Old World tropics. Some of the species are mimics of Danaidae. One of the most obvious genera of butterflies in Africa is *Precis* (Plate 11). These butterflies are abundant in gardens and cultivated land, the larvae feeding mainly on agricultural weeds. All the 29 species are distinctively patterned, and some develop striking seasonal forms that are associated with the alternation of wet and dry seasons.

Other genera of Nymphalidae contain many fewer species and there is a whole range of distinctive species that are the sole representatives of their genus. Many of these are soon encountered by collectors and observers as they often occur in gardens and disturbed land.

6. Acraeidae

Although Acraeidae occur in other tropical regions of the world, they are best developed in Africa. There is one large genus, *Acraea*, comprising 147 species that includes both forest and savanna butterflies. In almost all parts of Africa butterflies of this genus share with *Precis* (Nymphalidae) the distinction of being the most frequently encountered butterflies in gardens and similar habitats (Plate 13), but there are species of very restricted distribution, especially in East Africa. The twenty species of *Bematistes* are mainly larger butterflies and are restricted to forest. The females of many of them are conspicuously black and white while the males are black and orange. Both *Acraea* and *Bematistes* are unpalatable butterflies and act as models for Nymphalidae, Papilionidae, and Lycaenidae. The genus

Pardopsis contains only one species, a small orange butterfly with black dots that occurs in savanna.

7. *Libytheidae*

A small family of butterflies with much elongated palps which give rise to the common name of snout butterfly. The Libytheidae are often considered as a subfamily of the Nymphalidae and have even been assigned to the Riodinidae. There is one African species, *Libythea labdaca,* and another similar species on Madagascar. A third species, described from Mauritius, now appears to be extinct. At one time East African *Libythea* were thought to be specifically distinct from *Libythea labdaca* but this appears to have been incorrect.

8. *Riodinidae*

This is mainly a tropical American family with a few representatives in Africa and elsewhere in the world. There are only two African genera, *Abisara* (9 species) and *Saribia* (3 species). The Riodinidae are perhaps intermediate between the Nymphalidae and the Lycaenidae. They are small and brownish with white or blue markings and eye spots near the margins of the wings.

9. *Lycaenidae*

Africa is extremely rich in Lycaenidae. All three subfamilies, Lipteninae, Liphyrinae, and Lycaeninae occur and there is an enormous proliferation of species. Most are small butterflies and many are bright metallic blue with filamentous tails. Others are orange with dark markings and there are also white and pale yellow species. The larvae are woodlouse-shaped and in many species there is a 'honey' gland in the mid-dorsal line of the seventh segment which secretes a substance attractive to ants. The larvae of many species are in one way or another associated with ants (Plates 16 and 17).

The largest African genera of Lipteninae are *Pentila* (35 species), *Telipna* (28 species), *Liptena* (67 species), and *Epitola* (72 species). Some of the species in this subfamily are slow-flying forest butterflies and are involved in mimetic associations with Acraeidae and day-flying moths. The Liphyrinae are mainly forest butterflies and are extremely varied in superficial appearance; there are no large genera, and the larvae are carnivorous, feeding chiefly on Homoptera. The Lycaeninae include the blues and coppers and are well represented in Africa. Blues, reds, and browns are the predominant colours of these butterflies, and many have intricate lines and spots, including eye spots, on the underside. Some are mimetic and there are a remarkably large number of rare species, but this perhaps reflects little more than inadequate collecting. Although many species are confined to forest, the subfamily is also well represented in savanna and many are common garden butterflies. The genus *Anthene* alone contains 122 African species, and there are other large genera.

10. Hesperiidae

Skippers are not particularly well represented in collections from Africa. They are ignored by many collectors, partly because they are small and partly because compared with the American tropics they are not particularly diverse. As already mentioned, they are placed in a separate super-family from all other butterflies, and it could be argued that they are not butterflies but moths. Most species have a rapid darting flight and in the wet season in forest areas they are often common. Most of the African species are brown with paler markings. There are three subfamilies in Africa, Coeliadinae, Hesperiinae and Pyrginae. Various species of *Coeliades* (18 African species) are common garden butterflies.

The zoogeography of African butterflies

The northern limit of the African fauna is the Sahara desert; North Africa is zoogeographically part of Europe. The Ethiopian region is therefore surrounded by major barriers to animal movement, desert to the north and sea on all other sides. Madagascar and the associated islands may be included in the Ethiopian region for general discussion, but they form a distinct sub-region. It is possible to consider the African butterfly fauna as a relatively isolated unit and to assess its affinities with other major zoogeographical regions of the world. It should be emphasized however that the present occurrence and distribution of a genus or a species is unlikely to tell us much about the place of origin of that genus or species: distributions have undoubtedly undergone major changes in the past million years, even in the past ten thousand years.

No family of butterflies is peculiar to Africa; and with uncertainties over the definition of subfamilies, it is most fruitful to confine consideration of zoogeography to genera and species. Carcasson (1964) has surveyed the zoogeography of African butterflies and much of what follows, at least as regards factual information, is derived from his paper.

Affinities with other regions

Some large genera of African butterflies are found throughout the world. Examples are *Papilio* (Papilionidae), *Eurema* (Pieridae), and *Danaus* (Danaidae). A few genera are common to the Ethiopian and Palaearctic regions, including *Pieris, Pontia, Colias, Euchloe* (all Pieridae), *Pararge* (Satyridae), *Charaxes, Issoria, Melitaea* (all Nymphalidae), and *Apharitis* (Lycaenidae). In terms of number of species most of these genera can be regarded as predominantly Palaearctic, but *Charaxes jasius* (which also occurs in tropical Africa) is the only Palaearctic representative of a large

Ethiopian genus. *Lycaena phlaeas* (Lycaenidae) occurs in the Palaearctic, Nearctic and Ethiopian regions, which is a remarkable distribution for such a small butterfly.

There are few affinities between the South American (Neotropical) butterflies and the Ethiopian. One large South American tribe, the Eunicini (Nymphalidae), is represented in Africa by *Asterope*, but occurs in no other part of the world; indeed *Asterope* is considered by some to be congeneric with the South American *Eunica*.

Africa shares many genera and species with tropical Asia (the Oriental region). Carcasson (1964) points out that the species shared by the two regions are found mainly in drier habitats; forest butterflies in the two regions are often of the same genus, but the species are usually different. Hence the main zoogeographical distinctiveness of tropical Africa lies in its forest butterflies.

The butterflies of Malagasy

The Malagasy sub-region includes the main island of Madagascar, the Comoro Islands, the Mascarenes, and the Seychelles (Fig. 1.1). I have chosen to consider the zoogeography of Malagasy first because some special problems arise which come up again when the African mainland is considered, but are better understood with reference to Malagasy.

The island of Madagascar is separated from the African mainland by an area of sea which is nowhere less than 400 kilometres wide. The Comoros consist of four islands of volcanic origin surrounded by deep water and lying about half-way between Madagascar and the African coast at a point where the straits are about 640 kilometres wide. The Seychelles lie to the north-east of Madagascar and the Mascarenes to the east; both groups of islands are well isolated. Madagascar has been isolated from Africa for at least 60 million years and probably much longer. A chain of mountains runs from north to south of the island slightly west of centre. East of the mountains it is wet and forested (large areas of forest have now been destroyed by man), while the west side is relatively dry. The island is rich in flowering plants, but relatively poor in animals, especially when compared with other large islands such as New Guinea; but there are some striking endemic groups of animals, including butterflies.

The Malagasy sub-region became isolated before any major evolutionary development of butterflies had occurred, indeed probably before butterflies as we now know them had been evolved, and so the ancestors of all genera and species now present must have arrived there across the sea. One might guess that they came from Africa, but the presence of some typically Asian kinds suggests a more complex situation.

There are 301 species of butterflies in Malagasy of which 233 are endemic. Of the 81 genera, twelve (listed in Table 2.2) are endemic. Two

TABLE 2.2

Endemic genera of butterflies from the Malagasy sub-region

Genus	Family	Number of species†
Gideona	Pieridae	1
Heteropsis	Satyridae	2
Smerina	Nymphalidae	1
Saribia	Riodinidae	3
Trichiolaus	Lycaenidae	2
Hovala		5
Fulda		4
Arnetta		3
Malaza	Hesperiidae	3
Miraja		9
Perrotia		6
Ploetzia		1

† The number of species per genus is taken from Peters (1952).

genera, *Euploea* (Danaidae) and *Atroplaneura* (Papilionidae), are Asian and do not occur on the mainland of Africa. There are relatively few Lycaenidae in Malagasy (the Lipteninae are absent) and the sub-region is rather poor in Nymphalidae. Both the Satyridae and the Hesperiidae are well represented, and seven of the endemic genera are Hesperiidae.

Some widely distributed African butterflies (Carcasson (1964) mentions 26 species) occur as the same subspecies in Malagasy; others have formed distinct species. There are four species in the *Papilio demodocus* group of swallowtails on Madagascar compared with *Papilio demodocus* alone throughout mainland Africa. Many other mainland species are represented in Malagasy by single distinct species; an example is *Aterica galene* (Nymphalidae) which on Madagascar occurs as *Aterica rabena*.

Not all the endemic species of butterflies of Malagasy occur on the island of Madagascar. For example among the Papilionidae, *Graphium levassori* (Fig. 2.2) is confined to Grand Comoro, *Papilio phorbanta* to Reunion in the Mascarenes, and *Papilio manlius* to Mauritius, also in the Mascarenes. These and other species that are confined to small islands are probably in danger of extinction as their area of distribution is small and the islands are already overcrowded with people.

There has been much subspeciation within the Malagasy sub-region; this is to be expected as the various islands are well isolated from one another. *Papilio dardanus* (Papilionidae) has formed well differentiated subspecies on Grand Comoro and on Madagascar which differ in wing pattern (Fig. 2.3) and in the structure of the male genitalia (Turner 1963).

As already mentioned, all the butterflies of Malagasy must have crossed the sea from other land masses. A few species, notably *Papilio demodocus*

4. Cultivated hills in Uganda, with remnants of the original vegetation, including giant lobelias growing two metres high, in the foreground. (*Photo by Ministry of Information, Uganda*)

5. A forest clearing in Uganda. Another excellent site for observing and collecting butter-flies. (*Photo by C. H. F. Rowell*)

6. Coffee growing in partially cleared forest in Uganda. Many forest-edge and some savanna species move into this kind of habitat. (*Photo by C. H. F. Rowell*)

7. Savanna in western Uganda. In the foreground are *Euphorbia* trees. The Ruwenzori mountains are just visible in the background.
(Photo by Ministry of Information, Uganda)

(Papilionidae), have probably been brought over by man quite recently. Most of the species have affinities with African species, suggesting that they initially arrived from Africa, which is to be expected. Two genera are Asian

FIG. 2.2. *Graphium levassori*, confined to Grand Comoro. The butterfly is yellowish-white with black markings.

which suggests either that they arrived from Asia or that these genera were once present in Africa but are now extinct. The possibility of independent evolution in Asia and Malagasy cannot be entirely ruled out, but most

FIG. 2.3. Left: *Papilio dardanus humbloti*, Grand Comoro Island. Right: *Papilio dardanus meriones*, Madagascar. The butterflies are pale yellow with black markings. In these two subspecies the sexes are alike in colour and markings.

would agree that the same genus is statistically unlikely to be evolved more than once. Most of the endemic subspecies and species in Malagasy are quite similar to African species and probably represent colonization and subsequent evolution in isolation. The same principle applies to the occurrence within Malagasy of distinct but similar subspecies or species on different islands or groups of islands. No time scale can be suggested for this evolution as nothing is known about evolutionary rates in butterflies. Theoretically there is no reason why a subspecies or species should not evolve in as short a time as two or three thousand years.

There is also no reason why Malagasy species should not colonize Africa: *Graphium evombar* (Papilionidae) of Madagascar is replaced by a very similar species, *Graphium junodi*, on a narrow strip along the African coast facing Madagascar, but does not occur elsewhere.

The above considerations imply that from time to time butterflies travel great distances over the sea and form new populations. The distance between Madagascar and Africa and the distance between the Malagasy islands is so great that (1) colonization must occur infrequently and (2) there must be a considerable element of chance as to which species become established. This is presumably why the Malagasy butterfly fauna is rather poor in species but at the same time rich in endemics.

The butterflies of the African mainland

Forest. Rain forest can be broadly separated into two types: lowland and montane. Near the equator montane forest is confined to land higher than 1600 metres, but at higher latitudes it extends progressively to lower altitudes. There is of course wide overlap between lowland and montane forest in terms of the species of butterflies present; a few species, including *Charaxes candiope*, *Salamis parhassus*, and *Precis terea* (Nymphalidae), occur in both types. Moreover widely separated subspecies of the same species may differ as to whether they are montane or lowland forest butterflies; thus *Charaxes boueti* (Nymphalidae) occurs at 1500–2600 metres in Kigezi, Uganda, but in Sierra Leone I find it commonly at 300 metres.

The main area of lowland forest in Africa (Fig. 1.2) extends, with gaps, from Sierra Leone in the west to Uganda and western Kenya (where it is patchy) in the east. This is by far the richest area of Africa in terms of number of species, and a great many butterflies occur throughout the area. Check-lists and guides to groups of African butterflies give the distribution of numerous species as Sierra Leone to western Uganda or western Kenya. For some years I collected butterflies in the Budongo Forest in Uganda and when I moved to Sierra Leone I found that most of the species there were familiar.

In West Africa the western section of the forest is effectively isolated from the much larger section that extends from Nigeria to East Africa by the Dahomey Gap, a tongue of savanna that extends to the coast in eastern Ghana, Togo, Dahomey, and western Nigeria. This western section of forest has presumably been isolated for thousands of years, and although it contains many species that occur in the main area of lowland forest, it also contains endemic species and subspecies. Liberia is located in the middle of the western section and a detailed list of Liberian butterflies has been published by Fox *et al.* (1965). The list shows that 41 per cent of 64 species of Lipteninae are endemic to the western section, explicable because these butterflies are small and weak-flying and hardly ever leave the shade of the forest. About 13 per cent of 142 species of Nymphalidae are endemic to the western forest and 14 per cent of 36 species of Satyridae. In other families the percentage of endemics is low and there are no endemic Papilionidae, Pieridae, and Danaidae, which is to be expected as these butterflies are either strong fliers or are more often associated with open habitats. Taking the Liberian butterflies as a whole, about ten per cent of the species are endemic to the western forest.

Many species that occur in the main eastern section of the lowland forest appear to be absent from the western section. But it seems likely that the western section has been rather poorly studied as my own observations in Sierra Leone have revealed the presence of several species that were previously known only east of the Dahomey Gap. One such species is *Charaxes hadrianus* (Nymphalidae), a large and conspicuous butterfly recently collected for the first time in Sierra Leone and Ghana; undoubtedly it also occurs in the forests of Liberia and the Ivory Coast.

And then there are species that are thought to be restricted even within the western forest; thus Fox *et al.* (1965) state that *Najas francina* and *Najas perseis* (Nymphalidae) are confined to forests in Sierra Leone and Liberia, but I have recently seen specimens from western Ghana and so presumably these butterflies are more widespread. Many rare species have been reported from only one or two localities in the western forest, but this alone does not reflect a restricted distribution, as collecting in the area has rarely been intensive.

There is also some lowland forest on or near the East African coast from Kenya to Zululand. Such forest is now in isolated patches, but presumably during the past million or so years it was repeatedly joined and separated as the climate of Africa changed with the periodic glaciations to the north. The butterfly fauna of this forest is far less rich than that of the main forest area of western and central Africa. Many large genera such as *Euriphene* (Nymphalidae), *Epitola*, and *Liptena* (Lycaenidae) are absent, and other genera with numerous species in western and central Africa are represented by just a handful of species in the east; thus *Cymothoe* (Nymphalidae) with 56 species in the west has only three eastern lowland species. Moreover some western genera, *Kallima*, *Ariadne* (Nymphalidae), and *Elymnias* (Satyridae), also occur in India, but are absent from the lowland forest of the east coast of Africa. There are, however, some endemic species in the east; Carcasson (1964) lists four Papilionidae, one Pieridae, eighteen Nymphalidae, eight Acraeidae, one Riodinidae, nineteen Lycaenidae, and four Hesperiidae. Some of these species may not be strictly forest butterflies, but the evidence suggests relatively long periods of isolation of the extreme eastern from the main western block of lowland forest. The length of this isolation is a matter for speculation because, as already mentioned, it is impossible to predict rates of evolution, and therefore rates of speciation, in butterflies.

The montane forests of Africa are all in East and South Africa, with the exception of those on the Cameroon highlands (including Mount Cameroon), the islands in the Gulf of Guinea (especially Fernando Poo), and the Angolan highlands. The butterfly fauna of montane forest is relatively poor in species, but there are many endemics. Where there is a gradual transition from lowland to montane forest, as in Kigezi, Uganda, there are more species of montane butterflies, no doubt because of the continuity of the habitat. The East African montane forest is split into many isolated fragments including that on the Kivu-Ruwenzori mountains, the mountains of Abyssinia, and the numerous isolated mountains in Kenya, Uganda, Tanzania, and Malawi.

An important feature of the butterfly fauna of scattered blocks of montane forest is that although there is extensive geographical isolation between them many species of butterflies occur in most or all of the areas. Thus the following species listed by Carcasson (1964) occur in both the Cameroon and the East African highlands: *Papilio rex*, *Papilio zoroastres*, *Papilio charopus* (Papilionidae), *Mylothris sagala*, *Colotis elgonensis* (Pieridae), *Danaus formosa*, *Amauris echeria*, *Amauris albimaculata* (Danaidae), *Aphysoneura pigmentaria*, *Charaxes druceanus*, *Charaxes acuminatus*, *Antanartia hippomene*, and *Issoria excelson* (Nymphalidae). Indeed the Cameroon highlands have few endemic species, many of the lowland forest species ascend to a considerable elevation, and the butterfly fauna is in general more similar to that of the East African highlands than to any in West Africa.

In East Africa the richest area of montane forest is on the mountains in the Kivu-Ruwenzori block, which includes Ruwenzori itself, the eastern Congo, the Rwanda and Burundi highlands, the Kungwe and Mahare mountains to the east of Lake Tanganyika, and the mountains of the southern Sudan. In many of these areas montane forest is continuous with lowland forest, although the latter has been considerably altered and destroyed by man. The many endemic butterflies, as listed by Carcasson (1964), include: *Papilio leucotaenia*, *Graphium gudenusi* (Papilionidae), *Mylothris ruandana* (Pieridae), *Gnophodes grogani*, *Bicyclus aurivillii*,

Bicyclus matuta (Satyridae), *Charaxes opinatus*, *Kumothales inexpectata*, *Euryphura vansomererii* (Nymphalidae), *Acraea kalinzu*, *Acraea hamata*, *Acraea burgessi*, *Acraea amicitiae*, *Acraea alciopoides* (Acraeidae), and many Lycaenidae.

There is a considerable area of montane forest in Abyssinia (including northern Somalia). The Rift valley cuts through the mountains, so that the forest is divided into two sections (Fig. 1.2), and some species have evolved distinct subspecies on either side of the Rift. These include *Papilio echerioides* (Papilionidae) and *Charaxes brutus* (Nymphalidae). The Abyssinian montane forests are poorer in species than other montane forests in East Africa, but there is considerable endemicity. Among the endemic species Carcasson (1964) lists: *Papilio aethiops* (Papilionidae), *Mylothris mortoni* (Pieridae), *Bicyclus aethiops* (Satyridae), *Charaxes phoebus* (Nymphalidae), *Acraea oscari*, *Acraea ungemachi*, and *Acraea safie* (Acraeidae). There are also numerous endemic subspecies, some of them very distinct. Carcasson (1964) lists some widespread montane forest species that do not occur in the Abyssinian highlands, among them four species of *Papilio* and four species of *Charaxes*. Two genera with many species, *Cymothoe* and *Euriphene* (both Nymphalidae), that occur in both lowland and montane forest in the more equatorial parts of Africa are absent from Abyssinia.

Savanna. Most of the lowland and montane forest of Africa is surrounded by savanna (Fig. 1.2). There is evidence that savanna areas of one form or another are expanding at the expense of forest presumably because of human activities, especially burning. Most savanna butterflies are more widely distributed than forest species, and in addition there are fewer species. The most conspicuous savanna species are Pieridae, some genera of Nymphalidae, notably *Precis*, and Acraeidae, especially one or two common species of *Acraea*. Many species occur most abundantly where there is a forest–savanna mosaic or where forest borders on savanna. Some of these are essentially savanna species and include such widespread and common butterflies as *Papilio demodocus*, *Graphium pylades* (Papilionidae), *Precis terea* (Nymphalidae), *Acraea natalica* (Acraeidae), and *Axiocerses harpax* (Lycaenidae), while others are essentially forest species and include *Papilio nireus*, *Graphium policenes* (Papilionidae), *Leptosia alcesta* (Pieridae), and many species of *Charaxes* (Nymphalidae). In some savanna areas gallery forest extends along rivers and the species mentioned above (and others) occur in abundance.

One of the most characteristic savanna butterflies in Africa is *Graphium pylades* (Papilionidae). It occurs throughout the continent and shows considerable geographical variation in colour and in pattern. In southern Tanzania and Rhodesia there is a closely similar species, *Graphium taboranus*, while in South Africa there is another similar species, *Graphium morania*. This suggests that populations have several times been isolated in the southern savanna and that this isolation has been of sufficient duration for speciation to have occurred. In savanna north of 5° S. only *Graphium pylades* occurs and there are no similar species. The isolation of the two southern species probably occurred when forest was much more extensive than it is now. The two subspecies of *Graphium pylades*, and *Graphium taboranus* and *Graphium morania* are shown in Fig. 2.4.

FIG. 2.4. *Graphium pylades pylades* (upper left) occurs by itself north of approximately 5° S. *Graphium pylades angolanus* (upper right) occurs to the south with *Graphium taboranus* (lower left) in southern Tanzania and Rhodesia, and with *Graphium morania* (lower right) in southern Africa. The butterflies are white with black markings and some red on the underside.

Geographically isolated really dry areas of savanna (or subdesert as it might be called) as found in Somalia and the Kalahari, share a number of species. There appear to be relatively few endemic species in such areas, but thus far collecting in the dry savanna of Africa has not been extensive.

There are some peculiarities in the butterfly fauna of the extreme south of Africa. Several groups of butterflies with few species to the north are rich in species in the south, and a large proportion of these species is endemic. A few genera, notably *Durbania* (Lycaenidae), are endemic to South Africa.

A recent report on a collection of butterflies from Tibesti, northern Chad (Bernardi 1962), is of interest because the area is isolated well to the north of the savanna. The area is mountainous and the collection consists of a mixture of Palaearctic (North African and southern European) species and Ethiopian species. The Palaearctic species include *Pontia daplidice, Colias croceus* (Pieridae), *Vanessa atalanta,* and *Vanessa cardui* (Nymphalidae). Some of the Ethiopian species recorded, *Colotis evippe, Eurema brigitta,* and *Catopsilia florella* (Pieridae) occur in my garden at Freetown in Sierra Leone. Moreau (1966), discussing the bird fauna of Tibesti, mentions the same kind of mixture of Palaearctic and Ethiopian species.

FIG. 2.5. Male *Colotis evippe*. A white butterfly with black markings and a red bar in the forewing. Females are darker, extremely variable, and usually lacking the red.

The occurrence of *Colotis evippe* (Fig. 2.5) as a distinct subspecies in Tibesti provides evidence that the Sahara was in the past a much more favourable habitat for butterflies than it is now. *Colotis evippe* is one of the few species in the genus which is associated much more with forest edge than with true savanna, and in cleared forest in West Africa it is usually the only species of the genus present. Fig. 2.6 shows the northern limit of the species in Africa and the occurrence of the now isolated population in Tibesti.

Montane grassland and swamp. Montane grassland includes areas over 1600 metres that are not forested, such areas being chiefly in East Africa and always in proximity to montane forest. Some genera and species associated with montane grassland are essentially Palaearctic, including *Pieris brassicoides* and *Colias electo* (Pieridae), and the small copper butterfly, *Lycaena phlaeas* (Lycaenidae), a well-known European and North American species that occurs as three distinct subspecies in different parts of East Africa, including Abyssinia.

An astonishing variety of African butterflies are confined to swamps,

FIG. 2.6. Map showing the northern limit of distribution of *Colotis evippe* in Africa and the isolated population in Tibesti. From Bernardi (1962).

mostly at high elevations. The following species are listed by Carcasson (1964):

Mylothris bernice (Pieridae), confined to papyrus swamps throughout tropical Africa,

Eurema hapale (Pieridae), high level swamps in tropical Africa and Madagascar,

Ypthima itonia (Satyridae), high level swamps in tropical Africa,

Ypthima mashuna (Satyridae), high level swamps in Mashonaland,

Precis ceryne (Nymphalidae), high level swamps in southern and eastern Africa,

Pseudargynnis hegemone (Nymphalidae), wet meadows in tropical Africa,

Acraea ventura (Acraeidae), high level swamps in tropical Africa,

Acraea bettiana (Acraeidae), high level swamps in western Uganda, Rwanda, Burundi, and the eastern Congo,

Acraea rangatana (Acraeidae), high level swamps in Kenya,

Acraea rahira (Acraeidae), high level swamps in southern and eastern Africa,

Everes hippocrates (Lycaenidae), near streams throughout tropical Africa,

Cupidopsis cissus (Lycaenidae), wet meadows throughout tropical Africa,

Metisella meninx (Hesperiidae), wet meadows in South Africa,

Metisella midas (Hesperiidae), high level swamps in East Africa,

Pelopidas micans and *Kedestes malua* (both Hesperiidae), swamps in tropical Africa.

Derived savanna. In Africa cultivated areas are often abandoned and a succession of plants colonize the area. If the forest is cut down, the land cultivated, and then abandoned, many grasses, which do not occur in forest, colonize. Land originally forest and now under shifting cultivation is often called derived savanna. Gardens that have been developed in forest areas are also derived savanna as they are much more open than the original forest and contain grasses as well as a wide variety of native and introduced weeds, cultivated plants, and trees. In the more humid parts of tropical Africa derived savanna is fast becoming the most important butterfly habitat, and, as is to be expected, the species that occur are a mixture of savanna and forest species, and especially butterflies that are supposedly characteristic of forest edge. I say supposedly because there is little information as to what species really are characteristic of the natural edges of forest.

Derived savanna in the form of gardens provides one of the best habitats for butterflies. Thus in a garden at Freetown, Sierra Leone (Plate 22), I have recorded 26 species of *Charaxes* (Nymphalidae), including both forest and savanna species, a total higher than would be expected in undisturbed forest and considerably higher than would be expected in undisturbed savanna.

General zoogeographical considerations

The butterfly fauna of the Ethiopian region has many affinities with that of the Oriental region. Madagascar presents special problems, as it must initially have been colonized from the African mainland and to a lesser extent from Asia.

Forest butterflies show more endemicity at the generic, specific, and subspecific levels than savanna butterflies. There is abundant evidence that the distribution of forest and savanna in Africa has changed markedly in the past million years (Moreau 1966), and that in the past several hundred years the forest has become increasingly devastated by human activities. Derived savanna and cultivated land are fast becoming the most important butterfly habitats in Africa.

The repeated joining and fragmentation of the forest in Africa has undoubtedly stimulated speciation and subspeciation and has also resulted in spectacular alterations in the range of many species. The potential rate of speciation and subspeciation must be thought of in terms of the number of breeding generations in a period of time and not in terms of the number of years that have elapsed. Differentiation into species or subspecies could occur three or more times more rapidly in tropical Africa than in a temperate region where most species go through one generation a year.

Moreau (1966), summarizing Pleistocene changes in Africa during the last million years, emphasizes that the northern glaciations must have induced quite different climatic and vegetational conditions than those that now exist. In particular he postulates that during the glaciations essentially montane climates must have persisted throughout an area from Abyssinia to South Africa and that many lowland species (he is discussing birds, but the same would apply to butterflies) that were unable to withstand the montane conditions must have retreated to areas west of the Cameroons. This situation may have existed as recently as 18–25 000 years ago and the present pattern of montane and lowland forest and savanna was probably developed as recently as 8000 years ago. There is evidence (Moreau 1966) that the extent of the Sahara desert has varied during the Pleistocene: much of the western Sahara was covered with Mediterranean (not Ethiopian) vegetation as recently as 6000 years ago, and this undoubtedly allowed many butterflies to extend much further north than they do now. The isolated population of *Colotis evippe* (Pieridae) in Tibesti (Fig. 2.6) could easily have been joined to the main population of the species as recently as 6000 years ago. The extreme desert conditions of the present-day Sahara developed about 5000 years ago and with erosion caused by expanding human populations these conditions are undoubtedly still extending to the general detriment of the butterfly fauna of the Ethiopian region.

The lowland forests of West Africa were much reduced and (more importantly) fragmented about 22 000 years ago; those of the Congo basin underwent similar reduction and fragmentation about 50 000 and 12 000 years ago (Moreau 1966). The present Kalahari conditions must have been much extended, perhaps as far as the East Coast, at this time.

Thus Africa has been subjected to spectacular changes in climate and vegetation in the recent past, and one can be reasonably sure that most of the species of butterflies living in Africa have been affected in one way or another by these changes.

3

LIFE HISTORIES

BUTTERFLIES are insects that undergo a complete metamorphosis: there is a distinct larval and pupal stage and the adult butterfly is very different in appearance from the larva. Butterfly larvae are essentially consumers of green vegetation and flowers. There are a few exceptional species, to be discussed later in this chapter, but generally speaking a butterfly obtains its energy as a larva by feeding on living plants. The pupae are effectively immobile and it is only after the adult butterfly has emerged from the pupa (Plate 18) and taken its first flight that further feeding is possible. Larvae feed by chewing vegetation, but adults feed by sucking nectar from flowers and juices from rotten fruit and decaying animal remains, including faeces and urine. There are numerous reports of adult butterflies 'drinking' water from rain puddles, but these are almost certainly incorrect, as the butterflies were probably feeding on sugars or nitrogenous compounds in mammal (including human) urine that happened to have been deposited in a damp situation.

Relative to its body size a larval butterfly consumes an enormous amount of food, much of which is indigestible cellulose, so that large quantities of faeces are produced. Adult butterflies, in contrast, take nectar and juices in relatively small amounts. There are a few exceptions, especially *Charaxes* (Nymphalidae) whose abdomens become much enlarged as a result of apparently excessive feeding on rotten fruit (Plate 39). In many species it seems essential for adults to feed, but in some mating and egg-laying can occur without feeding. The extent to which feeding is essential for survival and reproduction in adult butterflies is not known; many species that take food in the wild will breed in captivity without feeding.

In any ecosystem there are several trophic (feeding) levels. Green plants produce organic material by employing radiant energy from the sun in the process of photosynthesis. Green plants are therefore called producers since they do not obtain energy by feeding. Plants provide energy for all other organisms. Organisms that feed directly on living plants are called primary consumers; those feeding on dead plants are called primary decomposers. Living primary consumers may be eaten by secondary consumers, and these in turn by tertiary consumers, and so on. Dead consumers are utilized by secondary, tertiary, and higher order decomposers. Since there is no long-term accumulation of organic matter on earth it follows that everything produced by the plants is ultimately utilized by other organisms. In a terrestrial ecosystem a relatively small fraction is consumed while the plants are still alive; most plant material is decomposed after the plant has died.

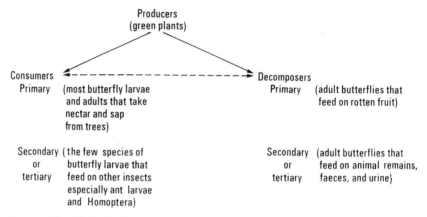

FIG. 3.1. Trophic levels in an ecosystem. Most butterflies can be classified as primary consumers, but a few fit into other categories. The broken line with arrows pointing in both directions indicates the possibility of, for instance, a secondary consumer eating a live primary decomposer or a secondary decomposer eating a dead primary consumer; but as far as butterflies are concerned these possible feeding relations can be ignored.

It is possible to construct a simple trophic diagram (Fig. 3.1) showing the feeding positions of butterflies in an ecosystem. Fig. 3.1 should not be interpreted too rigidly. An individual's trophic position may vary in its lifetime or even within a few minutes. Thus an individual swallowtail butterfly may feed on nectar from a flower (being therefore a primary consumer) and then move to feed on juices from a dead rat (thus becoming a secondary decomposer).

Butterflies are common in the tropics, but compared with other groups of primary consumers, such as moths and grasshoppers, their total consumption of living vegetation is small. Many young larvae feed on the buds and new leaves at the growing points of plants and to some extent inhibit plant growth. Occasionally the gregarious larvae of Acraeidae defoliate plants: in June 1969 at Akosombo, Ghana, I found that larvae of *Acraea eponina* had defoliated *Waltheria* plants that had recently colonized bare ground created by the construction of the Volta dam. Defoliation seems to be more frequent in disturbed than in undisturbed ecosystems where in all probability the populations are more balanced.

With these preliminary remarks about the trophic position of butterflies it is now possible to consider the four stages in a butterfly's life (egg, larva, pupa, adult) with special reference to selected African species.

Eggs and egg-laying

Soon after emergence from the pupa most female butterflies mate and begin laying their eggs a day or so later. An individual female may mate several times with different males and most males are capable of mating with more than one female. The sperm of male butterflies is enclosed in a membranous sac-like spermatophore which can be located after dissection in the bursa copulatrix of the female. Each spermatophore represents a separate mating and by counting the number of spermatophores in the female the number of matings can be determined. The spermatophores empty and tend to collapse as fertilization proceeds, but they are still identifiable in a dissected female. Burns (1966), using this method, has shown that the females of some North American butterflies mate up to five times, and this is also likely in many African species. By marking individuals with coloured ink it can be shown that males of *Acraea encedon* (Acraeidae) can mate with at least four different females (Owen and Chanter 1969).

Female butterflies usually lay their eggs on or near the food-plant of the larvae. Most species presumably locate the food-plant by scent, and many of the repellent chemicals elaborated by plants are undoubtedly used by butterflies as a means of finding the correct plant. Butterflies are remarkably good botanists and mistakes are rare; I have several times identified plants as belonging to the family Passifloraceae by first finding Acraeidae larvae on the leaves.

Many species lay their eggs singly, each on a different leaf or flower. The eggs are fixed to the plant by a sticky substance. Females fly from leaf to leaf and curve their abdomens so that the egg is deposited on the underside of the leaf. Some species, for instance *Catopsilia florella* (Pieridae), lay their eggs on the upperside of the leaf. A few, for instance *Acraea circeis* (Acraeidae), lay their eggs on the woody stems of the food-plant, or on hard objects (pieces of wood, stones, etc.) near the food-plant, as for instance does *Precis octavia* (Nymphalidae). When eggs are not laid directly on the leaves of the food-plant there is often some form of seasonal diapause or aestivation in the egg stage.

Although the majority of butterflies lay their eggs singly, some important groups lay their eggs in large clusters. Thus all species of Acraeidae lay their eggs in clusters either spread out on the underside of a leaf or piled in heaps on the stem.

Butterfly eggs are usually some shade of green or yellow and are often elaborately sculptured. In nearly all species the eggs darken and become conspicuous a day or so before the larva hatches. The first meal taken by a larva is normally its own chitinous egg shell. Butterfly eggs, especially those laid in clusters, are in general remarkably conspicuous against the

background on which they are laid. In the tropics many eggs are eaten
by ants, sometimes within seconds of being laid. In *Danaus chrysippus*
(Danaidae) and *Papilio demodocus* (Papilionidae) I estimate that more than
90 per cent of all eggs laid are eaten by ants.

Larvae

The larva is the main feeding stage in the development of a butterfly.
Butterfly larvae are quite variable in superficial colour and structure. Unlike the adult butterfly, they have biting mouth parts and no compound eyes.
There are more pairs of legs than in the adult but the number is variable.
In many species copious quantities of silk are produced by the labial
glands. Some larvae let out lengths of silk when they fall from the food-
plant and are thus able to climb up again. Silk is also used to spin a pad
during moulting from one instar to the next; this attaches the larva firmly
to the substrate. Young larvae of many species, especially the gregarious
Acraeidae, spin a silken web, presumably as a means of protection from
predators or to prevent them from falling off the food-plant.

The larvae of most Papilionidae (Plates 14 and 16), Pieridae (Plate 16),
Danaidae (Plate 15), Satyridae, and Hesperiidae are relatively smooth and
many are some shade of green with varying amounts of pattern depending
on the particular genus or species. Larvae of Satyridae resemble closely the
grass leaves on which they feed and the larvae of some Pieridae match
their background colour extremely well. The larvae of Lycaenidae (Plate
16) are woodlouse-shaped, the segments are well differentiated, and they
possess a 'honey' gland, which, as will be discussed later, is important in
their relationships with ants. The larvae of Nymphalidae and Acraeidae
(Plate 15) are usually spiny and are often black or brown marked with
paler colours, such as yellow. These larvae are conspicuous on the food-
plant and are presumably unpalatable to predators.

Butterfly larvae moult about five times during their development. At the
time of moulting they stop feeding and remain motionless on the food-
plant. The old skin (cuticle) is shed and some larvae eat this skin before
resuming normal feeding on the plant. During moulting the larvae are
probably more prone to predators as they cannot move and escape. Failure
to moult successfully invariably results in the death of the larva.

Larval foods

The chief food-plants of butterfly larvae are the leaves of angiosperm
plants and trees and there is abundant evidence that the evolution of feeding preferences by different groups of butterflies has taken place side by
side with the evolution and diversification of these plants in the Cretaceous
and Tertiary periods. There is little doubt that plants have undergone a
series of evolutionary adjustments that reduce their exploitation by primary

consumers, including butterfly larvae. Some of these adjustments are the development of thorns and hairs, the presence of a waxy layer over the surface of the leaves, and the elaboration of toxic compounds which play no part in the normal physiology of the plant but which act as deterrents to herbivorous animals. The leaves of many trees in tropical forests are bright red when young and this may be a further protective adaptation as most species of butterflies lay their eggs on green leaves. Much of the food-plant specialization among different groups of butterflies is undoubtedly an evolutionary adjustment to adaptations in the plants themselves. Thus some of the chemical compounds in plants are aromatic and it would appear that this is the way in which an egg-laying female or a larva 'knows' its own food-plant; larvae may be able to discriminate between chemical compounds that are indistinguishable to man's sense of smell. Indeed the choice of a particular food-plant is probably determined not only by the presence of chemical attractants in the plant but also by the presence of repellents in other plants.

Gregarious larvae of the Acraeidae will defoliate large areas of the food-plant, the larvae then moving to a new source of food. Solitary larvae occasionally eat a whole leaf before moving to the next, but very often the leaf is only partly eaten. Patterns of leaf eating tend to be characteristic of the species: some eat holes, others eat from one edge, and some eat symmetrically from both edges. Exactly why a larva should move from an unfinished leaf to a new one is not clear, but possibly the leaves not only serve as food but also as a cryptic background against which the larva is concealed from predators. Most species alternate periods of feeding with periods of rest. Some species feed only at night, others only by day.

Almost all larvae that feed on plants feed on dicotyledons. None is known to feed on ferns or bryophytes, but the Satyridae feed mainly on grasses and other monocotyledons. A few species of Nymphalidae, Lycaenidae and Hesperiidae also feed on grasses. *Acraea encedon* (Acraeidae) feeds on *Commelina*, a monocotyledon, but this is unusual for this family.

In Africa larvae of the Papilionidae feed primarily on Rutaceae (*Papilio*) and Anonaceae (*Graphium*). *Citrus*, which has been introduced into Africa from Asia as a crop, belongs to the Rutaceae, and a remarkable number of species of *Papilio* now utilize *Citrus* as a food-plant. In Sierra Leone I have recorded *Papilio demodocus*, *Papilio dardanus*, *Papilio nireus*, and *Papilio menestheus* larvae on *Citrus*, and other species have been found on it elsewhere in Africa. In tropical Africa the main food-plant of *Papilio demodocus* is now *Citrus*, but larvae are still occasionally found on *Fagara* and other wild Rutaceae which were presumably its original food-plants. *Papilio demodocus* also lays its eggs on cultivated marigolds and *Cosmos* daisies; the resulting larvae normally die in the third or fourth instar, but occasionally small adults are produced. It is probable that these garden flowers, which are quite unrelated to the Rutaceae, contain certain aromatic compounds also found in the Rutaceae and that the presence of such compounds induces some females to lay on the wrong plant. In South Africa, *Papilio demodocus* larvae feed on Umbelliferae as well as Rutaceae, the Umbelliferae-feeding larvae being more variegated in pattern than those on Rutaceae (Plate 16) (Clarke, Dickson, and Sheppard 1963). A large group of Papilionidae, unrepresented on mainland Africa, but with a single species, *Atroplaneura antenor*, on Madagascar, feed mainly on Aristolochiaceae, which includes Dutchman's pipe, a well-known climber grown in tropical gardens.

The larvae of the African Pieridae are very much associated with the Capparidaceae and to a lesser extent with the Cruciferae, a family of plants frequently utilized by temperate species of Pieridae. Members of the Capparidaceae are especially common in the savanna and indeed Pieridae are themselves more common in savanna. One very common species, *Catopsilia florella*, feeds on wild and cultivated species of *Cassia* (Caesalpinaceae), the larvae eating both the flowers and the young leaves, sometimes to such an extent that the growth pattern of the tree is affected. Indeed the damage caused by *Catopsilia florella* larvae to the growing points of the trees and the damage caused by goat moth (Cossidae) larvae which bore into the woody stems results in many ornamental *Cassia* trees dying. *Colias electo* larvae, like the larvae of temperate species of *Colias*, do considerable damage to clover and lucerne crops, especially in South Africa. Most members of the genus *Mylothris* feed on Loranthaceae and related families. The food-plant of *Pseudopontia paradoxa*, the very distinctive pierid confined to tropical African forests, was until recently not known. In January 1970 I found females laying on *Pseuderanthemum tunicatum* (Acanthaceae) and on another as yet unidentified plant of a different family in primary forest in Sierra Leone. Unfortunately it was not possible to rear them and the life history of this peculiar species remains unknown.

The Danaidae are virtually restricted to milkweeds, Asclepiadaceae, and the closely similar Apocynaceae, but many members of the Apocynaceae have waxy leaves and are probably not utilized as much as they might be if the leaves were not waxy. *Danaus chrysippus* larvae now feed extensively on *Asclepias curassavica*, which has been introduced into Africa from tropical America as a garden plant. *Amauris* feed chiefly on climbing milkweeds in forest and forest edge. Many milkweeds, including *Asclepias curassavica* and *Calotropis procera* (a native African species), contain heart poisons in their tissues, and most herbivores would presumably avoid eating these plants.

As already mentioned, the Satyridae are mainly grass feeders but, as in

8. *Lophira* savanna in Sierra Leone in the wet season. In the dry season the grass is burnt, but the *Lophira* trees are fire-resistant

9. Heavily grazed savanna in the Western Rift of Uganda. The protection of large mammals in national parks sometimes results in over-grazing. The clumps of vegetation originate from termite mounds. *Capparis*, one of the commonest bushes in the clumps, is the food-plant of several Pieridae. (*Photo by Jennifer Owen*)

most temperate satyrids, it is not known to what extent different species of butterflies are restricted to particular species of grass. Some species, such as *Melanitis leda*, seem to feed on any species of grass, including the leaves of cultivated cereal crops such as rice and maize. *Elymnias* feed on palms in tropical Asia, but I do not think that the food-plant of *Elymnias bammakoo*, the only African species, has been found. The food-plants of the Satyridae are extremely poorly known, possibly because tropical grasses have not stimulated a great deal of interest among naturalists. The life histories of many South African Satyridae have been described and figured by Van Son (1955).

There is much variation in the food-plants of the Nymphalidae, which is to be expected as the family is large and diverse. Butterflies of the genus *Charaxes* are among the best known African species, mainly because they are large and beautifully coloured and have therefore aroused the interest of collectors who know that the best way of getting good specimens is to rear them from larvae. The food-plants of about fifty African species of *Charaxes* are known. About 28 families of plants are utilized, nearly all dicotyledons, but several species feed on monocotyledons, including bamboo and cultivated sorghum. The species that feed on monocotyledons all appear to have alternative dicotyledon food-plants. Many of the common Nymphalidae found in gardens throughout Africa feed on weeds. Thus *Hypolimnas misippus* feeds on *Portulaca* (Portulacaceae) and *Blepharis maderaspatensis* (Acanthaceae) which are common weeds throughout West Africa, and several species of *Precis* feed on *Asystasia* (Acanthaceae) and *Solenostemon* (Labiatae), both common garden weeds.

The Nymphalidae as a whole feed on an enormous array of plants; indeed one or more species feeds on most of the families of tropical dicotyledons. Very little is known of the food-plants of the forest genera (*Najas*, *Euriphene*, etc.), and most of the published records are for species found in gardens and cultivated areas. Ehrlich and Raven (1965) have listed the known food-plants (by family) of the Nymphalidae of the world. The most important families utilized are Ulmaceae, Urticaceae, Moraceae, Convolvulaceae, Labiatae, Portulacaceae, Verbenaceae, and Euphorbiaceae.

The larvae of many species of Acraeidae feed on Passifloraceae; it is possible that all species of *Bematistes* are confined to forest climbers, *Adenia* and related genera, and some of the larger species of *Acraea* also feed on *Adenia* growing at the edge of forest and in cultivated land. There is however considerable variation in the food-plants of *Acraea*: at Freetown, Sierra Leone, I have found larvae on Tiliaceae (*Acraea bonasia* and *Acraea eponina*), Verbenaceae (*Acraea camaena*), Urticaceae (*Acraea circeis*, *Acraea parrhasia*, *Acraea lycoa*), Violaceae (*Acraea quirina*), Commelinaceae (*Acraea encedon*), Sterculiaceae (*Acraea eponina*), and Passifloraceae

(*Acraea egina, Acraea natalica, Acraea rogersi, Acraea zetes*). Although it is sometimes stated that the Acraeidae are effectively confined to the Passifloraceae, there are obviously numerous exceptions in the genus *Acraea*.

The single species of Libytheidae found in Africa, *Libythea labdaca*, and the related species on Madagascar, presumably feed on Ulmaceae as do all other *Libythea* in the world.

The food-plants of the African Riodinidae are apparently not known, but one African genus, *Abisara*, occurs in tropical Asia and the larvae feed on Myrsinaceae.

The Lycaenidae are the most varied family of African butterflies as far as larval food is concerned. Members of the subfamily Lipteninae feed on lichens, the forest species feeding on lichens growing on the trunks of trees, while *Durbania*, a genus confined to South Africa, feeds on lichens growing on rocks in open places. Other food-plants, including grasses, have been listed for the Lipteninae, but I am doubtful of the validity of these records. The Liphyrinae are entirely carnivorous, feeding on ant larvae and Homoptera; the relationships between ants, Homoptera, and Liphyrinae are discussed in more detail later in this chapter. Most species of Lycaeninae are also associated with ants, but the larvae feed on plants. A great many species feed on the flowers and inside the green pods of Leguminosae, and some species are destructive to bean crops. The food-plants of tropical African species are poorly known, but there is detailed information on the life histories of some South African species (Murray *n.d.*). There is a tendency in this subfamily for genera to be restricted to particular plant families: *Myrina* to Moraceae and *Iolaus* to Loranthaceae, for example.

The Hesperiidae also utilize a wide variety of food-plants, but records are scanty for tropical Africa, except for the genus *Coeliades* whose conspicuous larvae have been found on a wide variety of plants, including cultivated lilies. Pinhey (1965) lists the food-plants of many South African species, and records *Coeliades forestan* on as many as five different families of plants.

It is difficult to generalize about the food of butterfly larvae. Satyridae are more or less restricted to grasses and Danaidae to milkweeds. The Pieridae are especially associated with the Capparidaceae, the Acraeidae to some extent with the Passifloraceae, and the Papilionidae with Rutaceae and Anonaceae. No broad associations can be detected in the Nymphalidae and Hesperiidae. One subfamily of Lycaenidae is carnivorous and another feeds on lichens. The association of many Lycaenidae with ants is of considerable interest and luckily there are careful observations on these associations in some of the West African species. Since these observations are not well known I propose to go into the topic in some detail.

Associations with ants

Ants are extremely abundant in the tropics. A dead insect is almost immediately discovered and eaten by ants, and initially it is hard to see why living butterfly larvae are not attacked and eaten by ants to any great extent. It appears that many small herbivorous insects have in one way or another come to terms with the ants. There are two main ways in which this is achieved: by defensive mechanisms including behaviour that deters potential ant predators, or by the secretion of compounds that are so attractive to the ants that the insect is protected rather than eaten. Many small plant bugs (Homoptera) live in close association with ants, some even inside the nests of large species such as the tailor ant, *Oecophylla*, which constructs tents of leaves in trees. But some ants are undoubtedly very destructive and are not easily deterred. Thus driver or safari ants are often seen in hundreds of thousands moving in a fixed direction; these ants seem to attack anything they meet and there are probably few insects that can defend themselves from them.

Although ants are predators, there exists in the Lycaenidae a series of apparently symbiotic relationships with ants that are far removed from the usual predator–prey relationship that one might expect. The most detailed account of the associations of African Lycaenidae with ants is in two lengthy papers based on observations made in southern Nigeria more than fifty years ago (Lamborn 1913, Farquharson 1921). These two papers, which are hardly ever cited, consist in part of numerous letters sent by the authors to E. B. Poulton and others; both are extensively edited and annotated by Poulton. Lamborn and Farquharson made detailed and painstaking observations in the field, often under most difficult conditions, and sent notes and specimens, including the butterflies, their larvae, and the associated ants and Homoptera, to Poulton who in turn identified the specimens and stimulated further observations. Reading these papers one is impressed by two things in particular: first, the incredible patience and dedication that both men put into their field observations, and secondly, the nowadays non-existent luxury of being able to publish field notes and letters in a scientific journal.†

Fifty years ago the taxonomy of the African Lycaenidae was poorly known and many of the scientific names used in these two papers are no longer valid, and so in the account that follows I have used in part the nomenclature proposed by Clench in Fox *et al.* (1965).

All the subfamilies of Lycaenidae are involved in associations with ants, but there are important differences between them. The Lipteninae are mainly forest butterflies, but in South Africa there are species that

---

† Farquharson's paper, which includes an editorial by Poulton, and a systematic and descriptive appendix by 13 specialist entomologists, is 212 pages long.

inhabit rocky open country. As far as is known the larvae of most species feed on lichens and similar plants growing on the trunks of trees and on rocks. It is likely that the larvae of all species are associated with ants. The larva of *Teratoneura isabellae*, discovered by Farquharson, is quite unlike the larva of any other butterfly (Fig. 3.2). It bears a strong resemblance

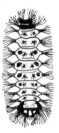

FIG. 3.2. Larva of *Teratoneura isabellae*. The larva is about 18 mm long.

to larvae of lymantrid moths. On each segment there are lateral and dorsal rows of tubercles from each of which arises a tuft of fine hairs. On segments five to eight there are dark patches made up of masses of urticating spicules. The larva is brightly coloured red, green, and yellow, and these colours enhance its lymantrid appearance. The adult butterflies and the larvae seem always to be found in association with trees containing nests of ants, *Crematogaster*, which often build large and conspicuous nests in forest trees. Farquharson reports seeing adult butterflies drinking the secretion of Coccidae (Homoptera) which live in association with the ants, the ants also drinking the coccid secretions. The larvae live among the columns of ants that move continually up and down the ant tree to and from the nest.

Farquharson reports having seen larvae moving down the tree to pupate meeting ant columns coming up, the ants moving aside to let them pass. He also pushed larvae away from the ant column but they returned immediately and were obviously closely attached to the ants. *Teratoneura isabellae* evidently does not feed on either ant larvae or coccids; all Farquharson's observations were of larvae feeding on vegetable matter on the tree trunk, particularly lichens.† The larva of a lymantrid moth, *Naroma signifera*, also lives in association with the ants and is found together with *Teratoneura isabellae* larvae; indeed it looks very like the lycaenid larva and has (like many lymantrid larvae) urticating spicules and spines. It is probably thus protected from the ants and the possibility exists that *Teratoneura isabellae* larvae are mimics of the moth larvae and are so not

† Farquharson examined microscopically the faeces of *Teratoneura isabellae* for fungal spores and similar material. In 1917 he wrote to Poulton, 'I am ashamed to confess that I do not remember whether any group of lichens has a brown mycelium.' I wonder how many biologists working in Africa today would feel similarly ashamed at their lack of knowledge?

attacked by the ants. There seems no evidence in this case of the ants obtaining secretions from the lycaenid larvae.

Farquharson worked out many aspects of the life history of other Lipteninae associated with ants. In many species his initial observation was of the adult butterfly drinking the secretions of the associated coccids. He followed this up with a search for the larvae on the ant tree. It appears that all the species he observed feed on plant material, chiefly lichens, and that the larvae are more or less lymantrid-like and live in close proximity to ants which do not molest them in any way. Much of the area of southern Nigeria where Farquharson was working was being planted with cocoa. This planting has continued in Nigeria and elsewhere in West Africa, especially Ghana, and the forest has been extensively cut down to make room for cocoa trees which are often grown among the remnants of the original forest. *Crematogaster* nests are destroyed in this process and the lycaenids associated with them may have become much reduced in numbers in the past fifty years. In some areas ant trees are probably so isolated from each other that the associated lycaenids now occur in discrete populations centred around such trees and isolated from other populations.

The association between ants and the next subfamily, the Liphyrinae, is somewhat similar, except that the Liphyrinae are undoubted carnivores. For detailed information, again with introductory notes by Poulton, the paper by Lamborn (1913) can be considered as a classic in African entomology. One species of Liphyrinae, *Euliphyra mirifica* (Fig. 3.3), looks

FIG. 3.3. *Euliphyra mirifica.*

superficially like a skipper (when I first collected an adult butterfly of this species in Sierra Leone I mistook it for a skipper). Its larvae are associated with tailor ants, *Oecophylla*, which construct leaf nests in trees (*Alstonia*, *Citrus*, cocoa, and others) by weaving the leaves together. Almost all *Oecophylla* nests contain Homoptera and the ants drink the secretions of these plant bugs. Lamborn describes how he first found *Euliphyra mirifica* larvae by cutting a 'window' in the ant nest and seeing larvae inside. The larva has a hard leathery cuticle into which the head is normally withdrawn. At times, however, the head is thrust out and the larva is seen to have a long 'neck'. When moving the larva will swing the head from side to side as if seeking food. Lamborn observed (to his astonishment) that the lycaenid larvae thrust their heads into the jaws of ants returning with food for their own larvae, and so obtain food. Large ants feeding smaller ants sometimes broke off and fed lycaenid larvae. When disturbed the ants pick up the lycaenid larvae and carry them to safety as if they were their own larvae. These observations show that *Euliphyra mirifica* larvae are treated by the ants as if they were ant larvae or young worker ants, but it is not clear what the ants obtain in return, if anything.

The genus *Aslauga* includes several species that also live in association with *Crematogaster* ants. The ants obtain secretions from coccids (but evidently do not eat them) while the lycaenid larvae feed on the coccids. *Megalopalpus zymna* lives in close association with *Pheidole* ants which attend and obtain secretions from Homoptera of the families Jassidae and Membracidae. The female butterflies lay their eggs near the ant shelter which is almost invariably centred around a group of Homoptera. Lamborn observed adult butterflies feeding from the Homoptera secretions. He also thought that *Megalopalpus zymna* larvae simulated the caresses of ants by vibrating their legs on the Homoptera and by so doing were able to approach closely. He describes how larvae thus engaged suddenly move forward and seize the Homoptera, biting them behind the head. Jassidae and Membracidae are relatively active and so *Megalopalpus zymna* has to 'catch' its prey, unlike *Aslauga* which feeds on immobile coccids. *Megalopalpus zymna* larvae eat both nymphs and adults of the bugs and the attendant ants evidently do not molest the butterfly larvae. The larvae of *Lachnocnema bibulus* also prey on Jassidae that are attended by ants. In Sierra Leone I have seen females of *Lachnocnema bibulus* laying eggs on the stems of *Sarcocephalus esculentus* (Rubiaceae), a savanna shrub that has colonized areas of cleared forest. The females lay their eggs just below colonies of adult and immature jassids, and the young larvae, which are extremely active, move up to the growing point of the stem where the jassids are aggregated. Both young and adult jassids are seized and eaten by full-grown *Lachnocnema bibulus* larvae, but I could never ascertain what the young larvae feed upon, although I suspect they take some jassid eggs. Ants are in constant attendance upon both the jassids and the butterfly larvae. On numerous occasions I saw ants take something from the mouth of the larvae (Plate 17); I could never be sure what was exchanged but it appeared to be regurgitated liquid food. Full-grown larvae pupate on the leaves of the plant and for the first two days are constantly attended by ants; later the ants ignore them. Around Freetown, *Lachnocnema bibulus* has become a common garden butterfly and is always associated with new growths of *Sarcocephalus esculentus* upon which the jassids occur abundantly. The species of ant in attendance seems to depend on the site of the nearest ant nest; I have seen six or seven different species of ant in attendance, but usually no more than one species on a plant. It may be noted that in West Africa the habit of gardeners of cutting back *Sarcocephalus esculentus* stimulates fresh growth, which leads to favourable conditions for the jassids and of course for the butterflies.

The association with ants is different again in the subfamily Lycaeninae. Here the butterfly larvae feed on plants but are attended by ants. Homoptera, although often present and attended by ants, play no part in the life history of the butterfly. In many genera (for instance *Deudorix*, *Myrina*) the ants seem to obtain secretions from the butterfly larvae. The larvae of *Myrina* feed on the new leaves of fig trees, *Ficus*, *Chlorophora*, and others, and are invariably attended by ants; I have seen twenty or more ants of at least four different species attending a single larva. My own observations and those of Lamborn (1913) indicate that the ants obtain a secretion from the dorsal gland of the larva (Plate 16), but Murray (*n.d.*) thinks that the ants feed on the latex from the leaves of the tree which appears as the larvae feed. In this connection it may be noted that ants are in constant attendance upon the larvae of *Catopsilia florella* (Pieridae) as they feed on *Cassia* leaves; these ants undoubtedly take juices from the freshly eaten edges of the leaves as the larva does not produce a secretion and the ants are never seen actually on the larva (Plate 16). Numerous observations on other Lycaeninae strongly support the view that there is a symbiotic relationship between the larvae and ants in which the larvae obtain some degree of protection from predators (including ant predators) and the ants obtain the sugary secretion from the dorsal gland. Indeed one of the best ways to find Lycaeninae larvae is to search for groups of ants on plants suspected of being the larval food-plant.

Predators and parasites of butterfly larvae

Most passerine birds and most lizards and amphibians are insectivorous and undoubtedly eat many butterfly larvae. There are numerous scattered records of these vertebrates eating larvae but such records lack detail and usually describe isolated observations. Predatory insects such as reduviid bugs also eat butterfly larvae. Some of the paper wasps, such as *Polistes* (Vespidae), capture butterfly larvae and chew them up before taking them to the nest for the larval wasps; the adult wasps obtain their own nutrients from the nectar of flowers. Spiders are probably also important predators.

Three large groups of Hymenoptera, the Ichneumonidae, Braconidae, and Chalcidoidea, are often referred to as parasites of other insects, but are really predators as the host always dies. The word 'parasitoid' has been coined to describe these predators. Female ichneumonids and braconids

lay their eggs on the larvae (sometimes on the eggs or pupae) of other insects. The predatory larvae feed inside the host on its body tissues and the
host eventually dies, sometimes first pupating prematurely. Most ichneumonids and chalcids and many braconids live on Lepidoptera larvae and it
is likely that all species of butterflies are affected although, at least in
Africa, host records are few. It was at one time thought that each species
of predator was restricted to one host, or at least to a group of similar
hosts, but it now appears that many of the species occur on many kinds of
host. Very little is known about the biology of these Hymenoptera in
Africa, indeed most of the species present in Africa are probably undescribed. From July 1964 to June 1965 I collected 1291 individuals of
232 species of ichneumonid in a garden at Kampala, Uganda. The collection was sent to Dr. Henry Townes, a specialist in the group, who found
that most of the species and some of the genera were new to science.
Townes (1969) estimates that 1618 species of ichneumonid have been
described from the Ethiopian region but thinks that this represents no
more than 15 per cent of the total number of species present in the region.
He thinks that there are some 60 000 species of Ichneumonidae in the
world, more than the total number of species of vertebrates; hence with
the possible exception of the beetle family Curculionidae these insects are
the largest family of animals. Probably all butterfly larvae are utilized by
ichneumonids, but the prospects for a better understanding of the importance of this family in the biology of African and other tropical butterflies
are at present remote as few people nowadays have the patience and skill
to undertake such a task.

Flies of the family Tachinidae have a similar predatory relationship with
the larvae of butterflies and other insects. The adult flies visit flowers for
nectar but lay their eggs on insect larvae or on the food-plant of the host
larva, which when infected always dies, the fully fed tachinid larvae leaving the dying host and pupating on or near the ground. Some species of
tachinid are effectively viviparous and deposit small larvae on the cuticle
of the host. In Sierra Leone the larvae of *Danaus chrysippus* (Danaidae) are
almost 100 per cent infected by tachinids at certain times of the year,
particularly at the beginning of the dry season. It would seem that these
flies must play an important part in the regulation of population size in
Danaus chrysippus and other species similarly infected.

Butterfly larvae are sometimes found to contain parasitic nematode
worms in their tissues. They are also subject to infection from viruses and
bacteria. Larvae reared in captivity sometimes die suddenly, especially if
crowded in a humid environment, and it would appear that viruses are
responsible. In Sierra Leone I have occasionally found the larvae of *Acraea
encedon* (Acraeidae) with red mites, Trombidiidae, attached; such larvae
slowly die, the mites probably extracting nutrients from their tissues.

Graphium tynderaeus (emerald green with black markings)	*Graphium latreillianus* (leaf green with black markings)
Graphium adamastor (black and white)	*Graphium leonidas* (pale blue with black markings)

2 cm

Papilio menestheus
(black and yellow)

10. Some Papilionidae of West African forests. All these species may be found feeding at patches of mammal urine. *Graphium leonidas* is frequently found in gardens, but the other species are effectively confined to the forest

Antanartia delius
(red with black markings)

Precis terea
(yellow and brown)

Byblia acheloia
(orange and black)

Precis octavia
(orange and black wet-season form)

Precis cloanthe
(orange with black markings)

Precis oenone
(black with iridescent blue patches
in hindwing and white subapical bar
in forewing)

Vanessa cardui
(salmon pink with black and white
markings)

Precis octavia
(dark brown, blue, and red dry-season
form)

11. Some common African Nymphalidae

Catuna crithea	Cynandra opis, female
Catuna oberthuri	Euriphene gambiae, female
Catuna angustata	Euriphene probably caerulea, female

12. Brown and yellow forest Nymphalidae. A remarkable number of species are brown with intricate yellow markings, as shown. In the three related species on the left the males and females are alike; in the three species on the right the males are quite different in appearance. In Sierra Leone *Catuna crithea* is the only member of the genus in most forests, but in the extreme east of the country the other two species also occur. A fourth species is known from Liberia. Slightly enlarged

Acraea zetes, male	*Acraea natalica*, male
Acraea egina, male	*Acraea bonasia*, male
Acraea camaena, female	*Acraea pharsalus*, male
Acraea circeis, male	*Acraea circeis*, female

13. Common West African members of the genus *Acraea* (Acraeidae). Many species are orange with black markings. Of those shown, *Acraea camaena* is brown and yellow, and the male of *Acraea circeis* yellow and black with a semi-transparent forewing. Until recently the male and female of *Acraea circeis* were regarded as distinct species, but rearing larvae and eggs obtained in gardens at Freetown, Sierra Leone, has shown that the two are of one species

Defensive mechanisms of larvae

Butterfly larvae are presumably protected to some extent from predators by their general shape and texture. Birds evidently avoid the spiny larvae of Nymphalidae and Acraeidae, but will eat large numbers of smooth larvae, such as those of *Catopsilia florella* (Pieridae). Some larvae live in clusters enclosed in a silk web, and this probably affords them some degree of protection. The larvae of Pieridae, Satyridae, and Lycaenidae are often green and blend remarkably well with the leaves on which they feed. Gregarious larvae will jerk the front parts of the body when disturbed and when this is done synchronously by a group of larvae it probably deters predators.

The larvae of Papilionidae possess a gland, the osmeterium, located mid-dorsally just behind the head. The gland consists of a two-horned invagination of the neck membrane and is normally hidden beneath the cuticle. If a larva is prodded the gland is suddenly everted and a strong odour is produced from the two horns which appear to glisten with secretion. Eisner and Meinwald (1965) found that the secretion produced by the larvae of *Papilio machaon* (a northern temperate species) contains isobutyric and 2-methylbutyric acid, and that the secretion deters ants. In *Papilio machaon* the same secretion is found if the larval food-plant is changed and it is therefore evidently synthesized by the growing larva and not obtained from the food-plant. The secretion can easily be collected on small squares of filter paper and if these are sealed in a tube the contents can later be chemically analysed. Dr. T. Eisner suggested that I should collect the secretion from *Papilio demodocus*. This was done and we found that the same two compounds were present but in different proportions from those found in *Papilio machaon*. It is known that the secretion deters ants, but it probably also deters ichneumonids and tachinids from laying their eggs on the larvae.

There has been much speculation about the supposedly toxic or repellent properties of some butterfly larvae, but only recently have biologists and chemists got together and initiated investigations into the nature of the chemical compounds. There are two general possibilities: first, that the larvae obtain toxic compounds directly from the food-plants (many plants contain the requisite compounds), and secondly, that the larvae synthesize their own compounds. Most of the investigations thus far have been on European and North American species, but the compounds in one African butterfly, *Danaus chrysippus* (Danaidae), have been investigated, together with those in the closely similar American species, *Danaus plexippus* (Reichstein, von Euw, Parsons, and Rothschild 1968). Heart poisons were found in adults of both species and these are also present in the larval food-plants, Asclepiadaceae. Thus the larvae obtain their unpalatable qualities from the food-plant. Another consequence of being able to feed on toxic milkweeds is that these plants are unpalatable to most herbivores and so Danaidae tend not to suffer from food-plant deprivation.

Pupae

Almost all butterfly pupae are protectively coloured and are attached in some way to vegetation (twigs, tree trunks, leaves) or to rocks or the walls of buildings. The larvae of Pieridae, Satyridae, and Hesperiidae often pupate without moving away from the food-plant. Lycaenidae associated with ants pupate in or near the ant nests. Papilionidae, Danaidae, Nymphalidae, and Acraeidae usually leave the food-plant and travel considerable distances in search of a suitable site.

Some species have become adapted to pupating on buildings and similar structures erected by man. Thus in 1961–3 the larvae of *Acraea pentapolis* (Acraeidae) were defoliating the *Musanga* trees, at that time about ten metres high, that had been planted in the Science Quadrangle of Makerere University College, Uganda. When fully fed the larvae left the trees and climbed the walls of adjacent buildings and pupated under window ledges. No pupae were found at any other site. In Africa *Musanga* trees are confined to secondary forest and only rarely are they planted near buildings. What happens to the pupae in a more natural site is not known.

In captivity the larvae of *Acraea encedon* and other species of Acraeidae tend to cluster in one part of the breeding cage at the time of pupation; this clustering does not seem to occur in the wild, and it would be of interest to know what stimulates this unusual behaviour in the laboratory.

Presumably the pupae of *Danaus chrysippus* and other Danaidae are unpalatable to predators, but they are green or brownish and not warningly coloured like the larvae and adults. The pupae of *Bematistes* (Acraeidae) and some Nymphalidae are quite spiny and this is presumably a protective device, but in general it would appear that butterfly pupae are protected by their colours and patterns and by the tendency of the larvae to seek out and pupate in relatively safe sites. In many African butterflies the pupal stage lasts only a very short time (a week or two), but a few species have a longer pupal period, and in some the pupal stage is when seasonal aestivation occurs.

Adult butterflies

Food and feeding

All butterflies have a sucking proboscis and most species feed. Different families of butterflies have somewhat different feeding habits which may be classified as follows:

Papilionidae. The swallowtails feed mainly at flowers, and are evidently able to utilize species of flowers that other butterflies ignore. Such flowers include *Hibiscus* and *Bougainvillea*, garden shrubs that are also visited by sunbirds in Africa and by hummingbirds in tropical America, and so the possibility arises of birds and butterflies competing for nectar. Swallow-tails regularly visit red flowers, which are not attractive to most other butterflies. Thus *Delonix regia*, a tree grown in gardens throughout the tropics (it is a native of Madagascar), flowers at the beginning of the rains, and its abundant red flowers attract numerous swallowtails. Some individual swallowtails become so covered with red pollen from these flowers that in flight they appear to be different exotic species, and sometimes an individual is hardly able to fly because so much pollen is attached to the wings and body. Many forest swallowtails, especially species of *Graphium* (Plate 10), visit patches of mammal urine and faeces and decomposing animals. In Africa patches of human urine often occur along roads and tracks and a passing vehicle will crush a great cluster of butterflies feeding at the urine. *Graphium policenes* is often attracted to the crushed body of another butterfly, including a member of its own species, and will feed at the exposed tissues.

Pieridae. Most species visit flowers and in the savanna many species also feed from patches of urine and from animal remains. At certain times of the year and at certain places great clusters of *Belenois* and *Eurema* may be seen feeding on urine, while at other times of the year urine is ignored. Presumably this has something to do with the availability of other attractive substances. In the primary forests of Sierra Leone *Pseudopontia paradoxa* sometimes congregates and feeds at the flowers of species of Rubiaceae and Acanthaceae growing on the forest floor.

Danaidae. The monarchs are mainly nectar feeders and in particular visit the flowers of weeds, such as *Tridax*, that grow in open places. *Danaus limniace* at times feeds on urine; I once saw hundreds of this species at patches of urine on roads in the Budongo Forest, Uganda. I also observed an unusual feeding association between *Danaus chrysippus* and the grasshopper *Zonocerus variegatus* at Cape Coast, Ghana. The grass-hoppers were feeding on the leaves and stems of *Heliotropium indicum* and the butterflies had congregated to feed on plant juices that appeared where the grasshoppers chewed the leaves and stems. Up to forty butterflies were seen around a single plant where the grasshoppers were abundant.

Satyridae. Almost all species visit flowers and most feed from rotten fruit. A few species visit animal remains, but this seems unusual in the family. Two of the largest species in Africa, *Melanitis leda* and *Elymnias bammakoo*, hardly ever visit flowers, but are immediately attracted to decaying bananas and similar fruit.

Nymphalidae. There is considerable variation in feeding habits between genera. *Charaxes* hardly ever visit flowers but obtain exceptionally large quantities of liquid food from rotten fruit. Many *Charaxes* collected at fruit have their abdomens so distended (Plate 39) that with incautious handling the abdomen breaks and the fruit juice floods out. In Sierra Leone I have found that most species of *Charaxes* that visit fruit will also come down to animal remains. *Charaxes paphianus* seems exceptional in that it does not come to fruit but instead is a frequent visitor to faeces and decaying animals. *Charaxes* will also feed from sap oozing from a damaged tree. Dr. Malcolm Edmunds tells me that he has observed thirteen species feeding at the sap coming from a damaged *Delonix regia* tree at Legon, Ghana. The overall impression is that *Charaxes* take on much larger quantities of liquid food than other butterflies; this might be necessary refuelling in view of their extremely powerful and sustained flight.

Two other large genera of African Nymphalidae, *Najas* and *Cymothoe*, are also fruit feeders. In the forest they move on to any fruit that becomes available, always feeding from fruit that has fallen to the ground. At Kasewe, Sierra Leone, I once found very large numbers of *Najas* and related genera feeding from *Musanga* fruits that had been knocked to the ground by red colobus monkeys that were feeding in the trees above. Some butterflies, especially forest species, are in my experience virtually impossible to find except at fallen fruit or at fruit that has been deliberately put out to attract them. Thus in Sierra Leone two species of *Asterope* are attracted in large numbers to fruit at particular times of the year, but otherwise are rarely seen. Many other Nymphalidae, especially forest species, are attracted to fruit, but most of these also feed at flowers. The daisy family, Compositae, is particularly attractive to nymphalids, and large numbers can be seen in gardens planted with ornamental daisies, some butterflies evidently flying considerable distances from the forest to visit garden flowers.

Acraeidae. All species seem to feed from flowers, especially the Compositae, and evidently do not visit fruit. In the Budongo Forest, Uganda, I have seen several species of *Acraea* feeding from chimpanzee faeces, but in West Africa I have rarely seen *Acraea* butterflies at anything but flowers. The forest *Bematistes* seem to visit flowers rarely, but they will fly into gardens to feed from ornamental daisies.

Libytheidae. These butterflies sometimes occur in immense numbers at mammal urine, and occasionally at rotten fruit and animal remains, but I do not think they ever visit flowers.

Riodinidae. I have no information on the feeding habits of these butterflies in Africa, but they probably visit flowers as they do elsewhere in the world.

Lycaenidae. Lipteninae and Liphyrinae seem to feed relatively rarely. Some species, for instance *Megalopalpus zymna* (Liphyrinae), feed on secretions from Homoptera. *Pentila* (Lipteninae) may not feed at all. The Lycaeninae are primarily flower visitors, but some species will also visit mammal urine and faeces, often in company with Pieridae, and sometimes in immense numbers. *Myrina silenus* occasionally visits rotten fruit, but this seems to be exceptional in the subfamily.

Hesperiidae. All species seem to be flower visitors, but occasionally *Coeliades* will visit rotten fruit. In January 1970 in the Kambui Hills of Sierra Leone, G. D. Field and I observed a *Coeliades* produce a drop of fluid from its anus at the same time curving its abdomen forward so that the fluid was deposited within reach of the proboscis. The butterfly then fed on the fluid. Presumably this behaviour resulted from extensive feeding for a short time from a limited resource, but it might have been associated with maintaining a water balance.

Enemies of adult butterflies

The first few hours after emerging from the pupa is probably the most difficult time in a butterfly's life. Its wings are still soft, and although large and conspicuous, it is incapable of flight. It seems highly likely that many butterflies are eaten by predators during this critical period. Once capable of flight a butterfly can evade a predator, and it can also seek out a sheltered and protected place if pursued or in dull weather and at night.

Many adult butterflies visit flowers for nectar and on these flowers, particularly in the tropics, lurk a wide variety of predators. Some of these predators remain motionless on the flower head until a butterfly alights and then they attack. Such predators include praying mantids (Plate 19), which are abundant everywhere in the tropics, crab spiders (Plate 19), and chameleons. Some praying mantids and crab spiders resemble very closely the colour of the flower on which they sit and wait. When the butterfly alights it is seized by the head and then slowly eaten. Not a great deal is known about African crab spiders but all common species of flowers seem to have their spiders which match to a remarkable degree the colour of the particular flower. It is possible that some species of crab spider change their colour to match the flower on which they rest. The extent to which chameleons eat butterflies is not known; these lizards are perhaps more important predators of flies, grasshoppers, and bugs than of butterflies. Web-building spiders are also predators of butterflies. In some areas, notably on the islands in Lake Victoria, large spiders (*Nephila*) that build enormous sticky webs catch very many butterflies. Smaller web-building spiders in gardens and in the forest catch many lycaenids and satyrids.

Some vertebrate predators hunt down butterflies by chasing after them. These predators include the more active lizards and skinks which are everywhere abundant in Africa, especially in gardens and similar open spaces. Birds also take many butterflies, but seem to avoid the distasteful Danaidae and Acraeidae (Carpenter 1941). Beak marks are fairly often found on butterfly wings, suggesting unsuccessful attacks in which the butterfly escaped or was rejected because it was unpalatable.

Dead or dying butterflies are quickly found and eaten by ants. It is probable that most butterflies eventually fall victim to a predator, but possibly in many cases not until mating and egg-laying have been completed and the life cycle is effectively at an end.

Defensive mechanisms

Although butterflies are often brightly coloured the underside of the wings is in many species intricately patterned with browns, yellows, and similar colours, so that when at rest the butterfly is often extremely difficult to detect. Each species tends to have a particular kind of resting place and the underside pattern of the wings serves to conceal the butterfly most effectively. *Melanitis leda* (Satyridae) rests among dead leaves and is almost impossible to see until it takes flight.

It has long been supposed that the eye spots on the edges of the wings of Satyridae and Lycaenidae, and the elongate tails of some of the Lycaenidae, are associated with deflecting the attention of predators from the vital parts (head, thorax, and abdomen) of the butterfly. Butterflies can survive and fly well with quite badly damaged wings and it is thought that a predator's attention is often attracted by eye spots and moving tails so that when it strikes the butterfly escapes with no more than a piece torn from the wing. The behaviour of many of the tropical Lycaenidae with elongate tails strongly supports this contention. On alighting they move the tails slowly and conspicuously from side to side so that a casual observer has the impression that he is looking at moving antennae. These movements cease after a short period, presumably once the butterfly has come fully to rest.

Species of Acraeidae and Danaidae are known to be unpalatable or distasteful to predators. As already mentioned, Danaidae obtain toxic heart poisons from the food-plant as larvae and there is evidence, discussed more fully in Chapter 9, that these butterflies are avoided by predators. Most, probably all, species of Acraeidae secrete from the thorax a yellow, often foamy, fluid which in *Acraea encedon* gives off hydrogen cyanide upon decomposition. Acraeidae and Danaidae are brightly coloured and slow-flying and they act as models for a wide variety of mimetic species in other families.

Forest is generally rather gloomy near the floor but there are often penetrating shafts of bright sunlight. Many forest butterflies, especially Acraeidae, have transparent or partly transparent wings and as a consequence seem to disappear and reappear as they fly. The characteristic pattern of most species of *Najas* (Nymphalidae), which involves iridescent blues and conspicuous white or yellow bars on the wings, may also be associated with living in forest. These butterflies fly rapidly when disturbed and are extremely difficult to follow with the eye. The colours of butterflies are also involved in functions other than protection, such as temperature regulation and behaviour; these are discussed later.

Flight activity

Butterflies are essentially diurnal and most species are fully active only in bright sunshine. *Melanitis leda, Gnophodes,* and some other Satyridae fly mainly at dusk and dawn and not at all during the day unless disturbed. Some species of *Coeliades* (Hesperiidae) are also crepuscular. An astonishing number of species that are normally active in bright sunshine are from time to time attracted to artificial lights. These include representatives of all the major groups; the significance of this behaviour is obscure, although in the north temperate regions migrant butterflies have sometimes been recorded in large numbers at lights, suggesting that at times of movement the normal diurnal flight behaviour is abandoned. There is considerable evidence that species that are attracted to rotten fruit (which may not always be easy to locate) will remain feeding at the fruit until long after sunset; such species include forest butterflies of the genera *Najas* and *Charaxes* (Nymphalidae).

Species of butterflies that fly only in bright sunshine during the dry season, when there is more sunshine, will fly even in light rain in the wet season, when there is often little sunshine. In addition many butterflies that in the dry season never leave the shade of the forest will move into gardens and other open areas in the wet season. Thus although in the dry season *Bematistes* (Acraeidae) are common inside the forests in Sierra Leone and are rarely seen in the open, in the wet season they are common in open habitats and are rather rare in the forest.

The height at which butterflies fly varies with the species and also depends on the availability of nutrients at different levels. A great array of Nymphalidae are forest floor butterflies and a few savanna species, such as *Hamanumida daedalus*, hardly ever fly higher than a few centimetres. The majority of butterflies, however, fly at heights ranging from half a metre to three or four metres and they are thus within the range of normal human vision. Some Lycaenidae and *Papilio antimachus* (Papilionidae) seem to be effectively confined to the forest canopy, descending only to feed from mammal urine and similar nutrients. Needless to say the canopy species are extremely poorly known and the extent to which species are restricted to the canopy is largely a matter of speculation. Jackson (1961) has reported on a collection of butterflies obtained at various levels from a 37-metre tower erected in the Mpanga forest, Uganda. Many of the Lycaenidae were collected only at about the 18-metre level and one species, *Teratoneura isabellae*, only above the canopy.

Life cycles and breeding generations

In tropical Africa most common butterflies occur in all months of the year, but each species tends to reach peak numbers at certain times of the year. This suggests that breeding is continuous all the year round, but that certain times of the year are better for breeding than others, a topic to be discussed more fully later. Leaving aside species with some form of seasonal delay in development, and generalizing considerably, it can be said that many African species remain only a few days as eggs, two or three weeks as larvae, and a week or two as pupae. Thus in *Acraea encedon* (Acraeidae) the generation time (egg to egg) is only 41 days in Sierra Leone; while in Uganda, where it is cooler, the same species takes 60 days to complete a generation. This means that in Sierra Leone *Acraea encedon* completes about nine overlapping generations in a year and in Uganda about six generations. Throughout much of tropical Africa *Danaus chrysippus* (Danaidae) completes its life cycle in slightly less than a month which gives twelve breeding generations a year. These figures contrast markedly with temperate species which breed only once (in some species twice) a year. The evolutionary and genetic implications resulting from short breeding generations are discussed in later chapters of this book.

4

SPECIES DIVERSITY

THERE are more species of butterflies in the tropics than in the temperate regions; there are also more species of birds, mammals, and indeed of all major groups of animals. The vegetation is more complex than in temperate regions: a tropical forest is characterized by the large number of species of trees, none of them really common, whereas a temperate forest is usually dominated by two or three species. Naturalists have long been puzzled as to why there is increased organic diversity in the tropics. Not only are there more species compared with temperate regions, but many tropical species are relatively rare while temperate species tend to be abundant.

The butterflies of Liberia and Michigan

Table 4.1 shows the approximate numbers of species of butterflies recorded in two relatively large and roughly comparable areas: Liberia in West Africa and Michigan in the northern United States. Liberia is at about 5–8° N. and Michigan at 42–48° N. Both areas have been much altered by man. Liberia was originally covered by rain forest, and large patches still remain; southern Michigan was once deciduous woodland, but is now mainly cultivated, while the northern part is largely coniferous with extensive areas of swamp.

TABLE 4.1

Approximate number of species per family recorded in a large temperate area (Michigan, U.S.A.) and a tropical area (Liberia, West Africa)†

Family	Michigan	Liberia
Papilionidae	6	23
Pieridae	13	27
Danaidae	1	5
Satyridae	10	38
Nymphalidae	34	152
Acraeidae	—	30
Libytheidae	1	1
Riodinidae	1	2
Lycaenidae	26	271
Hesperiidae	44	171
Total	136	720

† The Michigan list is from Moore (1960) and the Liberian list mainly from Fox *et al.* (1965).

All families of butterflies that occur in Liberia, except the Acraeidae, also occur in Michigan. As shown in Table 4.1, in Liberia there are between two and ten times as many as in Michigan of each of the families shared by the two areas. Apart from the absence of the Acraeidae from Michigan, the most striking difference is in the Lycaenidae with just over ten times as many species in Liberia as in Michigan. As is to be expected almost all species and most genera are different in the two areas. One species, *Vanessa cardui* (Nymphalidae) is shared, while *Precis orithya* (Nymphalidae), which is found in Liberia, is probably conspecific with *Precis lavinia*, which is found in Michigan.†

Although the total of 720 species of butterfly recorded from Liberia contrasts markedly with the 136 species recorded from Michigan, comparison with the British Isles is even more striking. About 68 species occur in Britain, less than one eleventh of the number on the Liberia list. The British Isles, however, have a considerably impoverished fauna, and that is why I have chosen Michigan as an example of a temperate continental area for comparison with Liberia.

Three small areas compared

Table 4.2 shows the number of species of Papilionidae, Pieridae, Danaidae, and Nymphalidae recorded in my garden at Freetown, Sierra Leone, compared with the number recorded in an area surrounding a garden in Michigan and an area of mixed deciduous woodland and farm-

TABLE 4.2

Approximate number of species in four families of butterflies in a garden at Freetown, Sierra Leone, and in two small temperate areas, one in Michigan, U.S.A., and one in Berkshire, England†

Family	Garden at Freetown	Garden and surrounding woodland and swamp, Michigan	Deciduous woodland and cultivated land, Berkshire
Papilionidae	12	4	—
Pieridae	15	7	6
Danaidae	3	1	—
Nymphalidae	85	21	10

† The records for each locality are my own, but the list for the Michigan area has been supplemented from Moore (1960).

land at Wytham, Berkshire, England. I collected and observed in the garden at Freetown for four years, in the Edwin S. George Reserve in

† Fox *et al.* (1965) give a record of two *Pieris rapae* (Pieridae) taken at sea off the Liberian coast. This butterfly, which does not occur in tropical Africa, has been introduced into North America from Europe and has spread to Michigan. It has been excluded from both lists in Table 4.1.

Michigan for four years, and at Wytham for six years. Both temperate areas are considerably larger (each about five square kilometres) than the Freetown garden, which is about one square kilometre. The impoverishment of the Berkshire locality, with no Papilionidae or Danaidae, is striking. The Freetown garden has over three times as many species in these four families as the area in Michigan and over six times as many as the area in Berkshire. Indeed there are more Nymphalidae in the Freetown garden than there are species of butterflies on the British list. I do not know how many species of Lycaenidae and Hesperiidae occur in the Freetown garden, and I have only incomplete information on the Satyridae, but I estimate that there are about 300 species in the garden. It is therefore certain that there are more species in the garden than in the whole of Michigan and possibly more than in the whole of the eastern United States.

Tropical gardens and tropical forest

The idea that the tropical rain forest is the richest environment in the world in terms of the number of species of animals appears in numerous papers and books, indeed some scientific writers become poetic when describing the richness of the forest. I suspect, however, that another type of habitat is richer. In Africa and elsewhere in the tropics, gardens cultivated in areas that were once forest have some unique features. A few old trees are often left standing and many ornamental trees (usually with conspicuous flowers or decorative leaves) are planted. These trees come from all parts of the world and there are similarities not only between gardens in widely separated parts of Africa but also between gardens in Africa and other tropical areas, such as Central and South America and tropical Asia. In my garden at Freetown (Plate 22) there are trees and shrubs that originate from Madagascar, India, New Guinea, the Pacific Islands, Mexico, Australia, Peru, Brazil, and other places. A similar variety of trees and shrubs, including many of the same species, were present in the garden I owned at Kampala, Uganda. Tropical gardens usually have a lawn or some similar grassy area and keen gardeners will plant a wide variety of flowers that come from all parts of the world. Weeds spread into flower beds and some of the commonest species are not indigenous. This kind of habitat provides many of the features of the forest and is attractive to forest butterflies, especially if, as is often the case, there are abundant flowers and fruit from which adult butterflies can obtain nutrients. Because grass is present there are many Satyridae (whose larvae feed on grass) in contrast to primary forest where grass is scarce or absent. Open spaces in gardens provide conditions suitable for savanna butterflies which do not occur in forest, but by far the most important garden species are those associated with forest-savanna mosaic. These include most species of *Precis* (Nymphalidae) and many species of *Acraea* (Acraeidae).

In my garden at Freetown there are nine species of *Precis* while in nearby secondary forest one, possibly two, of these species are absent. Primary forest in Sierra Leone supports only one species, *Precis stygia*, which evidently does not often leave the forest as I have never seen it in gardens. Two of the garden species, *Precis cloanthe* and *Precis hierta*, are savanna or grassland butterflies. There are 26 species of *Charaxes* (Nymphalidae) in the garden. Two of these do not occur in nearby secondary forest, but all species known from either primary or secondary forest in the immediate vicinity have been recorded in the garden. The genus *Najas* (Nymphalidae) comprises species of butterflies that are mainly associated with the forest floor. I have recorded ten species in the garden while in the surrounding forests there are about twenty species. These butterflies are more or less confined to deep shade and the garden list is remarkably long when one considers that the garden is relatively exposed. There are 24 species of Acraeidae in the Freetown area. Of these 16 are found in well-grown secondary forest, but only eight occur in primary forest. All 24 species have been recorded in the garden. Gardens also attract many Lycaenidae, especially those associated with leguminous plants (both ornamental and weed species). I do not know if there are more Lycaenidae in the garden than in nearby forest, partly because so many species seem to be rare and some may be confined to the forest canopy, but even as I write we are adding new Lycaenidae to the garden list at the rate of about one every two weeks.

I have made similar observations in Uganda. Gardens that were once forest, especially those within easy flying distance of forest, are remarkably rich in butterflies, and I think that further observation will show that tropical gardens are now the richest habitat for butterflies in the world. One difficulty is that it is much easier to obtain an idea of the species of butterflies in one's garden than in forest, especially primary forest, and as a consequence I have much more detailed records available from gardens than from forest. I suspect that butterflies are not the only group richer in species in gardens than in forest. It would be of interest to examine other groups of animals, and I suggest that woodlice, millipedes, and molluscs would be most revealing in this regard.

Measurements of species diversity

The word 'diversity' means variety of kinds and does not necessarily refer to great numbers of kinds. This meaning could be used when speaking of species that differ fundamentally from all other species. Thus butterflies of the family Pieridae, which includes *Pseudopontia paradoxa*, structurally very different from all other butterflies, may be regarded in this sense as a diverse family. In contrast the family Acraeidae comprising butterflies that are structurally similar is not well diversified.

But notwithstanding these preliminary remarks, the term *species diversity* is used by ecologists as a measure of the number of species in the area. There are various mathematical ways in which species diversity can be measured. One convenient method has been suggested by Fisher, Corbet, and Williams (1943). This method involves the empirical assumption that the distribution of the number of species represented by different numbers of individuals fits a logarithmic series. This distribution is defined by two parameters, x, a property of sample size only, and a, a property of the populations sampled, which can be regarded as a measure of species diversity, and which, following Williams (1964), I shall refer to as Diversity. The method of estimating Diversity, together with its standard error, is given by Fisher *et al.* (1943). Observed values of N (the number of individuals in the sample) and S (the number of species) are required. The calculation of Diversity and its standard error is somewhat tedious and is best done on

TABLE 4.3

Number of individuals and number of species in a large sample of Nymphalidae, Papilionidae, Acraeidae, and Danaidae from a garden at Freetown, Sierra Leone, October 1968–September 1969

Individuals per species	Number of species	Individuals per species	Number of species
1	26	28	1
2	10	31	2
3	8	32	1
4	3	34	1
5	6	37	1
6	7	40	1
7	1	48	1
8	1	62	1
9	—	102	1
10	3	106	1
11	—	128	1
12	1	145	1
13	—	153	1
14	1	157	1
15	—	159	1
16	2	173	1
17	1	210	1
18	3	246	1
19	—	266	1
20	—	298	1
21	1	302	1
22	1	503	1
23	1	691	1
24	—	741	1
25	—	785	1
		856	1
		960	1
		1624	1

This gives a total of 9342 individuals of 105 species.

a digital computer; I am extremely grateful to Mr. D. O. Chanter for help in the calculations that follow.

From October 1968 to September 1969 I caught (with an ordinary butterfly net), marked, and released random samples of butterflies of the families Nymphalidae, Acraeidae, Papilionidae, and Danaidae in my garden at Freetown, Sierra Leone. All captures and recaptures (which however are not used in the calculation of Diversity) were identified and recorded. The entire sample consists of 9342 individuals of 105 species.

Table 4.3 shows the number of individuals and the number of species in the entire sample. The important features of Table 4.3 are that 26 (a quarter) of the 105 species recorded were taken only once and that five species, *Precis oenone*, *Precis terea* (Nymphalidae), *Acraea circeis*, *Acraea eponina*, and *Acraea egina* (Acraeidae) account for 4966 (or 52 per cent) of the sample of 9342 butterflies taken. Just over half the species taken contribute only 1·2 per cent of the total sample. Thus a few species are very abundant, but the majority are relatively rare.

The computed value of Diversity for this sample is 16·57 with a standard error of 0·63. The distribution of N and S in this sample approximates the logarithmic series except that there were rather too many rare species. Thus 26 species were recorded once only, about ten more than would have been expected on the basis of the logarithmic series. This computed value of Diversity is not especially useful unless it is possible to compare the figure with results from other areas, particularly temperate areas. Unfortunately no such estimates are available for butterflies. In view of this the sample was broken down into twelve parts each corresponding to a month of the year. Diversity was then computed on a monthly basis which gives some indication of seasonal change. The results are given in Table 4.4. The lowest value of Diversity occurred in February at the height of the dry season. In this month only twenty species of butterflies appeared in the sample and of these just over 62 per cent were of one species, *Precis oenone* (Nymphalidae). In no other month did any one species dominate to this extent. The greatest increase in Diversity occurred between March and April at a time that marked the onset of the wet season. Diversity then remained high throughout the rains, reaching a peak in June and falling slightly by September. The overall picture is that Diversity in the families of butterflies selected for study is considerably higher during the wet months than during the dry months of the year. Many of the common garden butterflies occurred in all months of the year but numbers fluctuated, each species having one or more peaks of abundance. Rare species were far more likely to appear during the wet season than during the dry season. Butterflies were also more common during the wetter months but the method of collection does not permit a numerical analysis of abundance and so no correlation between abundance and Diversity has been possible.

TABLE 4.4

Monthly values of Diversity computed from samples of butterflies collected in a garden at Freetown, Sierra Leone

	N	S	Diversity ± standard error	N_1†	Observed N_1
Oct. 1968	348	24	5·85 ± 0·63	5·75	5
Nov.	412	28	6·79 ± 0·68	6·68	8
Dec.	635	38	8·87 ± 0·74	8·75	13
Jan. 1969	530	34	8·10 ± 0·73	7·98	12
Feb.	530	20	4·11 ± 0·43	4·08	5
Mar.	564	25	5·36 ± 0·52	5·31	6
Apr.	634	44	10·75 ± 0·86	10·57	13
May	589	48	12·35 ± 0·98	12·10	15
June	688	55	14·07 ± 1·04	13·78	18
July	767	52	12·61 ± 0·92	12·40	18
Aug.	2041	69	13·79 ± 0·77	13·70	26
Sept.	1604	56	11·28 ± 0·70	11·20	16

† N_1 is the expected number of species recorded once only and observed N_1 is the actual number of species recorded once only. There is a tendency for more species to be recorded once than would be expected on the basis of the logarithmic series; thus in August nearly twice as many species were recorded once only as would be expected.

It can be shown that the higher values of Diversity recorded in the second half are statistically significant.

In the hawkmoths, Sphingidae, it has been possible by trapping to show that Diversity is negatively correlated with abundance, the peak numbers of hawkmoths in Sierra Leone occurring at the onset of the rains in April–June when Diversity is lowest (Owen 1969a).

In the period February 1969–June 1970 a trap baited with banana was operated continuously in the garden. The most frequently taken butterflies were *Charaxes* (Nymphalidae), a total of 1485 individuals of 26 species being taken in the seventeen-month period. This sample provides an opportunity for measuring Diversity within a single large genus of butterflies.

Table 4.5 shows the number taken of each species. Slightly less than half the sample is composed of three species, *Charaxes castor*, *Charaxes pollux*, and *Charaxes boueti*, while 13 species (half the number taken) make up just over five per cent of the sample. Thus within this genus we have the usual pattern of a few common and many relatively rare species. The overall value of Diversity for the sample is 4·48 with a standard error of 0·37.

One advantage of trapping as compared with hand netting is that a more accurate idea of abundance and seasonal change can be obtained. As shown in Table 4.6, between 37 and 154 *Charaxes* were trapped each month. In 1969 numbers rose with the onset of the rains in April and May, a peak was reached in June, and from then onwards until April 1970 numbers fluctuated irregularly. There was then a decrease and the rise in numbers with the onset of the rains that occurred in 1969 was not repeated in 1970.

TABLE 4.5

Charaxes *butterflies taken in a baited trap in a garden at Freetown, Sierra Leone, February 1969–June 1970*

Species	Number taken	Species	Number taken
Charaxes castor	333	Charaxes ameliae	20
pollux	192	anticlea	14
boueti	178	fulvescens	10
eupale	151	etheocles	8
tiridates	120	candiope	7
brutus	92	achaemenes	6
varanes	88	jasius	4
etesipe	77	viola	2
zingha	46	pleione	2
cynthia	45	nichetes	2
lucretius	36	imperialis	2
numenes	25	smaragdalis	2
cedreatis	22	mycerina	1

The computed values of Diversity and its standard error for each month are also shown in Table 4.6. Diversity fluctuated between 3·61 (February 1969) and 7·64 (December 1969), but there are no trends: Diversity does not appear to be associated either with changes in abundance or with season. A fall in numbers did not lead to a proportional fall in the number

TABLE 4.6

Monthly values of Diversity computed from samples of Charaxes *butterflies taken in a baited trap in a garden at Freetown, Sierra Leone*

	N	S	Diversity $\pm$ standard error	N_1†	Observed N_1
Feb. 1969	40	9	3·61 ± 0·92	3·31	2
Mar.	74	16	6·28 ± 1·17	5·79	3
Apr.	100	17	5·88 ± 0·98	5·55	6
May	137	15	4·29 ± 0·66	4·16	2
June	154	17	4·88 ± 0·71	4·73	1
July	103	15	4·83 ± 0·81	4·61	2
Aug.	129	18	5·69 ± 0·86	5·45	4
Sept.	93	19	7·22 ± 1·21	6·70	7
Oct.	103	15	4·83 ± 0·81	4·61	5
Nov.	68	14	5·35 ± 1·05	4·96	4
Dec.	73	18	7·64 ± 1·42	6·91	5
Jan. 1970	70	14	5·26 ± 1·02	4·89	7
Feb.	105	14	4·34 ± 0·73	4·17	4
Mar.	102	16	5·33 ± 0·89	5·06	7
Apr.	50	10	3·76 ± 0·86	3·50	2
May	37	10	4·50 ± 1·17	4·01	3
June	47	11	4·52 ± 1·05	4·12	1

† N_1 is the expected number of species recorded once only and observed N_1 is the actual number of species recorded once only. There is a tendency for fewer species to be recorded once than would be expected on the basis of the logarithmic series.

2. *Papilio menestheus* (Papilionidae). A young larva about 15 mm long. It looks very like a bird dropping being soft, white, and brown. The bent position enhances this appearance

1. *Charaxes castor* (Nymphalidae). About 50 mm when full grown. The head shield is smooth, hard, and green with red on the spikes. The rest of the body is rough and green speckled with black and white. The eye spot has some red.

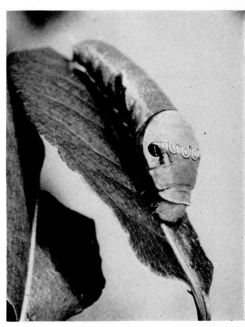

3. *Papilio nireus* (Papilionidae). Dorsal view of full grown larva about 40 mm long. The larva is smooth and green

4. *Papilio nireus* (Papilionidae). The same larva seen from the front. The swollen thoracic area is conspicuous and both the markings and the posture might be associated with threat against potential predators

14. Butterfly larvae. (*Photos by Jennifer Owen*)

1. Larvae of *Bematistes macaria* (Acraeidae) on *Adenia* sp. The larvae are about 40 mm long when full grown. They are gregarious, spiny, and maroon in colour with black markings

2. Larvae of *Danaus chrysippus* (Danaidae) on *Gomphocarpus* sp. When full grown they are about 35 mm long, cream with black bars, solitary, and conspicuous

15. Butterfly larvae. *(Photos by Jennifer Owen)*

1. Larva of *Catopsilia florella* (Pieridae) feeding on *Cassia alata*. These larvae, which when full grown are about 40 mm long, will defoliate the young leaves of *Cassia* trees. An ant is feeding on juices that appear at the chewed edges of the leaf. The larva is green with a black and white stripe. (*Photo by Jennifer Owen*)

2. Two colour forms of larvae of *Papilio demodocus* (Papilionidae). On the left is the form usually found feeding on *Citrus* (this one happens to be feeding on Umbelliferae), while on the right is the form usually found on Umbelliferae; this form is found only in South Africa. From Clarke, Dickson, and Sheppard (1963)

3. Larva of *Myrina silenus* (Lycaenidae) attended by an ant. The ant is taking secretions from the dorsal gland of the larva, which is about 15 mm long. (*Photo by Jennifer Owen*)

16. Butterfly larvae

1. Immature Homoptera attended by ants and an unattended butterfly larva. The Homoptera are eaten by the butterfly larvae

2. Ant stimulating a larva with legs and antennae

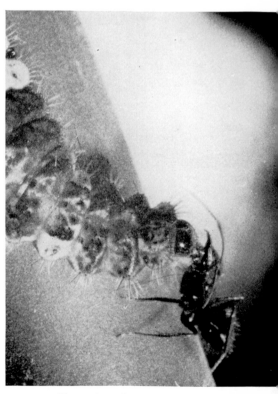

3. Larva feeding ant

4. Closer view of the larva feeding the ant

17. Predatory larvae with ants and Homoptera. The larvae are *Lachnocnema bibulus* (Lycaenidae); they are about 14 mm long when full grown. The Homoptera feed on *Sarcocephalus esculentus*, a shrub that grows on waste land and in gardens in West Africa.
(*Photos by D. O. Chanter*)

of species recorded. This result for *Charaxes* contrasts markedly with the figures in Table 4.4 in which there is a clear seasonal trend in Diversity in samples of butterflies obtained in the garden by hand netting.

From March to June 1969 and during the same period in 1970 another baited trap was operated in a second garden about 300 metres away. The trap was operated by Mr. G. D. Field and as in my own garden all butter-flies trapped were marked and released. This garden is bordered by secondary forest and is not as open as my garden. The results of trapping *Charaxes* in the two gardens (here called Gardens 1 and 2) in the two four-month periods are shown in Table 4.7. In each year more than twice as many *Charaxes* were taken in Garden 2 than in Garden 1, but the number of species taken is about the same. In both gardens about twice as many *Charaxes* were taken in 1969 as were taken in 1970, but again the number of species is about the same. As shown in Table 4.7 all but three species, *Charaxes mycerina, Charaxes pleione,* and *Charaxes smaragdalis,* occurred in both gardens during the periods of sampling. Relatively more forest

TABLE 4.7

Charaxes butterflies in baited traps in two adjacent gardens at Freetown, Sierra Leone, March–June 1969 and 1970†

	Relative frequency (%)			
	Garden 1		Garden 2	
	1969	1970	1969	1970
Charaxes ameliae	1·5	1·7	1·9	1·3
anticlea	0·9	0·8	1·7	1·5
boueti	12·5	6·4	5·2	4·5
brutus	6·7	3·0	2·7	1·3
candiope	0·2	0·4	0·6	—
castor	18·3	41·2	12·7	21·2
cedreatis	2·4	0·4	2·7	1·2
cynthia	5·4	2·1	10·9	11·3
etesipe	1·9	5·5	2·5	4·2
etheocles	0·9	—	0·9	—
eupale	10·5	7·6	11·6	10·3
fulvescens	0·4	0·8	1·7	2·4
jasius	0·4	—	0·1	0·2
lucretius	3·9	2·6	0·8	1·2
mycerina	—	0·4	—	—
nichetes	0·4	—	0·1	1·2
numenes	2·4	2·1	2·5	4·5
pleione	—	—	0·2	—
pollux	10·1	8·5	13·9	11·1
smaragdalis	—	0·4	—	—
tiridates	11·0	8·9	10·5	11·0
varanes	5·4	6·8	6·3	4·2
zingha	4·9	0·4	10·5	7·4
Total taken	465	236	1016	594
Species	20	19	21	18

† By applying 2 × n contingency χ^2 tests it can be shown that all four samples differ significantly from each other.

species, notably *Charaxes zingha* and *Charaxes cynthia*, were taken in Garden 2, and relatively more savanna species, *Charaxes boueti*, and forest edge species, *Charaxes castor*, were taken in Garden 1. This is presumably because Garden 2 is closer to forest and Garden 1 in a more open situation. Comparing the two years there was an overall decline in numbers between 1969 and 1970, but *Charaxes castor*, the commonest species, was relatively more common in 1970 than in 1969. *Charaxes etheocles*, taken in both gardens in 1969, did not appear at all in 1970, and *Charaxes zingha* was much scarcer.

These four samples, taken in two adjacent gardens during the same periods of two different years, demonstrate that species composition within a large butterfly genus may vary between similar habitats and also between years.

Theoretical reasons for variations in species diversity

The most striking variation in species diversity is latitudinal. There is a gradient of decreasing diversity from the equator to the poles. Many tropical species are relatively much rarer than temperate species. This gradient was first appreciated by Alfred Russel Wallace towards the end of the nineteenth century and it has given rise to a great deal of speculation and the formulation of numerous hypotheses. Curiously enough the phenomenon has still not been satisfactorily explained.

There are certainly more species in the tropics and butterflies are no exception to the rule. Animals such as butterflies depend largely on plants, and there is a marked tendency for species and genera to be confined to particular plants or groups of plants. There are more species of plants in the tropics than in the temperate regions and thus it is not astonishing that there are more species of animals all of which ultimately depend on plants. Tropical areas also offer a greater variety of habitats. Thus in Uganda there exists almost every conceivable kind of habitat from low altitude forest to high altitude boreal conditions. At higher latitudes some of these habitats disappear because the climate will not allow the establishment of plant and animal communities at high altitudes: land 2000 metres high in Uganda supports flourishing communities but in the Arctic there is no significant life at that altitude.

But the problem of special interest is why within a single tropical habitat can more species coexist than in a comparable temperate habitat. The figures in Table 4.1 illustrate the differences, but what is the explanation?

The longer favourable season in tropical areas could allow more species to exploit the available resources: the edible parts of plants are available over longer periods in the tropics than in temperate areas. Biotic interactions between species are possibly more important in regulating numbers than climatic factors. This could lead to smaller ecological niches in the tropics, which in butterflies might result in increased specialization in larval food-plants, but whether this is so is a matter of speculation.

Another view is that temperate regions are impoverished as a result of recent climatic catastrophes such as the Pleistocene glaciations. If this is so the re-invasion of species that have become extinct at high latitudes is not yet complete.

Other views have been put forward, but I suggest that in the case of butterflies the answer is to be sought in the plants they depend upon. There is a much greater diversity of plants in the tropics and many species of plant are rare. This alone could account for the diversity of butterflies and also the rarity of many of the species. But no one knows why the plants are more diverse.

The seasonal changes in diversity shown in Tables 4.4 and 4.6 represent a new approach to the problem as far as tropical animals are concerned. Somewhat similar data have been obtained for temperate moths (Williams 1964), but not for temperate butterflies. On a monthly basis butterflies may be quite rare in a tropical habitat. To give one example: a single (marked) specimen of *Precis cloanthe* (Nymphalidae) was present in my garden for over two months from September to November 1969, and no other member of the species was recorded despite careful searching. The butterfly was obviously rare during this period, although at other times of the year it is quite common. I suspect that rarity, including seasonal rarity, is even more marked in the forest environment. Thus intensive collecting in secondary forest near Freetown over four years has yielded only one specimen of *Pseudaletis leonis* (Lycaenidae) and similar collecting at a forest edge locality near Lake Victoria in Uganda yielded only one specimen of *Pseudaletis ugandae*, the second specimen ever collected. It is difficult to see how such very rare species maintain themselves, but of course it is always possible, especially in the forest, that the collector never obtains access to the precise places where these species fly. Excluding the rather special case of rare migrants or vagrants, no similar situation seems to occur in temperate butterflies, each species tending to be fairly common in restricted areas at particular times of the year.

5

SEASONS

IN most of Africa and elsewhere in the tropics biological events follow a seasonal pattern that is quite different from that at higher latitudes. In the temperate regions the annual cycle of biological activity is associated with a clearly defined winter and summer and a rather less clearly defined spring and autumn. The main environmental factors that determine seasonal cycles in the temperate regions are the incremental changes in day length and changes in air temperature. Much biological activity is reduced in the winter when temperatures are low and days short. As a result each species, including each species of butterfly, has a life cycle that is closely adjusted to seasonal change.

The situation is more complicated in the tropics. Here, especially towards the equator, days are of nearly constant length all the year round and temperature changes throughout the year are often small. In many equatorial regions daily differences between maximum and minimum temperatures are greater than seasonal differences. As one proceeds north or south from the equator seasonal changes in temperature become greater, but within 15° N. and S. these changes are quite small. Throughout Africa, and especially in the equatorial part, rainfall is the most important event that determines seasonal change. In many parts of Africa rainfall occurs regularly at specific times of the year and nearly everywhere there are one or two wet and dry seasons in the year. In areas where the annual rainfall is small the seasonal occurrence of rain becomes less predictable. In some savanna regions the dry season may extend from five to nine months during which ecological conditions may be very harsh for animals such as butterflies.

Since temperature is not an important environmental event affecting the seasonality of tropical butterflies there is a marked tendency on the part of many species to occur as adults in all months of the year. But in almost every species there is a seasonal peak of abundance that in one way or another is associated with the alternation of wet and dry seasons. It appears that for many species it is possible to complete the life cycle at almost any time of the year, but that certain times are much better than others. A more clear-cut seasonal cycle exists in the drier savanna than in the forest. In the savanna butterflies may be very scarce for much of the dry season, becoming extremely abundant with the onset of the first rains. In the dry season large areas of savanna grassland burn. Usually the fires are started by people, supposedly to improve grazing by promoting the growth of new grass, but very often for no particular reason. Savanna fires now occur on such a scale and with such regularity that they must constitute a major ecological event for butterflies. In at least one species of *Lepidochrysops* (Lycaenidae) emergence from the pupa occurs only after the grass has been burnt; if the grass is not burnt the butterflies are evidently unable to emerge. The pupae are formed underground and the larvae feed on *Becium* (Labiatae) which remains dormant unless there is a grass fire (Carcasson 1964).

In forest regions, or regions now cultivated that once were forest, rainfall is more evenly distributed throughout the year than in savanna, but in nearly every place there is at least one conspicuous peak per year. The butterflies of the forest are considerably less seasonal than savanna species, but in almost all species studied there is some evidence of seasonality.

The seasons at Freetown

Freetown, on the coast of Sierra Leone, is at 8° 28′ N. and is within the area of the western equatorial forest. By far the most striking climatic event is the alternation of wet and dry seasons. The wet season usually starts in April and May with severe thunderstorms, sometimes accompanied by strong winds, and as these moderate steady and continuous rain sets in and persists until September. There are further thunderstorms at the end of the rains in October and November. The dry season is quite severe, and there is little or no rain in the period December to March. Fig. 5.1 shows the mean rainfall at Freetown and the actual rainfall in 1969, a very wet year. During 1969, 1295 mm of rain fell in July, which is more than twice the average annual rainfall in London.

There is little seasonal change in temperature, the hottest months being February to April (mean maximum daily temperature 29°C) and the coolest July and August (mean maximum daily temperature 25°C). Mean minimum daily temperatures average about 7°C less than mean maximum daily temperatures. It is thus hot all the year round. The humidity is nearly always very high, readings of 100 per cent relative humidity being common; it is rather more humid in the wetter months. The humidity may fall for prolonged spells during the dry season when the harmattan wind blows from the north, but the effects of the harmattan at Freetown are small compared with areas inland. In the dry season there may be much dust in the air, but this varies from year to year; extensive burning of grasslands well to the north may also reduce visibility if the wind brings the haze to Freetown.

Most plant production occurs in the wet season, especially towards the end of the rains. Many trees and plants are at least partly deciduous in the dry season and many weeds and small plants die back completely. The

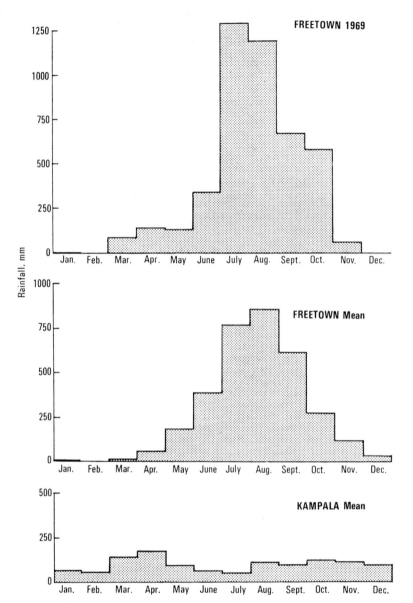

FIG. 5.1. Monthly rainfall at Freetown, Sierra Leone, and at Kampala, Uganda. The two lower figures show the mean rainfall at the two localities; the upper figure shows the rainfall at Freetown in 1969, an exceptionally wet year.

flowering cycles of almost all the common trees and plants are in one way or another associated with the alternation of wet and dry seasons. Flowers are relatively rare in the forest at the height of the rains and many common garden flowers are at their best at the beginning of the rains.

The number of hours of sunshine in each month varies with the rainfall. The sunniest months are December to March and the least sunny July and August, when there may be no sunshine at all for days or even weeks. The intense sunshine in the dry season often results in soil temperatures of 45°C at the surface, which must have a considerable desiccating effect on plants growing in the open. The forest is probably less affected by seasonal changes than open places; in the wet season the forest is dark and quite cool and there may on occasion be little sign of butterfly life.

The contrast between the wet and dry season is remarkable. Anyone who has not experienced tropical storms and tropical rainfall will find it difficult to imagine the scene. In July 1969 there was virtually continuous heavy rain at Freetown, as much as 269 mm being recorded in one period of nine hours. At my house, 300 metres above sea level, we were in almost continuous cloud throughout the month and there was scarcely any sunshine. And yet during this month butterflies were abundant in the garden.

The seasonal pattern of climatic change described above is fairly typical of coastal West Africa, although the rainfall at Freetown is rather higher than in most other areas. In other parts of tropical Africa, especially in the forested areas, the pattern is similar, but in many savanna areas and some forest areas there is a strongly bimodal distribution of rainfall. Fig. 5.1 also gives the mean rainfall for Kampala, Uganda (0° 20′ N.). The rainfall is more evenly distributed than at Freetown, but two wet seasons, one in March and April and one in October and November, can be distinguished in most years.

It is to be expected, then, that all aspects of seasonality in butterflies will depend mainly on the seasonal distribution of rainfall and also perhaps on the hours of sunshine. Temperature may become more important at higher latitudes in Africa, but the effects of temperature are small compared with those in the temperate regions.

Seasonal changes in numbers of butterflies

Causal observations and collecting indicate that there are fluctuations in the overall numbers of adult butterflies flying in an area; but these fluctuations cannot be estimated by mere observation and collecting. Some kind of systematic trapping is needed. One kind of trap, designed especially to take Nymphalidae and Satyridae, and described in Chapter 15, depends upon the provision of bait, usually fermented fruit. If operated over a period of months some indication of seasonal fluctuations in numbers can be obtained, but there is the possibility that the bait provided will not be equally effective at all times of the year; in particular if rotten fruit is abundant locally the trap will be competing with natural resources and will be less effective. Fig. 5.2 gives the number of Nymphalidae caught (marked

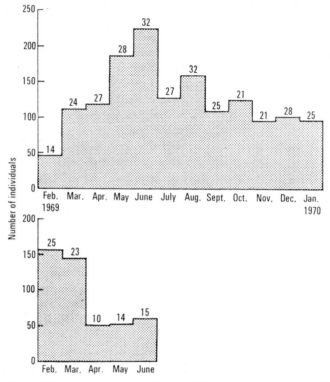

FIG. 5.2. Seasonal changes in numbers of Nymphalidae entering a baited trap in a garden at Freetown, Sierra Leone. The number of species taken in each month is given at the top of each column of the histogram. In 1969 numbers rose with the onset of the rains, but in 1970 numbers fell. The reasons for this difference are not known, but compared with 1969 butterflies in general were much scarcer in the early part of the 1970 wet season.

and released so that no individual is scored more than once) in a baited trap in my garden at Freetown. The peak number of butterflies entering the trap in this period occurred in June 1969, a month when dry season conditions had ended and the wet season had set in. The lowest numbers occurred in February 1969 and April and May 1970. The siting of the trap is important. Thus another trap operated in an adjacent garden during March to June 1969 and 1970 produced more individuals, but not conspicuously more species, as shown in Fig. 5.3. In 1969 the peak occurred in May, but June numbers were also high, while in 1970 the peak occurred in March and numbers fell as the wet season developed.

2 cm

1. Butterfly on the point
of emergence and empty
pupal case below

2. Pupa splits

3. Butterfly pushes
itself out

4. Clings to pupal case

5. Climbs up stem, wings
expanding

6. Wings continue to
expand

7. Wings nearly fully
expanded

8. Wings fully expanded

18. The emergence of a *Danaus chrysippus* (Danaidae) butterfly from its pupa. (*Photos by Jennifer Owen*)

1. Yellow crab spider on *Cosmos* daisy holding a male *Hypolimnas misippus* (Nymphalidae) by the head. The head will be eaten and the rest of the butterfly discarded. The colours of crab spiders match exactly the flowers on which they lurk. They are most abundant in the wet season and attack bees and moths as well as butterflies. Slightly enlarged

2. Praying mantis with *Amauris niavius* (Danaidae). Many species of praying mantis sit near flowers and seize butterflies and other insects as they come to feed. Reduced

19. Predators of adult butterflies. (*Photos by Jennifer Owen*)

The Malaise trap, also described in Chapter 15, does not depend on the provision of bait and thus probably gives a better idea of seasonal changes in numbers. Malaise traps are tent-like structures into which butterflies, and other insects, wander and eventually are caught in a killing bottle. These traps operate best in sunny weather when the butterflies are most active and so quantitative information obtained on a monthly basis is probably slightly biased during the sunnier months of the year, although, as will be discussed later, some butterflies actually reduce their activity during the sunniest months.

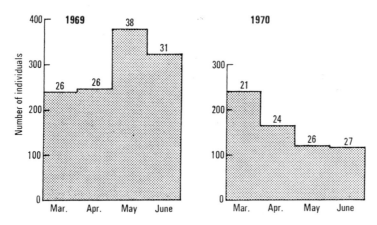

FIG. 5.3. Changes in numbers of Nymphalidae entering a baited trap in another garden at Freetown, Sierra Leone, during March–June, the period of maximum transition between the dry and wet seasons. The differences between the two years are striking and seem associated with the general scarcity of butterflies in the early part of the 1970 wet season. The number of species taken in each month is given at the top of each column of the histogram.

In 1965 I operated a Malaise trap in a garden at Kampala, Uganda (Plate 37). The trap collected insects continuously for a period of twelve months both by day and by night. I repeated the operation, using a slightly different design of trap, in my garden at Freetown in 1967. The total number of butterflies caught in these two traps is plotted on a monthly basis in Fig. 5.4. The most striking feature of Fig. 5.4 is that at both localities the peak numbers occurred at the end of the wet season. At Kampala, the heaviest rainfall occurs in March and April (Fig. 5.1) and the peak number of butterflies occurred in May and June. At Freetown the heaviest rainfall occurs in July and August (Fig. 5.1) and the peak number of butterflies in September and October. As shown in Fig. 5.4, butterflies entered the traps all the year round and the overall fluctuations in numbers are not conspicuous, the May peak at Kampala being only five times the number recorded in August, the poorest month, while at Freetown the September

peak is less than three times the number recorded in April, the poorest
month.

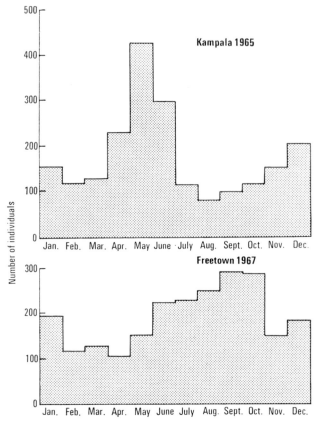

FIG. 5.4. Seasonal changes in total number of butterflies entering Malaise traps in gardens
at Kampala, Uganda, and Freetown, Sierra Leone.

But although overall numbers do not fluctuate markedly there is striking
seasonal fluctuation in the occurrence of different families of butterflies. As
would be expected this fluctuation is most clear at Freetown where the
wet and dry seasons are quite distinct. In Fig. 5.5 the main families of
butterflies taken in the Malaise trap are shown as a percentage of the total
butterflies taken. Families not shown contained too few individuals for
quantitative treatment. The records are here extended into the next year,
1968, for five months to show that the pattern is repeated. As shown in
Fig. 5.5, Lycaenidae were by far the most common butterflies taken, but
they were effectively confined to the dry season, reaching a peak in March
in 1967 and in February in 1968. The Satyridae were almost confined to the
wet season, reaching a peak at the end of the rains in November. The

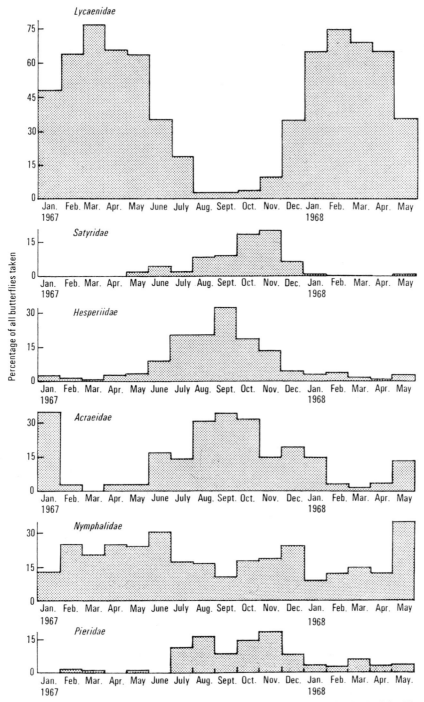

FIG. 5.5. Seasonal changes in relative frequency (as percentage of total taken) of families of butterflies entering a Malaise trap in a garden at Freetown, Sierra Leone.

Hesperiidae were also mainly wet season butterflies, the peak occurring in September. The Acraeidae look a little more complicated, but they were in general most abundant in the wet season, with a peak in September, the January 1968 peak being caused by what appeared to be a sudden immigration of large numbers of *Acraea bonasia* (Plate 13). No clear trend occurred in the Nymphalidae, but the samples consisted mainly of two species, *Precis terea*, which was abundant in the wet season, and *Precis oenone*,

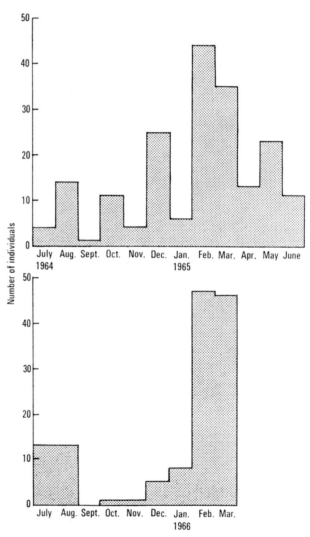

FIG. 5.6. Seasonal changes in numbers of *Acraea bonasia* entering a Malaise trap in a garden at Kampala, Uganda, during 21 consecutive months.

which replaced *Precis terea* in the dry season. Numbers of Pieridae were rather low, but there was a peak, possibly bimodal, in the wet season.

Within each family the species also fluctuated in numbers, similar common species tending to reach their peaks of abundance at different times of the year. Most common species occurred in the traps in all months, but reached peaks once a year. Fig. 5.6 shows the seasonal fluctuations in one of the common species, *Acraea bonasia* (Acraeidae), taken in the Kampala trap. The records extend over 21 consecutive months and the continuous occurrence of the butterfly and its seasonal peak in February and March in both years is typical of the kind of seasonality present in many common butterflies at Kampala and at Freetown.

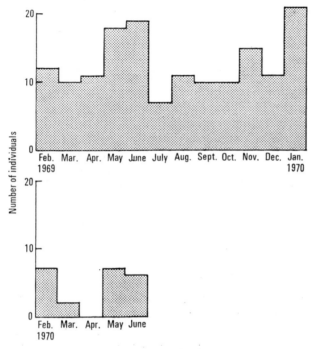

Fig. 5.7. Monthly totals of *Charaxes boueti* entering a baited trap in a garden at Freetown, Sierra Leone.

Fig. 5.7 shows the seasonal distribution of 178 specimens of *Charaxes boueti* (Nymphalidae) trapped over 17 consecutive months in a baited trap in my garden at Freetown. The butterfly occurred in all months except April 1970, but never became really common. This species is something of an exception as in almost all common species there is a well marked seasonal peak of abundance occurring at least once in the year.

The causes of seasonal changes in numbers

Here we come to an unresolved problem. But first it should be remembered that seasonality in butterflies is usually measured by fluctuations in the numbers of flying adults and that these fluctuations also indicate seasonal cycles in the larvae and pupae. Indeed it is possible that most seasonal cycles in numbers are simply an indication of variations in the availability of suitable larval food. Notwithstanding these considerations there are two possible causes of seasonal changes in numbers. First, the entire population of a species may be undergoing fluctuations to such an extent that it is regularly reduced to very small numbers and then increases again as ecological conditions improve. Secondly, overall numbers may not really be changing markedly, but there is instead some form of seasonal delay in development. This could take place in the egg, larval, pupal, or adult stage, depending on the species and the locality, and could take place in two or more of these stages as in some temperate butterflies that hibernate. Curiously neither of these possibilities, which are very different, has been investigated in tropical species, except in *Acraea encedon* (Acraeidae), which undoubtedly undergoes fluctuations in population size, as discussed in Chapter 7.

There is however considerable evidence of reduced activity, which may take the form of seasonal aestivation, in the dry season; whether overall numbers change is not clear. Thus the pupae of several Papilionidae, including *Papilio nireus*, undergo a prolonged aestivation during the dry season at Freetown. The larvae of *Papilio nireus* that feed on *Fagara* are deprived of food in the dry season, as *Fagara* is deciduous, and it appears that the pupae aestivate until the onset of the rains and the production of new leaves on the food-plant. Adults of *Precis octavia* (Nymphalidae) (Plate 11) seek out crevices in rocks or dark bushes and there shelter throughout the dry season, flying only when disturbed or if there is unseasonal rain. The seasonal adaptations of this species are discussed more fully in the next section of this chapter. Aestivation probably occurs in a wide variety of African butterflies whose food-plant becomes seasonally unavailable. At Freetown, *Acraea circeis* (Acraeidae) (Plate 13) passes the dry season in the egg stage while *Acraea zetes* may aestivate on a leaf as a full-grown larva. In both these species the food-plant is scarce or absent in the dry season.

Seasonal adaptations of species of animals to heavy tropical rainfall have received little consideration, and yet it would appear that for some butterflies the wet season is the least suitable time of the year. Mention has already been made of the disappearance of many Lycaenidae in the wet season. At Freetown *Graphium policenes* (Papilionidae) breeds continuously throughout the dry season, but with the onset of the rains in May fully fed larvae pupate and the pupae do not produce butterflies until the end of the rains in September or October. Development is thus suspended in the pupal stage for three or four months through the wet season, while in the dry season the pupal period is not more than about seven days. A few individual *Graphium policenes* adults occur in the wet season indicating that at least some pupae do not undergo arrested development.

The word aestivation is widely used to describe arrested development in the dry season and the word hibernation for similar events through a winter. Neither word is applicable in the case of arrested development through a tropical wet season, and I therefore suggest *pluviation* as an appropriate term. Lack of evidence for pluviation in tropical animals is probably because it is generally assumed that the wet season is always favourable, but this widely held view may be wrong for some animals, including some butterflies. It is however unlikely that pluviation is an adaptation to the scarcity of larval food; more probably the critical resource is food for the adult butterfly. Thus *Graphium policenes*, whose pupae pluviate, is mainly a forest butterfly and with the seasonal scarcity of flowers in the forest it may be disadvantageous for adults to fly in the wet season.

Seasonal forms

A considerable number of Satyridae and some Nymphalidae have seasonal forms that are environmentally determined. The frequency of these forms in each month of the year seems to depend largely on the rainfall and the humidity. At the height of the rains all members of a species may be of the wet season form while at the height of the dry season all will be of the dry season form. During transitional periods both wet and dry season forms may fly together at the same time.

Precis octavia (Nymphalidae) is the best known African butterfly with seasonal forms. The wet season form is bright orange with black markings, while the dry season form is intricately patterned with dark markings and blue spots and has hardly any orange. In addition (at least in West Africa) the dry season form is rather larger and the wing edges are more emarginated than in the wet season form. The two forms, drawn from Uganda specimens, are shown in Fig. 5.8 and specimens from Sierra Leone in Plate 11.

At Kampala, Uganda, the wet-season form of *Precis octavia* occurs throughout the year and in four years I did not see a single dry season specimen, although there are records of them. At Freetown, Sierra Leone, where the rainfall is more seasonal and where the wet season is much wetter and the dry season drier than at Kampala, the two forms replace each other as the seasons change. Table 5.1 shows the number of wet and dry season forms in each month in 1967, 1969, and 1970 in garden habitats near Freetown. The seasonal replacement is conspicuous: from July to

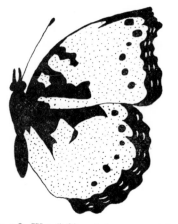

FIG. 5.8. Wet (left) and dry seasonal forms of *Precis octavia*. The specimens shown are
from Uganda.

TABLE 5.1

*Seasonal changes in the frequency of wet and dry season forms
of* Precis octavia *at Freetown, Sierra Leone*†

| | 1967 | | 1969 | | 1970 | |
	Wet	Dry	Wet	Dry	Wet	Dry
Jan.	—	—	1	5	2	3
Feb.	—	—	—	9	—	1
Mar.	—	—	—	36	—	3
Apr.	—	—	1	19	—	4
May	—	2	3	4	1	3
June	1	1	12	7	2	—
July	5	—	12	—	6	—
Aug.	24	—	27	—		
Sept.	22	—	33	—		
Oct.	18	4	13	6		
Nov.	4	10	4	5		
Dec.	—	3	2	3		

† All records are from gardens and include butterflies trapped and netted.

September, the wettest months, only wet-season forms occurred, while in
the dry months almost all the butterflies were of the dry-season form. The
butterfly seems to be rather rare in the dry season, but this is mainly because they seek out sheltered places and undergo a form of aestivation. Dry
season butterflies obtained in November are freshly emerged while those
in April and May are worn. By marking, releasing, and recapturing I was
able to establish that there is no breeding in the dry season and that the
November butterflies live for several months to reappear with the onset of
the next wet season. During the wet season the butterflies feed from flowers
and mate, but dry-season individuals, when seen, do not feed or show

signs of mating until about May. They spend the time on exposed bare ground or rocks in full sunshine. At Freetown, the larvae feed on *Solenostemon* (Labiatae), a common weed which itself has a clear-cut seasonal cycle. The seeds lie dormant through the dry season and begin to germinate in June, but germination is prolonged and some seeds remain dormant until almost the end of the wet season in September. The plants produce abundant foliage in September and after flowering in October die back completely. Seeds planted at intervals through the dry season and well watered failed to germinate, but did so when the rains were under way in June. The larvae of *Precis octavia* are abundant on the food-plant in September and October, but at no other time of the year. There is possibly an alternative food-plant (the species is known from other Labiatae in East Africa), as freshly emerged wet-season forms appear in May long before the known food-plant is available, unless, of course, there is pupal as well as adult aestivation. At Freetown the eggs of *Precis octavia* are laid on the ground and not on the food-plant, which perhaps suggests that aestivation may take place in the egg stage as well. The larvae travel over the ground from plant to plant, full-grown larvae often appearing on a plant which on the previous day had no larvae.

The ecological significance of seasonal forms in *Precis octavia* is not clear. In the laboratory intermediates can be produced by rearing the larvae under controlled conditions, but these intermediates are rare in the wild and in my experience are always effectively dry-season forms with traces of the wet-season coloration. McLeod (1968) concluded on the basis of some breeding experiments in Kenya that temperature was the main factor affecting pigmentation, and this could also be so in Sierra Leone as the wet season is slightly cooler than the dry. I suspect however that rainfall or humidity will be found to be the main stimulus affecting the production of seasonal forms, at least in equatorial Africa. As already mentioned, at Kampala the wet-season form occurs throughout the year and the dry-season form is rare. In Sierra Leone dry-season forms are produced in October, a month which is considerably wetter than even the wettest month at Kampala; this suggests that it is the amount of seasonal change that is taking place rather than the actual conditions of climate that stimulate the production of seasonal forms.

Possibly the dark dry-season form is better adapted to hiding and sheltering in dark places than the wet-season form, which is brightly coloured and conspicuous. Certainly aestivating butterflies are hard to detect against the rocky background on which they often rest. It is also possible that the seasonal forms are in some way associated with temperature regulation, the strikingly different colours and patterns being differently adapted to changes in air temperature that occur in the two seasons.

A parallel cycle of events occurs in *Precis pelarga*, a species which is ecologically very similar to *Precis octavia*. In *Precis pelarga* the wet-season form is small and the edges of the wings are less emarginated. There are two dry-season forms, one orange like the wet-season form and the other with an intense blue band in place of the orange. The difference in wing shape between wet and dry-season forms is shown in Fig. 5.9. In addition

FIG. 5.9. Wet (left) and dry seasonal forms of *Precis pelarga*. The specimens are from Sierra Leone.

both dry-season forms are extremely varied in the shades of brown and orange markings on the undersides of the wings. It appears that dry-season *Precis pelarga* aestivate among dead leaves and hence the underside variation would be cryptic as the resemblance to dead leaves is striking. Adults are common only in the wet season and like those of *Precis octavia* feed from flowers, while the few seen in the dry season show no signs of feeding or mating. The larvae of *Precis pelarga* also feed on *Solenostemon*, and they are common only in September and October when the food-plant is most available. The significance of the two dry-season forms, one orange and one blue, is obscure; it is sometimes suggested that the blue form is the result of very dry conditions, but this is doubtful as the blue form appears in about equal numbers with the orange at the beginning of the dry season when it is still quite wet.

In *Melanitis leda* (Satyridae) the wet season form has conspicuous eye spots on the underside and all individuals are alike. In the dry season form the spots are much reduced and are hardly visible, the wings are more emarginated, and the butterflies are larger. The dry season form is also much more variable, the underside of no two individuals being exactly alike. The larvae of *Melanitis leda* are grass feeders and I have successfully produced dry-season individuals in the wet season by rearing the larvae in the laboratory at 60 per cent relative humidity (Plate 23).

Many other Satyridae have seasonal forms. The general tendency is for the eye spots to become much reduced in size in the dry-season form, which in most species is also individually more variable.

Seasonal changes in frequency of colour forms

In the north temperate *Colias* (Pieridae) it has been shown that the two forms of the female, white and yellow, controlled by a pair of alleles, vary in frequency with the temperature and solar radiation. White females are more frequently found flying early and late in the day and early and late in the season, while yellow females are more active towards midday and are more frequent in the middle of the season when it is warmer (Hovanitz 1948).

A parallel situation exists in the African *Catopsilia florella* (Pieridae) in which there are also distinct yellow and white forms of the female, the males being white and all alike. At Freetown both female forms occur all the year round, but the yellow is much more frequent in the dry and the white in the wet season. The colour forms of *Catopsilia florella* are evidently genetically determined (unlike those of *Precis* and *Melanitis*), but details of the mode of inheritance have not yet been worked out.

The pupae of many Papilionidae exist in two forms, green and brown; intermediates are rare, and it appears that in at least some species these colour forms are inherited, although it is possible that there may also be environmental effects. Table 5.2 shows the frequency of green and brown

TABLE 5.2

Relative frequency of green and brown pupae of Papilio demodocus *at Freetown, Sierra Leone, and Kampala, Uganda*

	Green	Brown	Green (per cent)
Freetown			
Dry season (Nov.–Apr.)	48	74	39·3
Wet season (May–Oct.)	89	28	76·1
Kampala			
Six driest months (Dec.–Feb., May–July)	28	14	66·7
Six wettest months (Mar.–Apr., Aug.–Nov.)	43	22	66·2

pupae in *Papilio demodocus* reared from larvae at Freetown and Kampala. Early instar larvae were collected from *Citrus* and reared in glass jars under controlled conditions of temperature and humidity. The larvae pupated on the sides of the jars and there was thus no question of the pupae matching a background colour. The pupae obtained are divided into two groups in Table 5.2 corresponding with the wet and dry season at Freetown and the six wettest and the six driest months at Kampala. At Kampala there was no significant difference in the seasonal frequency of green and brown pupae, but at Freetown green pupae were significantly more frequent in the wet and brown in the dry season ($\chi^2 = 32\cdot4$, $P < 0\cdot001$). These differences are presumably due to the fact that the wet season at Freetown is very wet and green backgrounds are more available, while the dry season is very dry and the vegetation becomes much browner. At Kampala seasonal changes in the environment are less spectacular and the green and brown pupae occur at about the same frequency all the year round, green being more frequent than brown (Table 5.2). Brown pupae of *Papilio demodocus* are much more variable than green; a similar situation exists in some long-horn grasshoppers, Tettigoniidae, which are also either green or brown. Presumably this is because brown backgrounds are more variable than green.

6

POPULATION ECOLOGY

I N any habitat there are both common and rare species. Although as a
group butterflies are abundant in the tropics many species are relatively
rare as we saw in Chapter 4. Each female butterfly lays several hundred
eggs and it follows that over ninety per cent of these will fail to produce
adult butterflies if the population is to remain stable. The problem in
population ecology is therefore to determine what factors regulate numbers
and why some species are regulated in such a way as to be more common
than others.

A population comprises a group of interbreeding individuals. Members
of different species by definition belong to separate populations. Within a
species populations may be isolated from one another by geographical or
ecological barriers. Some species, such as *Acraea encedon* (Acraeidae), form
distinct populations that are confined to quite small areas, while others,
such as *Danaus chrysippus* (Danaidae), form large populations over vast areas.

There is some direct and much indirect evidence that the size of animal
populations is regulated in two ways: density-dependently, in which the
mortality rate varies with population density, in particular it is relatively
higher at high densities than at low densities; and density-independently,
in which the mortality rate does not vary with population density. Density-
dependent mortality is probably of widespread occurrence and will tend
to regulate a population whenever an essential resource (such as food) is in
short supply. Density-independent mortality is usually the result of non-
biological factors, such as weather, or, especially in the savanna of Africa,
grass fires. During catastrophic weather or fierce fires all individuals in the
population may be killed irrespective of their population density. It appears
however that many populations are regulated by a combination of
density-dependent and density-independent factors.

It has also been proposed that many animal populations have built-in
intrinsic self-regulating mechanisms which act density-dependently. Such
mechanisms would either be behavioural, in which breeding is regulated
by social or territorial interactions, or genetic, in which genetic factors
prevent the population from increasing. There is no direct evidence for
behavioural factors regulating density but there is an increasing awareness
that the genetic structure of a population may be important in the regulation of its size; an example from African butterflies is discussed in the next
chapter.

Populations and the availability of food

With a few exceptions butterflies are herbivores and the larvae of most species feed upon green leaves. Since green leaves are on only rare occasions depleted by herbivores it would appear on first impression that butterfly larvae are not food-limited. But appearances are deceptive as in many plants there are seasonal cycles of edibility; in particular the larvae of many butterflies seem able to feed only on new leaves, the older leaves evidently being unpalatable or even toxic. In the forest the production of new leaves follows a seasonal cycle, each plant tending to produce new leaves only at a restricted time of the year. Moreover a great many plants contain toxic compounds and there is evidence (mainly from research on cereal crops) that toxicity increases with the age of the leaf. Larvae feeding on what are sometimes called plant products (flowers, seeds, and fruit) are more likely to be food-limited than those feeding on leaves because plant products form only a small part of the biomass of the plant. But despite these considerations no one has yet attempted to measure the impact of butterfly larvae on plants or the extent to which larvae are food-limited. There is however abundant evidence that larvae are only able to utilize a small fraction of the total food-plant produced. This situation can be seen in *Catopsilia florella* (Pieridae) whose larvae feed on various species of *Cassia* (Plate 16). The female butterflies lay their eggs only on the new leaves of *Cassia* and the young larvae are able to eat only young leaves. New leaves are produced seasonally, but each species of *Cassia* tends to produce new leaves only at restricted times of the year. As a result the females move from species to species as the season changes. Young leaves may be covered with larvae and there may be much defoliation for a restricted period, but later when the leaves become tough there are no larvae, the females then laying on some other species of *Cassia*.

In situations where a larva is feeding on a small plant all the leaves may be eaten before the larva is full grown. It then moves and may or may not find another suitable plant. If sufficiently well grown it may be able to pupate prematurely and subsequently produce an undersized butterfly. Very small adult butterflies, sometimes only half the normal size, occur quite frequently among many species, especially in the dry season when food is more likely to be scarce, and all seem to be the result of poor feeding conditions for the larvae. The natural situation can easily be replicated in the laboratory by providing only just enough food to keep the larvae alive.

Competition and ecological segregation

Competition between individuals is likely to occur whenever resources are limited. A cluster of a hundred *Acraea* larvae feeding on an *Adenia* plant that can provide only enough food for fifty will sooner or later compete for food. Assuming that no other *Adenia* plant is available and that the larvae are not ready for premature pupation, two possibilities arise: they all die, or about half may die and the remainder survive. The second possibility is the more likely as the first demands that all the larvae are identical in terms of their ability to utilize the plant: some individual larvae may be less capable of exploiting the limited food supply than others and will then die of starvation.

If there are two species of *Acraea* larvae feeding on the same individual plant the chances are that one species will be better at utilizing the plant than the other. In this case there will be competition between species for the available food. The evolutionary consequences of interspecific competition for food are that similar species (1) tend to feed on different, although often similar, species of food-plant, (2) feed on the same food-plant but at different seasons of the year, or (3) feed on food-plants growing in different habitats or on different parts of the same food-plant. This kind of situation is an aspect of what is often known as the competitive exclusion principle, which stated briefly is that no two species have the same ecological requirements and so interspecific competition is minimized.

Unfortunately the ecology, including knowledge of larval food-plants, of groups of similar† species of African butterflies living in the same general area is inadequate, but an analysis of the butterflies of the British Isles shows that closely similar species tend to differ markedly in their larval food-plant, time of appearance, or habitat (Owen 1959).

The food-plants of many African butterflies are known, but most of the records come from widely separated geographical areas and there are likely to be regional differences in food-plant selection. What is needed is an intensive survey of the food-plants of a group of similar species in a restricted area. I have attempted such a survey in the genus *Acraea* in the vicinity of Freetown, Sierra Leone, but have not yet been able to find the food-plants of all the species present in the area. The results obtained thus far are given in Table 6.1. As shown, apart from three species on *Adenia lobata* (one of the species has an alternative food-plant), all feed on different plants, in many cases on plants belonging to quite different families. Only *Acraea rogersi*, a rather rare species, and *Acraea egina*, an extremely common species, seem identical in their choice of food-plants. It must be admitted however that the list of known food-plants is probably incomplete, and I would anticipate that some of the species, such as *Acraea bonasia*, which at present is only known to feed on a plant growing in swamps and yet is a common species in most open habitats, have alternative food-plants. Even so the information so far obtained supports the contention

† Similar species can be conveniently defined as those placed in the same genus by a competent taxonomist.

TABLE 6.1

Food-plants of the larvae of 14 species of Acraea *in the Freetown area, Sierra Leone*†

Species	Food-plants
Acraea bonasia	*Clappertonia ficifolia* (Tiliaceae)
camaena	*Premna hispida* (Verbenaceae)
circeis	*Urera oblongifolia* (Urticaceae)
egina	*Adenia lobata* (Passifloraceae)
encedon	*Commelina* sp. (Commelinaceae)
eponina	*Triumfetta rhomboidea* (Tiliaceae) and *Waltheria lanceolata* (Sterculiaceae)
lycoa	*Pouzolzia guineensis* (Urticaceae)
natalica	*Passiflora foetida* (Passifloraceae)
parrhasia	*Urera rigida* (Urticaceae)
pentapolis	*Musanga cecropioides* (Moraceae)
pharsalus	*Ficus exasperata* (Moraceae)
quirina	*Rinorea elliotii* and *R. subintegrifolia* (Violaceae)
rogersi	*Adenia lobata* (Passifloraceae)
zetes	*Adenia lobata* and *Smeathmannia laevigata* (Passifloraceae)

† The food-plants of the following species which also occur in the area are not known: *Acraea admatha, alciope, caecilia, cepheus, jodutta, perenna,* and *terpsichore.*

that closely similar species tend to be ecologically segregated as far as larval food-plants are concerned.

A more striking example of ecological segregation in the choice of larval food-plant occurs in the genus *Heliconius* (Nymphalidae) of tropical America. These butterflies are probably the ecological equivalents of *Acraea* in the American tropics. Table 6.2 shows the food-plants of nine similar species in Trinidad. In this instance all the species feed on vines of

TABLE 6.2

Food-plants of nine species of Heliconius *in Trinidad*†

Species	Food-plants (*all* Passiflora)
Heliconius isabella	*Passiflora serrato-digitata* and *laurifolia*
aliphera	rubra
melpomene	tuberosa and *laurifolia*
numata	lonchophora
erato	vespertilio, tuberosa, and *laurifolia*
ricini	laurifolia
sara	auriculata
wallacei	quadriglandulosa
doris	serrato-digitata and *laurifolia*

† From Alexander (1961).

the genus *Passiflora* and, as shown, there is a marked tendency for each species of butterfly to feed on different species of *Passiflora*. Only two species, *Heliconius isabella* and *Heliconius doris*, feed on exactly the same plants, but even here there are differences as *Heliconius isabella* eggs are

2 cm

2 cm

Elymnias bammakoo (Satyridae), the
black and white form

Elymnias bammakoo, the black and
orange form

Hypolimnas dubius (Nymphalidae), form
dubius, a black and white mimic of
several species of spotted Amauris

Hypolimnas dubius, form anthedon, a
black and white mimic of Amauris
niavius

Najas ceres (Nymphalidae), bluish-green
with black margins and a white subapical
bar

Euxanthe eurinome (Nymphalidae), black
and white with a yellow abdomen. The specimen is a female; the male is black and blue

Najas gausape (Nymphalidae), underside.
The uppersides of many species of Najas are
similar, but the undersides are often distinctive. Some have striking magenta patches;
in Najas gausape there is a broad magenta
band on the anterior of the hindwing

Palla ussheri (Nymphalidae), female. A
yellow, brown, and white forest butterfly.
The male is orange and black and quite
different from the female

20. Forest butterflies that feed on fruit

2. *Pseudaletis leonis* (Lycaenidae), upper- and underside. A rare species with a bold black and white pattern suggesting that it is a mimic of *Amauris niavius*

3. *Asterope boisduvali* (Nymphalidae), upper- and underside. A sombre brown butterfly bearing a superficial resemblance to a satyrid. This and other species of forest *Asterope*, although occasionally abundant, are rarely seen

4. *Pseudopontia paradoxa*, translucent white with no markings. The only member of a distinct subfamily of the Pieridae. It is extremely delicate and is confined to primary forest in tropical Africa

1. Four Nymphalidae that feed on rotten fruit

Cymothoe coccinata, brown and white female. A forest species

Hamanumida daedalus, grey with black-ringed white spots. A savanna species

Cymothoe caenis, black and cream male. A widespread species

Eurytela hiarbas, black and white. A forest species

⊢———⊣ 2 cm

21. Some West African butterflies

22. View of part of the garden at Freetown, Sierra Leone. There are probably about 300 species of butterflies to be recorded in the garden. In the right foreground are *Cosmos* daisy plants that have been deliberately encouraged to attract butterflies. (*Photo by D. O. Chanter*)

Wet-season male upperside   Dry-season male upperside | 2 cm

Dry-season female upperside   Dry-season male underside

Wet-season female underside   Dry-season female underside

Dry-season form of male produced in
the wet season by rearing the larva at
reduced humidity in the laboratory.
Upperside

Dry-season form of male produced
in the wet season by rearing the
larva at reduced humidity.
Underside

23. Seasonal variation in *Melanitis leda* (Satyridae). The butterflies are mainly brown and
orange and are similar to the European satyrid, *Maniola jurtina*

laid singly on the underside of the leaf while those of *Heliconius doris* are laid in clusters of up to fifty on the upperside. This means that *Heliconius isabella* larvae would occur as widely scattered individuals while those of *Heliconius doris* would be aggregated on single plants. In other cases where there is a food-plant in common another plant is also utilized, as in *Heliconius melpomene* and *Heliconius erato*.

In general tropical plants are relatively rare as species, with, of course, the exception of crops and their associated weeds. It is thus theoretically more likely that food would be a limiting factor to the growth of butterfly populations in the tropics than in temperate regions where plants of a species tend to be much more common. Compare for instance a butterfly whose larvae feed on oak in a north temperate forest with one whose larvae feed on a rain forest tree in Africa; oak trees tend to occur side by side in a temperate forest, but the rain forest tree may be the only individual of its species in an area of perhaps several square kilometres. A tropical forest butterfly is therefore more likely to be faced with food-plant scarcity, at least locally, than a temperate butterfly.

Competitive exclusion by choice of different habitat could also reduce the effects of interspecific competition. Evidence of this comes by comparing the habitats of closely similar species in different parts of their range. Thus *Charaxes acuminatus* (Nymphalidae) occurs in montane forest in the Cameroons, Uganda, Kenya, Malawi, and Rhodesia. Where *Charaxes acuminatus* and the very similar *Charaxes fulvescens* occur in the same area the former is above and the latter below 1600 metres altitude, but on the Kenya coast where *Charaxes fulvescens* is absent, *Charaxes acuminatus* extends down to 300 metres (Carcasson 1964). In West Africa, *Papilio demodocus* (Papilionidae) is a butterfly of open areas while the closely similar *Papilio menestheus* occurs in forest. The two occur together in gardens, but *Papilio demodocus* is much more common in this kind of habitat. Indeed whenever two or more closely similar species occur together there is usually one many times more abundant than the others. Thus three similar species, *Papilio nireus*, *Papilio sosia*, and *Papilio bromius* (Plate 33) occur in both forest and gardens in Sierra Leone. *Papilio nireus* is five times as common as *Papilio sosia* which in turn is twice as common as *Papilio bromius*. In Uganda I found *Papilio bromius* the commonest of the three.

Lastly, interspecific competition can be minimized if several closely similar species in an area have different cycles of seasonal abundance. As discussed in Chapter 5, almost all butterflies undergo seasonal cycles of abundance in the tropics, usually in association with the alternation of wet and dry seasons. But although climate may be directly responsible for these cycles there is also the possibility that the cycles have evolved in response to interspecific competition. Under this hypothesis common species in an area would tend to occur as adults at different times of the year, which in turn would mean that larvae would be feeding at different times of the year, an important consideration in situations where more than one species feeds upon a particular species of plant. But perhaps more important, closely similar butterflies reach their seasonal peaks of abundance at different times of the year and so competition for nectar and the juices of fruits is minimized.

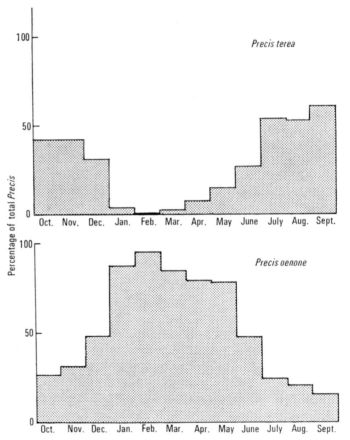

FIG. 6.1. Seasonal changes in relative frequency of *Precis terea* and *Precis oenone* in a garden at Freetown, Sierra Leone.

The results obtained from marking and releasing some groups of butter-flies in my garden at Freetown provide useful information on this point, especially when the seasonal peaks of groups of closely similar species are examined. Thus there are nine species of *Precis* (Nymphalidae) in the garden, but four are rare and were taken too infrequently to give reliable estimates of seasonal peaks of abundance. Two, *Precis terea* and *Precis oenone*, are extremely common and are often seen chasing each other from *Cosmos* flowers on which they feed. Fig. 6.1 shows the relative frequency (as a percentage of all *Precis* taken in each month) of these two species during the course of one year. Both species occur in all months, but *Precis terea* is far more abundant in the wet season and *Precis oenone* more abundant in the dry season. This means that competition for food among the adults is reduced as the two species (which together represent over 83 per cent of all *Precis* taken) replace each other as the season changes. Three other species, *Precis sophia*, *Precis octavia*, and *Precis pelarga* are moderately common in the garden. Their seasonal peaks are shown in Fig. 6.2. *Precis sophia* is relatively more frequent in December and again in

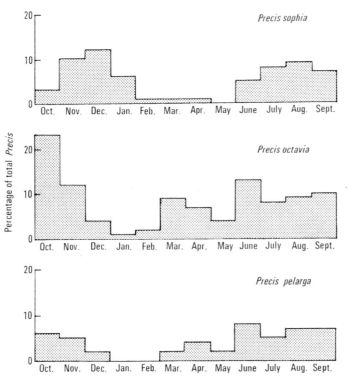

Fig. 6.2. Seasonal changes in relative frequency of **Precis sophia**, **Precis octavia**, and **Precis pelarga** in a garden at Freetown, Sierra Leone.

August and is rare or absent in the drier months of February to May. *Precis octavia* and *Precis pelarga* (which feed as larvae on the same food-plants) show an almost identical pattern of seasonal frequency, *Precis pelarga* being consistently less frequent than *Precis octavia*, but in these two species the situation is complicated by the occurrence of seasonal colour forms (Chapter 5) and, at least in *Precis octavia*, partial aestivation in the dry season. Indeed the life cycle and ecology of these two species is so similar that they appear to be an exception to the general idea of com-

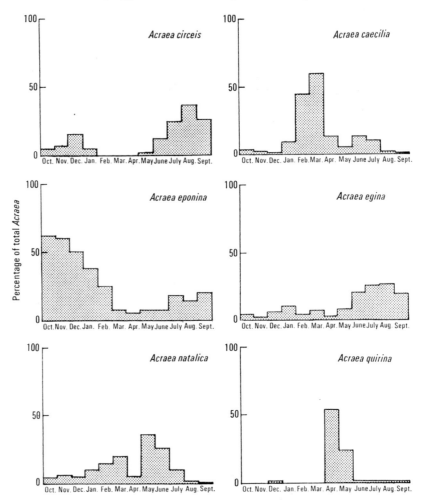

FIG. 6.3. Seasonal changes in relative frequency of *Acraea circeis*, *Acraea caecilia*, *Acraea eponina*, *Acraea egina*, *Acraea natalica*, and *Acraea quirina* in a garden at Freetown, Sierra Leone.

petitive exclusion; no obvious differences in the ecology of the two species seem to exist.

Fig. 6.3 shows the relative frequency of six species of *Acraea* in the same garden during the same year. Each of these six species reached a relative frequency of at least 25 per cent of the total *Acraea* butterflies flying in the garden in at least one month. As shown each species tends to reach a peak of relative abundance at a different time of the year, *Acraea circeis* and *Acraea egina* being the only two species that coincide. Fig. 6.4 shows the relative frequency of a further five species none of which exceeds in any one

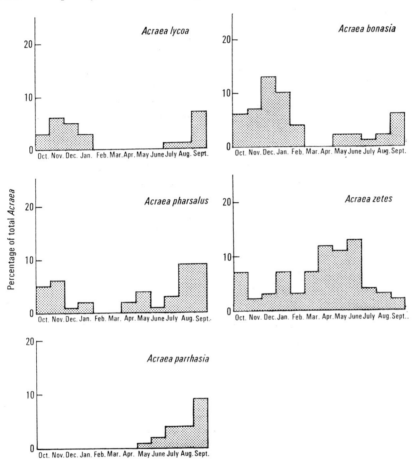

FIG. 6.4. Seasonal changes in relative frequency of *Acraea lycoa*, *Acraea bonasia*, *Acraea pharsalus*, *Acraea zetes*, and *Acraea parrhasia* in a garden at Freetown, Sierra Leone.

month a relative frequency of 15 per cent of all the *Acraea* butterflies flying. Here again the species tend to replace each other as the season changes. The remaining eight species of *Acraea* in the garden were relatively rare during the year and so no seasonal peaks could be established.

There is, then, evidence of ecological segregation among closely similar species of tropical butterflies. The evidence is far from satisfactory as it

depends upon observation of the contemporary scene. What is needed is
a thorough investigation into the population ecology of two or more similar
species living in the same area. When this has been done it may be possible
to obtain a better insight into competition and to see to what extent the
numbers of one species affect the numbers of another.

Brower (1961, 1962) has approached the problem in a subtropical area in
his study of the effects of population increase in *Danaus gilippus* (Danaidae)
on the numbers of the closely similar and migratory *Danaus plexippus*. In
Florida numbers of *Danaus gilippus* build up in June when *Danaus plexippus* is still present; *Danaus plexippus* then migrates northwards and breeds
north of the range of *Danaus gilippus*. The first instar larvae (both species
feed on the same food-plants) are egg cannibals and they also eat each
other's eggs. In *Danaus gilippus* the percentage of eggs cannibalized increases as the density of the eggs increases. This suggests a self-regulating
mechanism acting density-dependently. *Danaus gilippus* larvae are about
twice as cannibalistic as those of *Danaus plexippus*. But no difference has
yet been found in the extent to which the two species eat each other's eggs.
The possibility exists, however, that one species can adversely affect the
other by eating its eggs.

Concluding remarks

No mention has been made in this chapter so far of the effects of predators, parasites, and disease on butterfly numbers. This is because although
it is known that butterflies have many predators, parasites, and diseases,
nothing is known of the impact of these organisms on population size.

Most populations have a high capacity for increase and yet they remain
relatively stable. The stability is probably brought about mainly by
density-dependent events acting through competition. Most tropical butterflies are relatively rare, although butterflies as a whole are common
tropical animals. The larvae rarely deplete their food-plants, but this does
not necessarily mean that food is not a limiting resource. Mention has
already been made of the fact that many plants elaborate structural and
chemical defences against the attacks of herbivores and in this way the
growth of the herbivore population can be inhibited. Indeed plant resistance to the attacks of herbivores is probably so widespread that it has often
been overlooked. Cultivated crops with low resistance are sometimes
badly damaged by herbivores but when a resistant strain is developed the
herbivore population soon falls. In Africa some species of butterflies now
associated with crops and weeds and those that have gained by man's
devastation and alteration of the landscape have undoubtedly increased in
numbers quite recently, but there is no accurate documentation of such
increases.

The next chapter is devoted entirely to the population ecology of one species, *Acraea encedon* (Acraeidae), a species I have been studying in Africa for eight years. I initially started work on this butterfly because it seemed to be a highly variable mimetic species, but my interest developed along different lines as the existence of a highly unusual self-regulating mechanism came to light.

7

POPULATION ECOLOGY OF
ACRAEA ENCEDON

THE genus *Acraea* includes some of the most conspicuous butterflies in Africa. Many species have undoubtedly undergone recent changes in distribution as a result of human alteration of the landscape for they are now most abundant in cultivated areas, including gardens. *Acraea encedon*, a very distinctive member of the genus, occurs throughout tropical Africa south to the Cape. In Uganda the generation time (egg to egg) is about 60 days; in Sierra Leone it is about 41 days. This difference is probably due to the fact that Sierra Leone is considerably warmer than Uganda. In all probability there are between six and nine breeding generations a year in *Acraea encedon* in most parts of tropical Africa, with rather fewer in the south where, at least seasonally, it is cooler. These generations overlap and although there are marked fluctuations in numbers in different populations there is no evidence of any form of seasonal aestivation at any stage in the life cycle. Indeed the fluctuations in numbers are in some populations not associated with seasonal changes in the environment, in marked contrast to the situation in most other tropical butterflies.

Acraea encedon forms discrete populations in a wide variety of habitats, which include the tops of hills, lakeside forest edge, rice fields, weedy places near the sea shore, and cultivated land in general. It seems rare or absent in most tropical areas that have not in some way or other been altered by man, although it does occur in savanna in western Uganda and probably elsewhere. The adult butterflies fly slowly and are easily caught and marked. They are almost certainly unpalatable, as the yellowish secretion produced from a thoracic gland gives off hydrogen cyanide upon decomposition. The yellow eggs are laid in clusters of fifty to a hundred or more on the undersides of the leaves of various species of *Commelina*, an abundant weed of cultivation. Many different species of *Commelina* are utilized but the larvae refuse to eat the leaves of some species, including *Commelina capitata*, a forest plant that does not occur in the butterfly's usual habitat. In West Africa where there is a pronounced wet season and a relatively severe dry season populations of *Acraea encedon* are usually established in low-lying areas, especially irrigated rice fields, where *Commelina* does not die back in the dry season. In Sierra Leone some adult butterflies move on to higher ground in the wet season when certain species of *Commelina*† grow profusely, but evidently populations are not established in such habitats. In Uganda, which is much less seasonal than West Africa, *Commelina* is available all the year round, but the larvae of many hill-top populations feed on *Pseudarthria hookeri*, a tall woody weed that does not die back when the weather is dry.

All eggs of a cluster hatch together and the first instar larvae are highly gregarious. They first eat their own egg shells and then start on the surface tissues of the leaves of the food-plant. As they grow and moult into successive instars they spin communal webs, but become less gregarious by about the third instar and more or less solitary when full-grown. They eat entire leaves, flowers, and the thinner stems of the food-plant. In natural situations a cluster of a hundred or so first instar larvae is often reduced to a dozen or so by the last instar. The causes of death, or disappearance, are not known. Indeed there is little evidence of natural predators of the larvae, one braconid having been bred from a larva collected in the wild in Uganda, and a few tachinids from larvae in Sierra Leone. At Brimsu, Ghana, and Newton, Sierra Leone, I have found larvae feeding on *Commelina* growing out of water. Such larvae are presumably often isolated by surrounding water on small pieces of food-plant and in such situations may be deprived of sufficient food to survive. Larvae found on *Commelina* in two populations in Uganda refused to eat and died when transferred to *Pseudarthria*. But eggs laid in captivity on *Commelina* by butterflies from a *Pseudarthria*-feeding population produced larvae that fed successfully on *Commelina*. The larvae are black with paler stripes. They are spiny and extremely conspicuous, and one would suppose that they would be unlikely prey for vertebrate predators. In captivity they are easily reared but tend to die in large numbers from virus infections if crowded at high humidities. Larvae of *Acraea encedon* are shown in Plate 24.

Pupation takes place on or near the food-plant. In captivity the pupae tend to be aggregated on one side of the breeding cage. The pupae are variable in colour ranging from buff to black with all kinds of intermediates. Black pupae are more frequently produced in captivity, possibly in response to high densities in the breeding cages.

The butterflies usually emerge from the pupae in the early morning, later in the day if it is cool or if they are reared in an air-conditioned laboratory. If the weather is sunny the first flight is taken about midday and mating (Plate 24) can occur in the same afternoon. No mating takes place in the morning, but eggs are laid (provided there is sunshine) from about 10 a.m. onwards. Females lay a cluster of eggs, sometimes two or

† The systematics of the Commelinaceae is complex. There is much polyploidy and environmentally determined variation (Morton 1967), and I have not attempted to identify the species of *Commelina* upon which *Acraea encedon* feeds.

more clusters, 24 hours after mating and they are then ready to mate and lay further clusters of eggs. Males can mate with more than one female during the course of a sunny day and during their lifetime may mate with several different females.

A conspicuous feature of *Acraea encedon* is that in almost all populations there are a number of distinct genetically determined colour forms, some of which, in certain populations but not in others, are associated with mimetic assemblages of other butterflies. This topic is discussed in later chapters, but by far the most unusual feature in *Acraea encedon* is that although some populations have a normal 1:1 sex ratio in others there are hardly any males. The rest of this chapter is devoted to aspects of the ecology and genetics of these abnormal populations, but first it is necessary to consider briefly sex and sex ratios in butterflies in general.

Sex ratios in butterflies

In almost all sexually reproducing animals sex is an inherited trait. Although intermediates between the sexes (gynandromorphs) sometimes occur in butterflies (Ford 1945), most individuals are quite clearly either male or female. The sex of an individual is determined by its complement of sex chromosomes. All chromosomes, including sex chromosomes, occur in the cells of the body in pairs, one of each pair from each parent. In the Lepidoptera the pair of sex chromosomes in the male are identical and are written as XX. In the female there is only one X chromosome; its partner is not identical to it and so in the female the sex chromosomes are written as XY, which simply indicates that the two chromosomes are different. This situation is reversed in most other animals (including man), the male being XY and the female XX. Lepidoptera, birds, and caddis flies (which are probably related to Lepidoptera) are peculiar in having XY females.

When sperm are formed each receives a single X chromosome, but when ova are formed approximately one half receive X and one half Y chromosomes. Upon fertilization pairs of chromosomes are formed again, one half of the fertilized eggs having XX and the other XY, as shown in Fig. 7.1. This means that a female butterfly laying a hundred eggs should produce about fifty males and fifty females, a sex ratio of 1:1. Slight deviations from the expected 1:1 are normally the result of chance.

Fisher (1930) was the first to explain that no matter what the mechanism of sex determination an approximately 1:1 ratio of the two sexes would be maintained by natural selection. The almost universal occurrence of 1:1 ratios in sexually reproducing organisms had been taken for granted, and Fisher's explanation, which is widely accepted, becomes relevant if abnormal sex ratios of the sort that occur in *Acraea encedon* are discovered. Fisher's reasoning, usefully summarized by Hamilton (1967), is as follows:

Suppose male births are less frequent than female. A newborn male then has better mating prospects than a female and can expect to have more offspring. Any parent producing more males would tend to have more grandchildren. Since sex is inherited the male-producing tendencies spread and male births become more frequent in the population. As the 1:1 sex ratio is approached the advantage of the males is reduced. The same reasoning applies if females are substituted for males. Therefore the sex ratio is maintained at the 1:1 equilibrium.

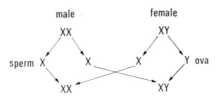

FIG. 7.1. Sex determination in butterflies. The pairs of chromosomes separate when sperm and ova are formed and rejoin (one from each parent) upon fertilization.

Extensive breeding of butterflies in all parts of the world has confirmed that in almost all species the sex ratio is 1:1. Field collections of adult butterflies often contain an excess of one sex over the other, usually in favour of the males. This is explained by differences in behaviour of the two sexes which affect the chances of each sex being collected. Thus if a collection of a species is made near the food-plant there will tend to be a bias towards females because females are more likely to be associated with the food-plant while egg-laying. Collections of butterflies feeding at mammal urine sometimes contain only males because males but not females of some species feed at urine. Large collections of *Acraea* and other butterflies in my garden at Freetown indicate that males are more active and are therefore more frequently seen and caught. Breeding these same species has confirmed that the true sex ratio is nearly always 1:1.

Sex ratio in *Acraea encedon*

As already mentioned, *Acraea encedon* usually occurs in discrete populations that are isolated from other populations. The butterflies fly slowly and it is possible when visiting a population to capture and mark (Plate 25) every or nearly every individual flying. Sufficiently large samples have been examined by this method to establish that there are in various parts of Africa populations with a normal 1:1 sex ratio. I know of three such populations in Tanzania, one in Ghana, one in The Gambia, two in Uganda, and two in Sierra Leone. Smaller samples and collections sent by correspondents indicate that normal sex ratios occur in populations in Zambia, Rhodesia, and Zululand. In marked contrast there are populations in the

Kampala–Entebbe area of Uganda, in Sierra Leone, and in Ghana where females outnumber males to such an extent that the populations are predominantly female. There is also evidence that predominantly female populations occur, or have occurred, in southern Nigeria (Poulton 1914). These predominantly female populations occur only in habitats disturbed by man in the more humid parts of tropical Africa; normal populations occur in drier undisturbed savanna.

TABLE 7.1

Overall sex ratio in predominantly female populations of Acraea encedon†

Population	Dates	N	Percentage of males
Kawanda	Feb. 1964–Mar. 1966	1739	3·9
Kololo	Oct. 1963–Mar. 1966	1647	3·5
Makerere	May 1964–Apr. 1966	1239	1·9
Lubya	May 1965–Apr. 1966	8627	2·5
Budo	Mar. 1965–Mar. 1966	2491	6·3
Kazi	Oct. 1963–Apr. 1966	1119	6·9
Nalugala	May 1965–Mar. 1966	367	3·0
Newton	Oct. 1968–Aug. 1969	1307	15·6

† From Owen and Chanter (1969) and Owen (1970).

Table 7.1 shows the overall frequency of males captured in eight populations in the Kampala–Entebbe area of Uganda and one in Sierra Leone. All the samples are large and each was obtained by repeated visits to the population for periods of a year or more. On each visit all or nearly all butterflies that were flying were captured, marked, and released. The extremely low frequency of males suggests a problem of genetic and ecological interest, especially as there are other populations where the sex ratio is normal.

In 1909–12, C. A. Wiggins, at the suggestion of E. B. Poulton, collected random samples of *Acraea encedon* from the Kampala–Entebbe area. The collection is preserved intact in the Hope Department of Entomology at Oxford University, and comprises 96 males and 54 females, suggesting a normal sex ratio. The apparent change in sex ratio between 1909–12 and 1963–6 is statistically significant ($P < 0.001$), as shown in Owen (1965, 1966). This suggests that the present abnormal sex ratios in *Acraea encedon* in the Kampala–Entebbe area are relatively recent in origin.

Inheritance of sex ratio

Many of the males found in the predominantly female populations are mated and in view of this it is clear that *Acraea encedon* is not entirely parthenogenetic. In both Uganda and Sierra Leone I have repeatedly obtained eggs from unmated females all of which proved to be infertile.

Reproduction by parthenogenesis (which is not known to occur in butter-flies) can therefore be ruled out. It also follows that with males sometimes occurring at frequencies of two or three to every hundred females, many females must remain unmated; I shall return to this later.

In Uganda I found that eggs obtained from four wild-taken females that had mated produced only female offspring. I also found that eggs obtained from three other females produced only females; but in Uganda I did not thoroughly investigate the genetics of sex ratio. When I came to Sierra Leone in 1966 I discovered another predominantly female popula-tion at Newton (Table 7.1). In 1968 I started a large-scale breeding pro-gramme from material obtained from this population and at the time of writing the work is continuing. It had been predicted (Owen and Chanter 1969) that there must be two sorts of females, one producing females only and the other males and females. Some old published records of breeding experiments with *Acraea encedon* by Lamborn in Nigeria also suggested the existence of two sorts of female: Lamborn reared 19 broods that con-tained only females and nine of males and females (Poulton 1914).

My laboratory stock of *Acraea encedon* was started from 28 clusters of eggs, each from a different wild female, collected at Newton from October 1968 to February 1969. These were reared, and 26 clusters produced only female butterflies and two males and females in approximately equal num-bers. There was no conspicuous mortality of the larvae or pupae. From this stock four successive generations were obtained in the laboratory. Three kinds of matings were made: brother × sister, male × female from all-female broods, and male × female, that were not sisters of the males, from male/female broods. The results are summarized in Table 7.2. Males

TABLE 7.2

Sexes appearing from different kinds of matings in Acraea encedon†

Kind of mating	Broods obtained	Sexes present in broods obtained
Brother × sister	24	Males and females
Male × female from male/female brood	5	Males and females
Male × female from all-female brood	17	Females only

† From Owen (1970).

mated to females from all-female broods produced only female offspring. Brother × sister matings and males mated to females not their sisters from male/female broods produced males and females. Four of the 29 broods that produced males and females contained a statistically significant excess of females, one an excess of males. In the remaining 24 broods there is no significant departure from the expected 1:1 ratio. One male was mated successively to three different females; two were its sisters and one a female from an all-female brood. The matings with its sisters produced males and females and the mating to the female from the all-female brood produced only females. Thus the existence of two kinds of females, one producing males and females and the other females only, is confirmed.

The larvae of *Acraea encedon* are gregarious and pupation takes place on or near the food-plant. Adult butterflies from a brood emerge from the pupae over a period of several days, the males appearing slightly earlier than the females, but with considerable overlap. Females can mate on the day they emerge. In view of this and because of the overall scarcity of males in a predominantly female population most matings that eventually produce males and females must be between brothers and sisters. Most matings, however, will be with females from all-female broods as these are the commonest kind of female in the predominantly female populations.

Survival of males and females and multiple matings by males

At three predominantly female populations, Lubya and Budo in Uganda, and Newton in Sierra Leone, enough butterflies were marked and re-captured five or more days after marking to test whether males and females have different chances of survival. The results are summarized in Table 7.3. At Lubya 15·8 per cent of all males marked were recaptured five or

TABLE 7.3

Survival of males and females for five or more days in three predominantly female populations of Acraea encedon

Population	Males		Females	
	Marked	Recaptured	Marked	Recaptured
Lubya	215	34	8412	317
Budo	157	14	2334	17
Newton	204	27	1103	26

more days later while only 3·8 per cent of the females were similarly re-captured; this difference is highly significant ($\chi^2 = 42\cdot4$, $P < 0\cdot001$). At Budo 8·9 per cent of the males but only 0·7 per cent of the females were recaptured five or more days later; this difference is also significant ($\chi^2 = 67\cdot8$, $P < 0\cdot001$). The higher percentage of recaptures of both sexes at Lubya is probably due to the fact that Lubya was visited more frequently than Budo; no biological effect is suggested. The situation at Newton was similar: 13·2 per cent of the males and only 2·3 per cent of the females were recaptured five or more days later, this difference also being highly significant ($\chi^2 = 113\cdot4$, $P < 0\cdot001$). These results show that males survive longer than females, or at least that they remain in the population longer than females. At one population, Kawanda in Uganda, a male is known to have lived for 41 days; no female is known to have lived more than 16 days. Thus it is possible that in the predominantly female populations males live two or three times as long as females.

In populations where males live longer than females there are increased chances of males mating with several different females. By marking and recapturing many instances of males mating with two different females were recorded and there was one record of a male mating with four different females. Evidently, then, males are capable of multiple matings, but it is questionable whether all the females in a predominantly female population could be mated. In such populations a male would have to mate with fifty to a hundred females if all females are to be mated, and this would seem impossible.

Aggregating behaviour

One of the most striking features of the predominantly female populations is the intense aggregating behaviour. On sunny afternoons females fly around each other as if in courtship and frequently settle in groups on vegetation. Later in the afternoon smaller groups join together to form one or two larger groups and eventually these settle on vegetation. Individuals are often so close together as to be clinging to each other. The same pieces of vegetation are used day after day and the same general areas are used for months or even years. Plate 26 shows part of an aggregation late in the afternoon and Plate 27 a small group of females clinging to grass stems and to each other. Aggregating behaviour does not occur in populations where the sex ratio is normal and it is conspicuously less intense when there is a temporary rise in the frequency of the males in a predominantly female population.

At sunset activity in the aggregations ceases and the butterflies remain together overnight. They disperse as soon as the sun is well up next morning and behave more or less normally, visiting flowers, etc., until early afternoon when the aggregations begin to form again. Males, if present, take part in the aggregations and mating often occurs in or near the centre of the aggregation.

During the aggregations unmated females lay eggs on plants that are not known as larval food-plants. The plants utilized appear to be those that happen to be growing in the areas selected for aggregating. None of these eggs hatch. Infertile eggs are also laid on the wings and sometimes on the bodies of other females. This usually occurs late in the afternoon when the butterflies are close together and often touching each other. Plate 28 shows part of the wing of a female *Acraea encedon* on which eggs have been laid by another female. Females with eggs attached carry them for days, but they seem eventually to fall off, possibly on contact with vegetation, leaving a small 'scar' on the wing where each egg had been attached. At Lubya in

Uganda about 0·5 per cent of all females examined had eggs attached. Usually there were only one or two eggs on each butterfly, but some carried large clusters, the maximum recorded being 56. Eggs have occasionally been found on the wings of females at Newton, Sierra Leone, but not nearly as frequently as in some of the Uganda populations.

The very low frequency of males in these populations and the production of infertile eggs under remarkable circumstances strongly suggests that in the predominantly female populations many females must remain unmated.

Fluctuations in sex ratio and in population size

In all predominantly female populations there are fluctuations in the frequency of males and in the size of the population. These fluctuations may occur quite independently of seasonal changes in the environment: in Uganda fluctuations in adjacent populations separated by no more than a few kilometres were often not synchronized.

It is possible to estimate the size of an *Acraea encedon* population with a high degree of accuracy because almost all butterflies present on any day can be captured and marked. D. O. Chanter and I made repeated estimates of the size of the Lubya population over a period of one year. I have repeated the exercise at Newton in Sierra Leone, but here I shall give only the results from Lubya as work in Sierra Leone is still in progress.

The population size at Lubya every tenth day (or nearest fine day) and the per cent males captured are shown in Fig. 7.2. In Uganda the generation time of *Acraea encedon* is about sixty days, hence the population size sixty days *after* the calculated sex ratio is shown in Fig. 7.2. By plotting the figures in this way the correlation between percentage of males and subsequent population size becomes evident. The most conspicuous correlations are as follows: the rise in frequency of males to just over three per cent by day 60 was followed 60 days later by an increase in population size to 141. Males then became infrequent or absent and the next rise in their frequency occurred around days 150 and 160 with a subsequent rise in population size to 250. A threefold increase in male frequency above the previous highest male frequencies around day 260 was followed by a high population of 574. It was not possible to continue observations after day 330 (10 April 1966) and hence it is not known what effect the nearly 13 per cent male frequency recorded around day 300 (not shown in Fig. 7.2) had on subsequent population size, but the frequency of males fell to just over 12 per cent on day 310, to under three per cent on day 320, while on day 330 no males were found. By day 330 the population had increased to more than a thousand, as shown in Fig. 7.2. Fluctuations in sex ratio were thus maintained and it appears that although males can increase in frequency over quite short periods the increase is not continued. Indeed two samples

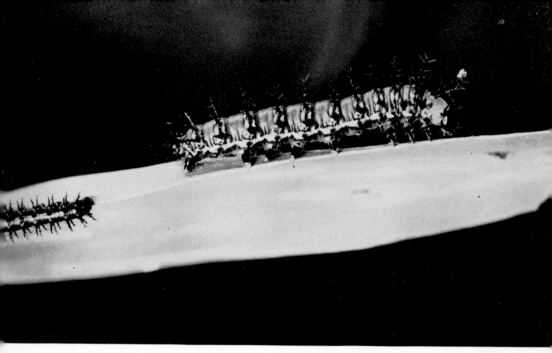

1. Larvae, which when full grown are about 35 mm long

2. Mated pair. The female is above. The pair may remain joined for three or four hours

24. *Acraea encedon* (Acraeidae)

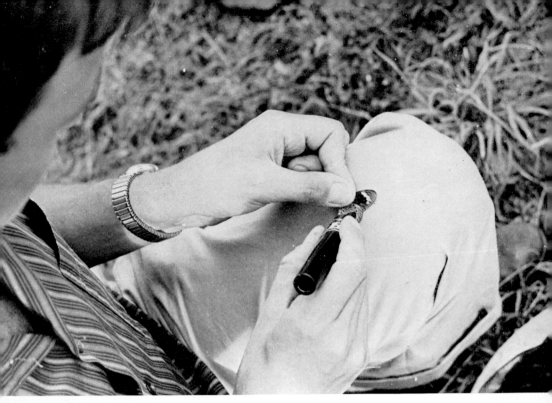

1. Holding a butterfly prior to marking

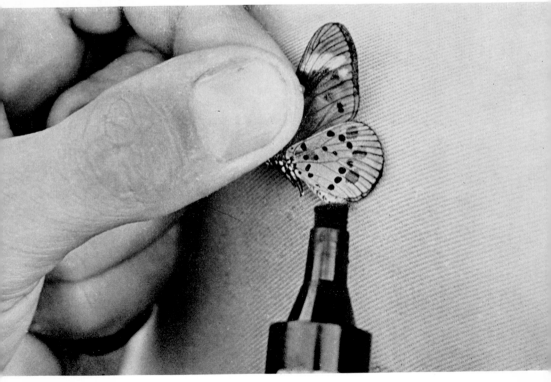

2. Three spots of ink placed on the hindwing

25. Marking *Acraea encedon* (Acraeidae)

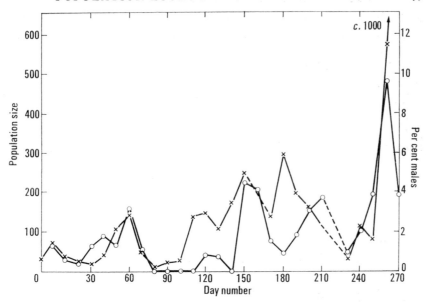

FIG. 7.2. Fluctuations in population size (crosses) and per cent males (circles) in *Acraea encedon* at Lubya, Uganda, 10 May 1965–10 April 1966. The figures for population size are brought forward 60 days in order that the correlation between them and per cent males may be seen. Broken line = no records. From Owen and Chanter (1969) in which details of sample sizes for the per cent male calculations are given.

of *Acraea encedon* collected on my behalf on single days nearly two years later showed that males made up only about one per cent of the population.

The general trend that emerges from Fig. 7.2 is for relatively high frequencies of males to be followed one breeding generation later by a high population and for relatively low frequencies of males to be followed by a low population size. This correlation is statistically significant ($P < 0.001$). Similar correlations have been obtained at other predominantly female populations of *Acraea encedon*. But in all these, as at Lubya, the sex ratio never approaches the expected 1:1 of a normal population; males are always rare but their frequency may double or treble within quite short periods of time.

An interpretation

The events described are of a highly unusual nature for butterflies and indeed for most species of animal. Most of the time it would be impossible for all the females in a predominantly female population to be mated, and the production of infertile eggs under unusual circumstances demonstrates that many females contribute nothing to succeeding generations. It is possible, however, that the aggregating behaviour increases the chances of multiple matings by males as all females tend to be in one place at the time of day when mating could be expected to occur. But male offspring are produced only from matings involving females from broods that also contained males; matings with females from all-female broods produce only females.

Two questions can now be asked and both can be partly answered. First, is it possible that the correlation between male frequency and subsequent population size (Fig. 7.2) is indicative of an intrinsic population regulating mechanism that has nothing to do with the external environment? A relatively high male frequency results in more matings and a larger population a generation later. This larger population contains relatively few males, matings are consequently relatively fewer and the population subsequently falls. It is possible that when the males are especially rare there is a tendency for matings to be non-random, the males (by some unknown mechanism) tending to mate with females from male/female broods rather than with females from all-female broods. This may partly explain the aggregating behaviour which is most intense when males are very rare. The males could then select particular females that will eventually produce broods of males and females. Such mate selection may not operate to the same extent when the males are more frequent. These events would result in population fluctuations that have little to do with the environment and in effect the population would be self-regulating. The danger with such a mechanism is that the population could easily become accidentally extinct if males were to disappear altogether for a period. One predominantly female population (at Entebbe in Uganda) did become extinct, while another (at Kawanda, also in Uganda) apparently became extinct, but was restarted perhaps by a stray fertilized female that was subsequently able to produce a brood of males and females.

The second question is how did the predominantly female populations arise? There is evidence that at least in the Kampala–Entebbe area the predominantly female populations arose recently, perhaps within the past fifty years (Owen 1965). It is possible that these populations changed as a result of hybridization of formerly isolated populations resulting from human disturbance of the environment. *Acraea encedon*, it will be recalled, is very much a butterfly of disturbed agricultural land, the larvae feeding on a common weed of agriculture. Many of the populations of *Acraea encedon* that I have examined must be of relatively recent origin because until recently the habitats they now occupy must have been covered with forest. There is moreover some evidence of movement of individuals between populations (Owen and Chanter 1969), but this only became apparent after marking and releasing, an event which itself could have resulted in movement.

As already mentioned the female has the XY complement of chromosomes. Suppose the Y chromosome has mutated in such a way that during fertilization it is 100 per cent successful and that no XX individuals are produced. The resulting offspring would be all females, and the trait would be transmitted generation after generation with nothing but females appearing from a mating. As the mutant spreads the sex ratio of the population will become more and more disturbed in favour of females, and the logical consequence is that extinction will eventually occur. This theory, which is explored in more detail by Hamilton (1967), can be referred to as the presence of a driving Y chromosome. Normally the effect of a driving Y chromosome would be covered up by other genes which suppress its expression; such genes could be located on other chromosomes. But when a female with a driving Y chromosome enters a new population, perhaps as a result of human disturbance of the habitat, the trait could spread rapidly as the new population may not have evolved the suppressing system. Under these conditions a population could become predominantly female in quite a short time, but the sex ratio should return to normal again once a suppressing system has been evolved. If the suppressors are not evolved the population could become extinct. This occurred in one population of *Acraea encedon* and may have occurred in another.

In 1969 I crossed male *Acraea encedon* from Ghana where the sex ratio is normal with females from all-female broods from Sierra Leone. All the offspring in 19 broods were females. Thus the experiment simulates what might have happened if these Sierra Leone females had spread into a normal population by natural means, and it is presumably in this way that the mainly female populations are started.

If in *Acraea encedon* the predominantly female populations result from a driving Y chromosome introduced into the population by females from elsewhere, then the population is only prevented from becoming extinct by the mating behaviour of the males. In particular, if at low frequency males mate mainly or only with females from male/female broods (that is, with females without the driving Y chromosome) the population is maintained and indeed regulated. In this sense the population regulation through the presence of abnormal sex ratios can be seen as an accidental consequence of the presence of driving Y chromosomes.

Some of what has been said in this section is highly speculative, but in general the facts fit the theory. I can envisage that the entire phenomenon has been generated as the result of man's alteration of the African landscape; in particular all the predominantly female populations so far discovered are in man-made environments and many of these environments are undoubtedly recent. Gene complexes that have been built up for centuries, perhaps over hundreds or thousands of breeding generations, have suddenly been thrown together and mixed. Indeed there is evidence of abnormal sex ratios in other species of African butterflies, including

Danaus chrysippus (Danaidae), but these have not been investigated in detail (Owen and Chanter 1968).

Finally it must be mentioned that I do not mean to imply that the population ecology of *Acraea encedon* as it is presently understood is in any way typical of butterflies: it is probably highly unusual. But remarkably little is known of the means by which butterfly populations anywhere are regulated. All that is really known, even in well studied species, is that populations tend to fluctuate within certain limits and that a high, but usually unspecified, percentage of eggs, larvae, and pupae die from equally unspecified causes.

The sex ratio phenomenon discovered in *Acraea encedon* might provide a clue as to how populations of insects of medical and agricultural importance can be controlled by genetic means and without the use of insecticides. Obviously if a population of an insect can be effectively converted to one sex, that population should rapidly decline and perhaps become extinct.

Work on the sex ratio in *Acraea encedon* is being continued at Newton in Sierra Leone. There are already indications that the situation at Newton shows some important differences from that described from Uganda. At Newton the habitat is altered periodically by man: weeds, including *Commelina*, are destroyed and a succession of crops is grown which are adapted more or less to the alternation of very wet and very dry conditions. These activities might well prove to be as important or even more important than the sex ratio phenomenon in regulating the size of the Newton population. We are also continuing laboratory breeding of *Acraea encedon* and in particular we are crossing isolated populations in an attempt to obtain a more precise idea of the genetics of sex ratio.

8

POPULATION GENETICS

IN Chapter 5 I discussed environmentally determined seasonal variation in several species of butterflies. As far as is known there is no direct genetic control of such variation, although there may be a genetic component to the capacity to develop seasonal forms in some areas but not in others. Apart from variation in adult size, which within limits is influenced by the availability of larval food, environmentally determined variation is rather unusual in butterflies.

No two individual butterflies are exactly alike and most of the differences between individuals are inherited from their parents. Individuals in some populations are extremely variable in colour and in pattern, and presumably also in less obvious biochemical and physiological features. A considerable number of African butterflies show geographical variation in the form of clines which is probably the result of genetic differences. Species that form discrete populations ecologically and geographically isolated from other populations often vary enormously in certain characteristics from one population to another.

Natural selection and genetics

The Darwinian idea of natural selection and its evolutionary consequences depends upon a series of propositions, all of which can be observed and tested. The first of these propositions is that organisms have an enormous capacity to increase in numbers, but that despite this capacity most populations remain relatively stable most of the time. Thus many female butterflies produce several hundreds of eggs, but if the population is to remain relatively stable the average number of offspring surviving per female will be one male and one female. Fluctuations in numbers do of course occur, but these are far less than the potential fluctuations. Secondly, it follows that since numbers remain relatively stable there must be an exceedingly high mortality rate, especially among the young and before the age of reproduction. There is no doubt that this occurs, although it is rarely apparent exactly what causes the high mortality. Thirdly, organisms are individually variable, no two members of a population are exactly alike, and many of these individual differences are heritable. Lastly, it follows that since individuals vary each will have a different probability of survival, which in terms of natural selection, means survival to reproduce. An individual's probability of surviving and reproducing is known as its fitness. Thus each individual because of its genetic constitution will tend to have a different probability of finding food, of being eaten by a predator or attacked by a parasite, and of dying of disease or through exposure to bad weather. Those that survive these hazards of nature will transmit their genes to their offspring, while the genes of those that die will not of course be transmitted.

Most of the time natural selection will tend to impart genetic stability to a population; that is to say, generation after generation the genetic structure of a population will remain more or less constant and there will be no conspicuous long-term change. But under the influence of an environmental change different individuals will stand a higher chance of survival and hence different genes will tend to be transmitted. Given time (in terms of the number of breeding generations that elapse rather than the number of years) the population will undergo a genetic change and will eventually become different from what it was originally. This is what is known as evolution.

Polygenic characters

Variation in a population may be discontinuous or continuous; that is to say, if a sample from a population is examined the individuals may fall into two or more discrete categories with few or no intermediates, or there may be a continuous range of possibilities around a mean value. Sex is the most obvious example of discontinuous variation and also included are the sympatric colour forms to be discussed later in this chapter. Continuous variation about a mean is usually determined by the combined effects of several genes, each having a relatively small effect on the observed character. Such polygenic characters can undergo rapid evolutionary adjustments to ecological conditions, especially if the population is isolated. These adjustments are achieved by a shift in the mean within the range of variation already present in the species. It is also possible for the existing range of variation to be extended through mutation and subsequent selection.

Ford (1964) has provided a good example of polygenic characters evolving in isolation in the European meadow brown butterfly, *Maniola jurtina* (Satyridae). The character studied was the distribution and frequency of spots on the underside of the hindwing which vary in number from one to six. Ford and his colleagues found that the distribution of these spots was constant over large and diverse areas of much of the English mainland, but that the spot distribution was quite different in the extreme south-west and particularly in the Isles of Scilly, where each island could be characterized by a particular spot distribution. It was also shown that the spot distribution could change within a few generations and that there were differences between laboratory-reared butterflies and those caught in the wild from the same population. Ford's analysis of polygenic characters in *Maniola jurtina* prompted me to search for a comparable situation in an African butterfly. Many African Satyridae have spots on the hindwing similar to those present in *Maniola jurtina*, but these are subject to environmentally determined seasonal variation and are thus not suitable for an analysis of polygenic characters.

Most species of African Acraeidae have a distinct arrangement of solid black spots on the underside of the hindwing which also appear, although less distinctly, on the upperside. In some species the spots are clustered in the region of the inner angle of the wing, but in others, including *Acraea encedon*, they are well dispersed and easy to distinguish. The spots vary in size and shape, usually between species, but there is also variation within species. Closely similar species have the spots in similar positions relative to the wing veins.

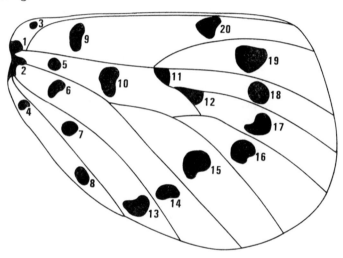

FIG. 8.1. Hindwing of *Acraea encedon* showing the distribution of the full complement of spots on the underside. From Owen and Chanter (1969).

In *Acraea encedon* the number of spots varies between individuals, while in *Acraea natalica* the number seems rather constant. Fig. 8.1 shows the full complement of spots in *Acraea encedon* and Fig. 8.2 the pattern of spots in *Acraea natalica*. The two species differ in that spot 17 seems always absent and spots 1 and 2 fused in *Acraea natalica*. (The spots can easily be seen in the photograph of *Acraea encedon* in Plate 28.)

Any of the twenty spots in *Acraea encedon* can be missing, although I have never seen a butterfly without spots; the nearest to this was a specimen from Makerere, Uganda, with only spots 11 and 12 present, but since these can be missing it is theoretically possible for there to be spotless

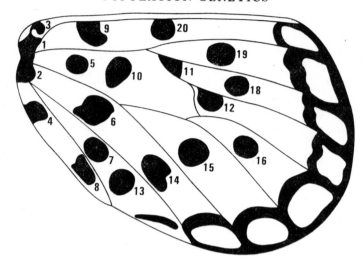

FIG. 8.2. Hindwing of *Acraea natalica* showing the distribution of the full complement of spots on the underside.

individuals. The presence and absence of spots is inherited, but the size and shape of spots appears to depend partly on development. Evidence for developmental factors comes from abnormal individuals with rayed spots, a character that is not transmitted to succeeding generations. Four rayed butterflies, all somewhat different from each other, have been found at Newton in Sierra Leone, and I have seen another specimen from Ghana.

Fig. 8.3 shows the frequency of spots in samples of *Acraea encedon* from populations at Makerere, Lubya, Kololo, Kazi, Entebbe, and Kawanda in Uganda, and from Bukoba in Tanzania. The location of the Uganda populations is shown in Fig. 8.5, the important point being that the populations are close together. Two samples were examined from Kawanda, one obtained in February to August 1964, the other in February and March 1966. Only the frequencies of spots 3–13 are shown in Fig. 8.3, as spots 1 and 2 and 14–20 were nearly always present in these populations. In all populations examined spots 3, 5, and 8 were most frequently missing.

Each population can be characterized by its own spot frequency. Thus Makerere differed† from Lubya in its lower frequency of 5 and 8, and Kololo from Makerere in its higher frequency of 3 and 8. The two populations on the shore of Lake Victoria, Entebbe and Kazi, differ in that 8 was more frequent at Kazi. Another lake-shore population, Bukoba, was like Entebbe, and differed only in a lower frequency of 3. But spots 3, 5, and 8 were all less frequent at Bukoba than at Kazi. Compared with other

† These differences are statistically significant and the levels of probability are given in Owen and Chanter (1969).

26. Part of an aggregation of female *Acraea encedon* (Acraeidae) late in the afternoon. The butterflies are clinging to grass stems and to each other. Budo, Uganda, 1965. (*Photo by Clive Spinage*). From Owen and Chanter (1969). Slightly reduced

27. A small part of a large aggregation of female *Acraea encedon* (Acraeidae). Some of the butterflies are touching each other and it is under these circumstances that infertile eggs are laid on the wings of other individuals. Budo, Uganda, 1965. (*Photo by Clive Spinage*).
From Owen and Chanter (1969)

1. Hindwing of female showing 14 infertile eggs laid by another female. The butterfly has been marked with four spots of coloured ink. Makerere, Uganda, 1965

2. Part of the underside of the hindwing of the specimen shown above much enlarged. From Owen and Chanter (1969)

28. Unusual egg-laying behaviour in *Acraea encedon* (Acraeidae). (*Photos by C. H. F. Rowell*)

29. The responses of blue jays to palatable and unpalatable butterflies. The bird attacks and eats a palatable butterfly (1–3), but when faced with an unpalatable *Danaus plexippus* (Danaidae) the bird eats only part of it (4 and 5) and reacts (6); it then vomits (7 and 8), but later recovers (9) and rejects subsequent butterflies of a similar coloration. From Brower (1969)

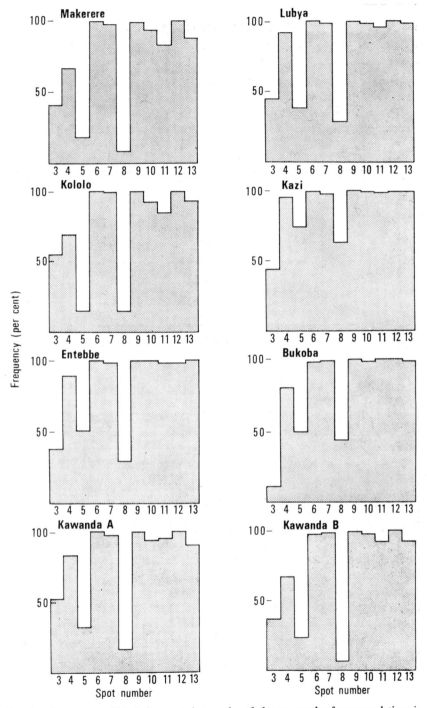

FIG. 8.3. Frequency of hindwing spots in samples of *Acraea encedon* from populations in the Kampala–Entebbe area of Uganda and from Bukoba in Tanzania. From Owen and Chanter (1969).

populations, which were all on hill-tops away from the Lake, the lake-shore populations were characterized by relatively higher frequencies of 5 and 8. The two most different populations were Kololo and Kazi. Five spots, 3, 4, 5, 8, and 11 differed significantly in these two populations as shown in Table 8.1. Except for 3, which was more frequently present at Kololo, the sample from Kazi was characterized by the presence of more spots.

TABLE 8.1

A comparison of spotting on the underside of the hindwing in two populations of Acraea encedon†

| | Percentage with spots | | | |
Spot	Kololo	Kazi	χ^2	P
3	54·9	44·0	5·6	<0·02
4	68·9	95·3	77·8	<0·001
5	14·6	73·8	166·1	<0·001
8	14·6	62·6	84·3	<0·001
11	84·1	98·1	42·4	<0·001

† From Owen and Chanter (1969).

Kawanda resembled Makerere, Lubya, and Kololo in relatively low frequencies of 5 and 8. Two samples were collected at Kawanda with an interval of about two years (approximately twelve breeding generations) between them. As shown in Fig. 8.3, in the later (1966) sample there was a decrease in the frequencies of both 3 and 4, but no change in any of the other spots.

These results from *Acraea encedon* are comparable with what Ford (1964) has described in *Maniola jurtina*. Adjacent populations differ in the frequency of spots and some spots can change in frequency within a population over a relatively short period. All the populations sampled are isolated from each other and there is probably only very restricted inter-change of individuals between even the nearest populations. Some movement does occur, because seven out of 1239 butterflies captured at Makerere had previously been marked at Lubya, 2·5 km away, while one of 1647 captured at Kololo had previously been marked at Makerere, 2·5 km away. As in *Maniola jurtina*, there is no clue as to the ecological significance of spot distribution in *Acraea encedon*, but it would seem likely that the differences are the result of natural selection acting on isolated populations. Indeed it is possible that the spots are merely an external manifestation of hidden traits and that selection is acting on the immature stages and not on the adult butterflies.

In large populations the differences described above would almost certainly be caused by adaptation brought about by natural selection, even though, as in this instance, the adaptive significance of the trait is not known. If the populations were small there is the possibility that random genetic drift is responsible. The idea of genetic drift is easily understood: if the population is small there may be chance elimination of certain alleles which after several generations will result in a different genetic structure of the population that has nothing whatsoever to do with adaptation and natural selection. But if the population is large chance will play a less important part and there will be considerably less risk of alleles being eliminated by chance alone. The populations of *Acraea encedon* are not large but the breeding generations overlap and there are nearly always some butterflies present. Whether the differences in spot distribution described above could at least in part be caused by the effects of drift cannot as yet be estimated. One approach would be to try and identify a selecting agent that is responsible for the spot distributions, but thus far this has not been possible.

There is also another possibility that must be mentioned. The subsequent genetic structure of a population, although perhaps influenced by natural selection, will depend on the genes present when the population was started. That is to say, what happens to a population after several breeding generations will depend upon the founders of the population. If a relatively small number of individuals start a population they will not contain all the possible alleles for a particular trait or traits and no matter how intense the selection there will be limits set by the genetic constitution of the founders, at least until the missing alleles arise by mutation or by further immigration of butterflies from elsewhere. In *Acraea encedon* there is evidence that many of the populations are of relatively recent origin, the butterflies having colonized habitats created by man. But it is not possible to say how many individuals are involved in founding new populations, nor is it possible to estimate the genetic constitution of these founders. An almost exactly parallel situation exists in the polymorphic African land snail, *Limicolaria martensiana*, which forms discrete populations that are often genetically different from each other, sometimes even when separated by only a few metres of unfavourable habitat.

Hence although polygenic characters provide evidence for evolutionary changes occurring in isolation, in butterflies the exact cause of these changes cannot be stated. There is no reason why selection, drift, and the effects of founders should not all be operating together in some populations, but to sort out the relative importance of each would be a mammoth task.

Multiple alleles and polymorphism

Polymorphism may be defined as the existence in a single population of two or more distinct genetic forms in such proportions that the rarest of them cannot be maintained by recurrent mutation alone. Differences due to age and sex are excluded. Intermediates may occur, but by definition at relatively low frequency. Polymorphic forms within a population are normally under the control of genes having clear-cut phenotypic effects. The existence of polymorphism reflects a balance of selective forces such that under certain environmental conditions one genotype is at an advantage in terms of chances of survival while under different conditions another genotype is at an advantage. Such a state of equilibrium occurs frequently, the ABO blood groups in man being a well known example.

Some polymorphic forms are very rare. Indeed some are so rare that they occur at frequencies close to the theoretical mutation rate. In butterflies the occasional occurrence of melanic individuals could be either a case of polymorphism or of recurrent mutation. Among the African butterflies, *Acraea egina* (Acraeidae) occasionally produces a melanic form, but insufficient sampling has been carried out on this species to determine whether it is frequent enough to constitute an example of polymorphism.

There are two general ways in which polymorphism can be maintained in a population. First, where the fitness of the heterozygote is greater than that of the homozygotes. Secondly, where the fitness of the alleles varies with their frequency in the population, that is to say, a given allele will be at a selective advantage over another so long as it does not exceed a specified relative frequency in the population. The frequency of polymorphic forms can change quite rapidly in a population and this situation is sometimes called transient polymorphism, but in most cases investigated the change is followed by stability at new frequencies.

Almost all cases of polymorphism known are under the control of multiple alleles. Multiple alleles are alternative forms of the same gene at a single locus, and usually there is a clear-cut order of dominance. A common situation is where there are two forms, one dominant and the other recessive. Polymorphism as a result of multiple alleles with dominance is of rather common occurrence in butterflies, especially in mimetic tropical species.

In butterflies the most common kind of polymorphism discovered so far is the existence within populations of two or more distinct colour forms. In many species these colour forms are mimetic, each being a mimic of an unrelated unpalatable species of butterfly that occurs in the same area. In an astonishing number of African species both mimetic and non-mimetic colour forms are found in the female only, the males being all alike. I know of no example among African butterflies of polymorphism confined to the male, although in *Pseudacraea eurytus* (Nymphalidae), one of the most polymorphic butterflies in the world, there are forms that occur only in the male as well as forms that occur in both sexes and in the female alone. Sex-limited polymorphism is usually determined by genes present in both sexes but which express themselves in the phenotype of one sex. No case of

Y-linked colour polymorphism is known among African butterflies, but its existence is possible because the black and yellow female forms of the North American, *Papilio glaucus* (Papilionidae) appear to be Y-linked (Clarke and Sheppard 1962*a*).

As already mentioned, there are two ways in which polymorphism can be maintained in a population, but although one of the ways, heterozygote advantage, has been frequently detected in other animals, including man, it does not seem to occur often in butterflies.

There is some evidence of heterozygote advantage in one polymorphic African butterfly, *Hypolimnas misippus* (Nymphalidae). In this species the polymorphism is limited to the female, the main colour forms being shown in Fig. 9.1 (Chapter 9). The *inaria* form of *Hypolimnas misippus* is recessive to the *misippus* form. Four crosses have given significant departures from the expected 3:1 ratio, which suggests a deficiency in the homozygous dominant *misippus* (Ford 1953, 1964). But since the number of crosses is small this result must be considered as tentative.

Polymorphism maintained by the fitness of the genes varying with their frequency in the population is probably of more general occurrence in butterflies. This is the most reasonable explanation of polymorphic mimicry in which within a population there is a series of mimetic forms, each bearing a resemblance to an unrelated unpalatable species. The frequency of each form depends upon the frequency of the unpalatable butterfly that it mimics: a mimetic form is common or rare depending upon the abundance or rarity of the unpalatable species. In the next chapter mimicry, including polymorphic mimicry, is discussed in more detail; here I simply want to mention mimicry under the general heading of the factors that are likely to generate polymorphism.

Polymorphism in *Acraea encedon*

Rather than undertaking a general discussion of polymorphism in tropical butterflies, I have decided to consider in detail polymorphism in *Acraea encedon* (Acraeidae), the species that has already been considered in regard to polygenic characters and sex ratios, and which will come in for further analysis under mimicry in the next chapter. As before, the field work on which this section is based consisted of capturing, marking, and releasing the adult butterflies. In the account that follows I have restricted myself to a discussion of the genetics of polymorphism, changes in gene frequency, and the effects of isolation on the genetic structure of polymorphic populations.

West African populations

It is convenient to consider polymorphism in West African populations first and then to turn to East Africa where the situation is more complicated because of the presence of more colour forms. Only four forms seem to occur in West Africa, and as with many other distinctive forms within a species, these have in the past received formal Latin names, which, for convenience, I shall continue to use. The four West African forms are shown in Fig. 8.4. Form *lycia* is black and white, as shown; *commixta* is a dull orange colour with the hindwing mainly dirty white; *infuscata* is dull orange marked with black; and *alcippina* is bright orange marked with black and with a mainly white hindwing.

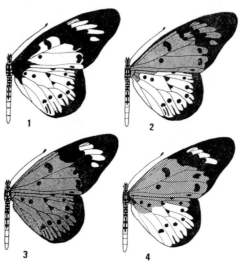

FIG. 8.4. Colour forms of *Acraea encedon* in West Africa. (1) *lycia*, (2) *commixta*, (3) *infuscata*, (4) *alcippina*.

Samples of twelve or more butterflies have been obtained from ten populations in West Africa as follows: The Gambia (1 population), Sierra Leone (4), Ghana (4), and Nigeria (1). The only large sample obtained in West Africa is 2517 individuals from Newton in Sierra Leone. In all but one of these populations *lycia* is the most frequent form. At Newton 68·3 per cent of the sample are *lycia*. Form *commixta* occurs in three of the Sierra Leone populations, in one population in Ghana, and in the Nigerian population, but *infuscata* has appeared only in three populations in Ghana. Form *alcippina* occurs as a rarity in two of the Ghana populations, while at Newton one has been recorded in the sample of 2517 individuals, a frequency that may not be above the theoretical mutation rate. At Gegbwema, Sierra Leone, 29 *alcippina* and no other colour forms were obtained in July 1970. Since *alcippina* is apparently rare in West Africa it is of interest to record that in 1912 Simpson recorded 39 *alcippina* at 'Gigbema' in Sierra Leone (Poulton 1914); 'Gigbema' is almost certainly an old spelling of Gegbwema.

The genetics of two colour forms

Extensive breeding has determined the mode of inheritance of *lycia* and *commixta*, the two common colour forms in Sierra Leone. All crosses that gave both phenotypes are summarized in Table 8.2. The broods for each

TABLE 8.2

Analysis of segregation ratios in laboratory reared broods of Acraea encedon *where the phenotypes of both parents are known*

Source	Inferred parental genotypes	Number of broods	Expected ratio	Phenotypic totals		χ^2
				Commixta	Lycia	
Sierra Leone	$Cc \times Cc$	12	3:1	466	170	1·01
Sierra Leone	$Cc \times cc$	3	1:1	40	40	0
Ghana	$Cc \times Cc$	4	3:1	197	57	0·26
Ghana	$Cc \times cc$	4	1:1	196	184	0·38
Ghana × Sierra Leone	$Cc \times Cc$	1	3:1	68	24	0·06
Ghana × Sierra Leone	$Cc \times cc$	6	1:1	144	141	0·03

type of mating are pooled because there is no evidence for heterogeneity, the calculations of which are given in Owen and Chanter (1971). The four matings between inferred heterozygous *commixta* from Ghana give a value of χ^2 that is just significant, but it is to be expected that when several values of χ^2 are calculated an occasional significant value will occur even when the null hypothesis is correct. The pooled result from each series of crosses was tested against the expected ratio, and, as shown in Table 8.2, there is no significant departure from the expected 3:1 or 1:1 ratios. These results demonstrate that the two forms are allelic, the *commixta* allele (which can now be written as *C*) being dominant to the *lycia* allele (*c*), so that individuals of the *commixta* phenotype are either of genotype *Cc* or *CC* and those of *lycia* phenotype are *cc*. The crosses that gave only one phenotype in the offspring do not contradict these results. Thus 46 *lycia* × *lycia* crosses gave a total of 3644 *lycia* offspring, one *commixta* × *lycia* gave 112 *commixta*, indicating that the *commixta* parent was of the *CC* genotype, and four *commixta* × *commixta* gave 357 *commixta*; in this latter case the *commixta* parents were either *Cc* and *CC* or *CC* and *CC*.

I have omitted from this analysis all wild-taken batches of eggs where the colour form of the male (and usually also the female) parent was not known. In general the results from these broods fully confirm the results obtained from controlled matings, but there was one important exception.

A wild female *lycia* taken at Legon, Ghana, produced 44 *commixta* and 136 *lycia*. This at first sight suggests a reversal of the order of dominance, but subsequent breeding from the offspring demonstrated that the female must have mated with two different males. In all probability one mating was with a male *lycia* and the other with a heterozygous male *commixta*. Assuming that the two males contributed equally to the brood of 180 obtained the expected ratio would be approximately 3 : 1 in favour of *lycia*, one mating resulting in *lycia* only and the other *commixta* and *lycia* in a 1 : 1 ratio. This case demonstrates the danger of predicting dominance and recessiveness when matings have not been rigidly controlled.

Fluctuations in the frequency of the lycia *allele at Newton*

The population at Newton in Sierra Leone is centred on some irrigated rice fields. The rice is planted in July after the onset of the rains and is harvested in the early part of the dry season in November and December. During the rest of the year, mainly in the dry season and early part of the wet season, a variety of other crops is grown in the rice fields. The area is subject to repeated modification by agricultural workers who from time to time remove large quantities of *Commelina*, the weed which is the only known food-plant of *Acraea encedon* in West Africa. Newton was visited once a week for fifty consecutive weeks (October 1968 to September 1969) and subsequently every two weeks until May 1970. Every individual *Acraea encedon* seen was captured, marked, and released, and the figures obtained from each visit provide an indication of fluctuations in population size as well as fluctuations in gene frequency. But before presenting and discussing the results of this sampling it is necessary to go into what is meant by gene frequency.

When the frequency of a polymorphic form in a population changes it is usual to analyse the data in terms of the frequency of the gene responsible for the polymorphism rather than the frequency of the phenotype itself. This is because a recessive allele can be hidden in a population, but actually be much more common than the occurrence of the occasional homozygous recessive phenotype would suggest. To illustrate the point, consider the *commixta* and *lycia* forms of *Acraea encedon*. As already shown *commixta* is dominant to *lycia*, and hence a *commixta* phenotype may be either CC or Cc, while *lycia* is always cc. Suppose a population of one hundred *Acraea encedon* is made up of four *commixta* with the genotype CC, 32 *commixta* with Cc, and 64 *lycia* which are cc. The allele c thus occurs once in each of the 32 heterozygotes and twice in each of the 64 homozygous *lycia*, a total of 160 times. The maximum possible number of times it could occur (if the whole population were *lycia*) is 200, that is, twice the population size. We can then calculate the gene grequency of c as 160/200 or 0·8. This can alternatively be expressed as 80 per cent.

Unfortunately when analysing field samples of *Acraea encedon* it is not possible to distinguish the homozygous from the heterozygous *commixta*, the only figures available being the number of *lycia* and the total number of both types of *commixta*. In consequence it is not possible to determine the frequency of *c* exactly. The best that can be done is to make the assumption that the frequencies of the three genotypes follow a mathematical pattern known as the Hardy–Weinberg ratio. This is equivalent in biological terms to making the assumptions that mating is random between the phenotypes and that there is no natural selection. It is then possible, given the frequency of any one of the genotypes, to estimate the frequencies of the other two. I shall omit details as to how this is done, but simply note that in this case the estimate of the gene frequency of *c* is obtained by taking the square root of the frequency of the *lycia* phenotype obtained in the sample. Thus for the figures given earlier the gene frequency of *c*, 0·8, is the square root of 0·64, the frequency of the *lycia* phenotype in the population.

The advantage of calculating gene frequencies is that the results provide evidence of genetic changes that are taking place in the population.

The results of sampling at Newton are shown in Table 8.3. Two periods when the population was small, weeks 19–29 (March and April 1969) and weeks 68–82 (February to May 1970) coincide with the driest time of the year, suggesting that fluctuations in population size may be seasonal. Before the first fall in population size the estimated frequency of the *lycia* gene showed small fluctuations about a mean of 83·2 per cent. At the beginning of the subsequent rise in population size, weeks 27–33 (end of April and May 1969), the average gene frequency was 70·1 per cent, a significant† difference from its former value. It is impossible to say whether this change was the result of a seasonal founder effect (see later), but as the population increased again the frequency of the *lycia* gene returned to its former level, the estimate for weeks 52–66 (October 1969 to January 1970) being 84·2 per cent, which is not significantly different from its original average of 83·2 per cent. It will be recalled that in *Acraea encedon* breeding generations overlap and that the mean generation time in Sierra Leone is 41 days, and it is therefore not possible to analyse the fluctuations in the frequency of the *lycia* allele with the techniques used by Fisher and Ford (1947) for a population of the moth, *Panaxia dominula*, the breeding generations of which are discrete. By taking the samples obtained in weeks 28–48 (the period of increase in the frequency of *lycia*) it is possible to show that this increase is significant, whereas the fluctuations from week to week can be explained by sampling effects (Owen and Chanter 1971).

Nothing is known of the adaptive significance of the *commixta* and *lycia* alleles, except that the phenotypes they produce are not mimetic. The

† Results of statistical testing are here omitted, but are given in Owen and Chanter (1971).

TABLE 8.3

Fluctuations in population size and in the frequency of the lycia *gene at Newton*

Week number†	commixta	lycia	N	Frequency of lycia gene (per cent)‡	Week number	commixta	lycia	N	Frequency of lycia gene (per cent)
1	23	61	84	85·2	42	7	25	32	88·4
2	25	36	61	77·3	43	6	7	13	73·4
3	13	18	31	76·4	44	2	21	23	93·5
4	15	29	44	80·3	45	19	41	60	83·2
5	19	46	65	84·9	46	11	52	63	91·1
6	13	42	55	87·3	47	5	42	47	94·2
7	22	38	60	79·6	48	10	28	38	85·8
8	11	19	30	77·1	49	15	18	33	75·6
9	9	16	25	79·3	50	45	39	84	69·5
10	7	20	27	87·1	51				
11	16	58	74	88·5	52	19	56	75	86·4
12	23	45	68	82·5	53				
13	26	57	83	82·1	54	11	44	55	89·4
14	37	99	136	85·9	55				
15	30	78	108	84·4	56	24	41	65	79·4
16	15	36	51	84·5	57				
17	11	7	18	67·1	58	18	42	60	83·7
18	4	12	16	86·6	59				
19	—	—	—		60	2	7	9	
20	—	1	1		61				
21	1	1	2		62	16	29	45	80·3
22	—	—	—		63				
23	—	—	—		64	9	25	34	85·7
24	3	4	7		65				
25	1	1	2		66	4	8	12	81·6
26	—	—	—		67				
27	2	4	6		68	7	2	9	
28	5	2	7		69				
29	3	2	5		70	1	2	3	
30	6	4	10	67·4	71				
31	5	7	12	76·4	72	—	—	—	
32	no data				73				
33	11	8	19	64·9	74	—	—	—	
34	3	7	10	83·7	75				
35	14	13	27	69·4	76	1	—	1	
36	9	16	25	78·4	77				
37	1	6	7		78	—	1	1	
38	7	8	15	73·1	79				
39	—	6	6		80	—	—	—	
40	1	7	8		81				
41	18	39	57	83·0	82	—	—	—	

† Commencing 23 October 1968 and ending 12 May 1970. The population was sampled every week for the first 50 weeks, thereafter every two weeks.
‡ Gene frequencies are not calculated for samples of less than 10.

Newton population of *Acraea encedon* seems to undergo fluctuations in numbers that are associated with the alternation of wet and dry seasons. There are two possible explanations of seasonal changes in adult numbers, as already mentioned in Chapter 5. The population as a whole may not fluctuate but at certain times of the year there may be a delay in the development of eggs, larvae, or pupae. In *Acraea encedon* such a delay obviously does not affect all individuals as there are usually some butterflies around. Secondly, the fluctuations in adult numbers could reflect real changes in the overall population size, which in effect means that the probability of survival varies with the season of the year. These two possibilities would have quite different effects on the genetic structure of the population. Thus if a population is reduced to very small numbers by the end of the dry season the effect of the surviving founders and subsequent gene frequencies would be considerable. There is no field evidence for dry season aestivation in *Acraea encedon* and in extensive laboratory breeding there was no suggestion of a developmental delay at any stage in the life cycle. At Newton the larval food-plant is available all the year round although the effects of weeding may on occasion reduce the amount of food-plant substantially.

Acraea encedon lays its eggs in batches of varying size, but usually between twenty and a hundred. The larvae are gregarious in the early instars. Although no figures are available it appears that many batches of eggs and young larvae disappear completely while in others survival is high. Hence the probabilities of survival of offspring of a single female may not be mutually independent, some batches contributing markedly to the next generation and others not at all. The effect of high survival in some batches could cause some or all of the fluctuations in gene frequency shown in Table 8.3.

This experiment shows that sampling over thirteen overlapping breeding generations detected significant genetic change in the structure of the population, but that at the end of the experiment the situation was effectively the same as at the beginning.

East African populations

Samples of *Acraea encedon* have been obtained from populations in Tanzania and Uganda. The Uganda populations are discussed in detail in Owen and Chanter (1969). Here I shall consider populations in the Kampala–Entebbe area (Fig. 8.5) where it was possible to obtain exceptionally large samples. The situation in East Africa in regard to polymorphism is much more complex than in West Africa. Thus in Uganda there may be twelve forms present in a single population.

The colour forms known from the Kampala–Entebbe area are shown in Fig. 8.6. Again Latin names exist for many of the colour forms and these are used sometimes in combination with descriptive English names. The following descriptions amplify the black and white illustrations in Fig. 8.6.

(1) *encedon:* the so-called typical form, with a bright orange ground colour, black markings, and a white subapical bar. The West African *infuscata* is similar, but duller orange.

(2) *alcippina:* like *encedon*, but with a white area in the hindwing that varies in size between individuals; in some specimens there is hardly any orange (as in West African *alcippina*) while in others the wing is mainly orange.

(3) *daira:* like *encedon*, but with the black and white wing tip absent and replaced by orange.

FIG. 8.5. The Kampala–Entebbe area of Uganda showing locations of the populations of *Acraea encedon*. From Owen and Chanter (1969).

(4) *lycia:* the orange is replaced by white, but the markings are as in *encedon*. This form does not differ from West African *lycia*.

(5) suffused *alcippina:* like *alcippina*, but with a blackish suffusion in the forewing and in the corner of the hindwing.

(6) *sganzini:* like *encedon*, but the orange and white replaced by lemon yellow; a few specimens with a dark suffusion in the forewing are included.

(7) suffused *lycia:* distinguished from *lycia* by a heavy black suffusion in the forewing.

(8) white *alcippina:* like *alcippina*, but with white areas in the forewing, and the remaining orange areas suffused as in suffused *alcippina*.

(9) and (10) *encedon-daira:* a variable form illustrated in Fig. 8.6 by two extremes. There is a continuous series of intermediates ranging from the replacement of the white subapical bar in *encedon* by orange, to the near absence of the apical markings as in *daira*.

(11) and (12) *alcippina-daira:* as in *encedon-daira*, but with the white hindwing of *alcippina*.

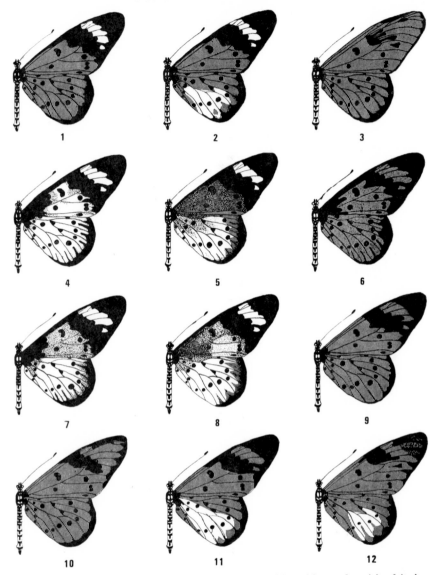

Fig. 8.6. Colour forms of *Acraea encedon* in East Africa. (1) *encedon*, (2) *alcippina*, (3) *daira*, (4) *lycia*, (5) suffused *alcippina*, (6) *sganzini*, (7) suffused *lycia*, (8) white *alcippina*, (9) and (10) *encedon-daira*, (11) and (12) *alcippina-daira*. From Owen and Chanter (1969).

Other forms occur as extreme rarities, but these are not figured, nor are they discussed in the section that follows.

Table 8.4 shows the relative frequency of colour forms in nine populations in the Kampala–Entebbe area. In all populations *encedon* is the most

TABLE 8.4

Relative frequency (per cent) of colour forms of Acraea encedon in the Kampala–Entebbe area

Colour form (see Fig. 8.6)	Population								
	Kawanda	Kololo	Makerere	Lubya	Budo	Kazi	Nalugala	Kagolomolo	Entebbe
encedon	67·1	69·0	64·1	65·7	65·5	51·6	47·1	34·9	43·8
alcippina	22·3	25·1	25·9	15·3	14·8	1·5	0·8	—	—
daira	4·8	1·3	4·0	10·3	8·1	14·3	18·3	28·6	15·1
lycia	1·1	0·4	0·6	2·1	5·7	22·4	24·3	22·2	24·7
suffused alcippina	0·2	0·3	0·1	0·2	0·3	—	—	—	—
sganzini	0·1	—	0·2	0·4	0·8	1·3	1·4	1·6	6·9
suffused lycia	0·1	0·1	0·1	0·3	0·2	2·4	1·6	1·6	4·1
white alcippina	0·6	0·5	0·9	0·5	0·4	—	—	—	—
encedon-daira	2·7	2·0	2·2	3·3	2·6	3·8	4·6	6·3	2·7
alcippina-daira	0·9	1·3	1·9	1·8	1·6	2·7	1·9	4·8	2·7
others	—	—	—	0·1	—	—	—	—	—
Number examined	1739	1647	1239	8627	2491	1119	367	63	73

frequent form, varying from 34·9 per cent at Kagolomolo to 69·0 per cent at Kololo. Form *encedon* occurs at higher frequencies in populations located on the tops of small hills (Kawanda, Kololo, Makerere, Lubya, and Budo) than in populations located on level ground near the shore of Lake Victoria (Kazi, Nalugala, Kagolomolo, and Entebbe). Form *alcippina* is next in frequency in the hill-top populations, but is rare in the lake-shore populations. Both *daira* and *lycia* vary in frequency from population to population, and both are more frequent by the lake shore than in the hill-top populations. All the other forms are relatively rare. Suffused and white *alcippina* occur only where *alcippina* is frequent, suggesting that these two forms are modifications of *alcippina*. Except at Entebbe where it reaches 6·9 per cent, *sganzini* is very rare. Likewise suffused *lycia* is rare and appears to be associated with high *lycia* frequencies. Specimens classified as 'others' in Table 8.4, all from Lubya, are mostly butterflies too damaged to be recognized, but also include rare forms not shown in Fig. 8.6.

It may be noted that in populations where the sample size exceeds 1000, and especially at Lubya, where the sample size is 8627, a low percentage in Table 8.4 is often based on a large number of specimens. Thus the figure of 0·3 per cent suffused *lycia* at Lubya is based upon 23 specimens. Many of the differences in relative frequency of the forms in different populations are statistically significant, as shown in Owen and Chanter (1969). Thus although Makerere and Lubya are separated by 2·5 km of cultivated land and are within easy flying distance of each other, there is a significantly higher frequency of *alcippina* at Makerere and a much higher frequency of *daira* at Lubya, while *lycia* is infrequent in both populations but is significantly more frequent at Lubya. Many other significant differences between populations exist and the reader is referred to the more detailed analysis in Owen and Chanter (1969).

The overall picture is that *Acraea encedon* is split into discrete populations by ecological and geographical barriers, with some possible gene flow between nearby populations, but with each population characterized by the frequency and occurrence of polymorphic forms.

The genetics of East African colour forms

No extensive breeding under laboratory conditions has thus far been carried out on East African *Acraea encedon*. Some provisional results indicate that *daira* is dominant to both *encedon* and *lycia*.

Survival in relation to colour form

There is evidence from marking and releasing that some colour forms are more likely to leave the population than others. It is not known whether some butterflies leave the population as a result of being marked, but this seems possible. However, it appears that if a butterfly is going to leave it does so immediately or soon after being marked. The term 'survival' is always difficult to interpret in an animal like a butterfly; in marking and releasing experiments survival more accurately means remaining in the population.

Table 8.5 shows the survival in relation to colour form at Lubya, one of

TABLE 8.5

Survival in relation to colour form at Lubya, Uganda

Colour form	Marked	Recaptured	Per cent recaptured
encedon	5533	225	4·1
alcippina	1259	36	2·9†
daira	881	41	4·7

† The tendency for *alcippina* to survive less well than *encedon* and *daira* is statistically significant ($\chi^2 = 4\cdot1$ and $4\cdot7$ respectively), as shown in Owen and Chanter (1969).

the populations in the Kampala–Entebbe area located on a hill-top. Only recaptures after five or more days are recorded and so the survivors are butterflies that remained in the population for five or more days after being marked. Form *alcippina* survived significantly less well than *encedon* and *daira*; the small difference between *encedon* and *daira* is not significant.

The tendency of like forms to aggregate together

As shown in Chapter 7 many populations of *Acraea encedon* are predominantly female. In these populations, as has already been described, there is intense aggregating behaviour, the significance of which is not fully understood. Casual observations suggest that in localities where more than one aggregation occurs there is a tendency for like forms to aggregate together. At Lubya in January 1966 the frequencies of colour forms captured and marked in two aggregations (between which there was repeated interchange) separated by 20 metres were compared. The results for *alcippina* and *daira* are shown in Table 8.6. The frequency of *encedon* in the two aggregations does not differ significantly, but one aggregation was characterized by a high frequency of *daira* and the other by a high fre-

TABLE 8.6

The tendency for alcippina *and* daira *to aggregate with themselves, Lubya, Uganda*

Aggregation†	alcippina	daira
1	70	8
2	16	47

The difference between the two aggregations is statistically significant ($\chi^2 = 59\cdot6$), as shown in Owen and Chanter (1969).

1. Madagascan female. Males and females from Madagascar are alike in colour and pattern and are yellow and black

2. South African female mimetic form. A black and white mimic of *Amauris niavius* (Danaidae)

3 and 4. Intermediate females resulting from crossing Madagascan butterflies with black and white mimetic forms. Unlike mainland females they have tails but the pattern incorporates elements of both Madagascan and mainland females

| 2 cm |

5. Another mimetic female from South Africa. An orange, black, and white butterfly, and a good mimic of *Danaus chrysippus* (Danaidae)

6. Intermediate female resulting from crossing Madagascan male with female like (5). This individual is more like the mainland parent

30. Genetics of *Papilio dardanus* (Papilionidae). (*Photos by C. A. Clarke and P. M. Sheppard*)

2 cm

1. On the left are upper- and undersides of *Najas themis* (Nymphalidae), and on the right upper- and undersides of *Najas janetta*. The two species are extremely similar. Both are remarkably variable, with or without red patches at the base of the underside of the fore- and hindwings. In *Najas themis* the subapical bar is white and is also conspicuous on the underside; there is a white patch on the blue-green area of the hindwing. In *Najas janetta* the subapical bar is the same blue-green as in the hindwing, and does not show on the underside. In Sierra Leone *Najas janetta* appears to be confined to the forest of the Freetown peninsula and is replaced in other forests by *Najas themis*

2. Sexual dimorphism in *Aterica galene* (Nymphalidae), a common butterfly of the forest floor throughout tropical Africa. The male (left) is small and the light patches in the hindwing are pale yellow. The female (right) is larger and the pale area of the hindwing is either white (as shown) or orange

2 cm

31. Geographical replacement of species, and sexual dimorphism

2 cm

Charaxes protoclea, male (black and red)

Charaxes lucretius, male (dark brown with red markings and purple reflections)

Charaxes castor, sexes alike (black and pale yellow with blue markings at edge of hindwing)

Charaxes protoclea, female (black and white with a red margin to the wings)

Charaxes lucretius, female (dark brown and pale yellow with orange margins)

Charaxes varanes, sexes alike (white with broad brown and orange borders)

32. Variation in the extent of development of sexual dimorphism in *Charaxes* (Nymphalidae) butterflies

Papilio nireus

Papilio sosia

Papilio bromius

2 cm

33. Three similar species of *Papilio* (Papilionidae). They can be distinguished by the width of the blue-green band across the wings and the development of spots in the margin of the forewing

quency of *alcippina*. I cannot say, however, whether the statistical tendency for like forms to remain together is due to a preference on the part of the butterflies or to slight differences in the environment to which the two phenotypes respond differently. The tendency of like forms to aggregate together and the fact that mating often occurs in the aggregations should result in a certain amount of assortative mating, but no evidence of this could be found in any population when matings were examined.

The significance of colour forms in Acraea encedon

More is now known about the population biology and ecological genetics of *Acraea encedon* than any other species of tropical butterfly. As regards polymorphism, the forms appear to be allelic and are not associated with sex. The effects of isolation on the genetic structure of the population can be seen not only in differences in the frequency of colour forms, but also in the frequency of hindwing spotting and in differences in the sex ratio. It has been shown that the gene frequency can change, but although natural selection probably determines changes of this sort, the precise mechanism of selection is elusive. Differences in behaviour and survival also occur between colour forms. Some of the forms are mimetic and this topic is taken up in the next chapter, but before doing so it is necessary to mention briefly a kind of natural selection, analysis of which, so far as butterflies are concerned, is only in the theoretical stage.

Apostatic selection

The word *apostatic* means standing apart in kind or quality. Apostatic selection has recently been suggested as a useful concept to explain polymorphisms where there are several contrasting colour forms that are neither mimetic nor cryptic. The concept depends upon the theory, for which there is some evidence, that visual predators such as birds develop a specific search image such that they successfully locate proportionately more of the most frequent types of prey in a population. If the prey are contrastingly polymorphic for colour, relatively rare forms will be at a selective advantage provided they remain relatively rare. As soon as they tend to become more frequent their selective advantage is reduced, and hence a balanced polymorphism is achieved, each form being maintained at a relatively stable frequency. The concept of apostatic selection does not depend on the forms necessarily being cryptic: the important quality is that they should contrast with each other thus restricting the learning abilities of the predators.

No one has yet investigated the possible action of apostatic selection in butterflies. However, they are the sort of animal in which one might expect apostatic polymorphisms to develop because they have conspicuous colours that are presumably easily learnt by predators.

Polymorphisms occur in many non-mimetic species and in many of these the colour forms are conspicuously contrasting. It is possible that such polymorphisms are maintained by apostatic selection. Fig. 8.7 shows the

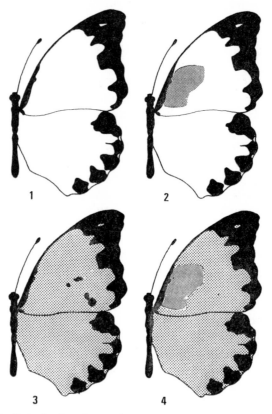

FIG. 8.7. Female-limited colour forms of *Nepheronia argia*. (1) white with black markings, (2) the same, but with an orange patch in the forewing, (3) yellow with black markings, (4) the same, but with an orange patch in the forewing.

female-limited colour forms in a single population of *Nepheronia argia* (Pieridae) in Sierra Leone. The males are not polymorphic, but the females may be bright yellow with or without red markings or white with or without red markings. The forms look completely distinct in the field, a necessary condition for apostatic selection. It would be of considerable interest if someone could devise an experiment to test the possible efficacy of this kind of polymorphism in confusing predators.

9

MIMICRY

NATURALISTS exploring the tropics of Africa, South America, and south-east Asia in the second half of the nineteenth century frequently observed that butterflies that looked similar in colour and pattern belonged to quite different families, while some butterflies that looked superficially very different were sometimes found mating and thus belonged to the same species. This situation initially led to confusion in naming and classifying tropical butterflies, but was eventually explained by the theory of mimicry. This theory is based on the assumption that some butterflies are unpalatable to predators such as birds and lizards while others are palatable. Potential predators are able to recognize and avoid unpalatable species by their conspicuous warning colours and patterns which are easily learnt and remembered. Some palatable butterflies resemble the unpalatable species closely in colour and pattern and it is assumed that predators often mistake them for the unpalatable species. Although there certainly are unpalatable butterflies, palatability is probably relative and occurs in all degrees.

It has long been the custom to refer to the unpalatable species as models and to the palatable species that resemble them as mimics. Two kinds of mimicry can be distinguished: Batesian† mimicry in which there is an unpalatable model and a palatable mimic, and Müllerian† mimicry in which several, often unrelated, unpalatable species resemble one another in colour and pattern. In practice it is often difficult to distinguish between these two kinds of mimicry, especially in tropical areas where there appears to be a complex assemblage involving both Batesian and Müllerian mimicry. In general mimetic and model species lack the intricate patterns of non-mimetic species. Models in particular tend to fly slowly and do not readily take evasive action when attacked; their bold markings make them conspicuous and easy to see in a green environment.

The idea that mimics are at an advantage because of their resemblance to models depends upon the assumption that predators such as birds learn to recognize boldly marked butterflies as being unpalatable and that on subsequent encounters butterflies with these patterns tend to be avoided. This does not of course mean that models and their mimics are never eaten by predators; they are often eaten, but presumably less so than palatable non-mimetic species. Indeed if mimetic resemblance is the result of natural

† Named after the nineteenth century English naturalist Henry Walter Bates and the nineteenth century German zoologist Fritz Müller.

selection by predators it could only be maintained if the mimics were constantly preyed upon.

From these considerations it follows that mimics must on the whole be less common than models. If they were not predators would quickly learn that many boldly marked butterflies are indeed palatable and the model-mimic relationship would break down.

Much has been written about mimicry in butterflies. Mimicry played an essential part in the early understanding of the theory of natural selection, and the phenomenon was frequently used as evidence for the occurrence of selection in the wild. How else, it was argued, could two unrelated species bear such a strong resemblance to each other except by the action of natural selection? There was however considerable controversy as to how mimetic resemblance first evolved, partly because the processes of natural selection and mutation were to some extent misunderstood, and, as discussed later in this chapter, it is only relatively recently that the origin of mimetic resemblance has been satisfactorily explained.

Poulton, among many others, repeatedly drew attention to mimicry as a means of understanding and appreciating evolution by natural selection which at the turn of the century was still regarded as a controversial issue (see in particular Poulton (1908) for a wide-ranging discussion of mimicry in butterflies). Poulton urged collectors in Africa to obtain large samples of mimetic and model butterflies in order that the phenomenon could be more thoroughly investigated. Many of these specimens are now in the Hope Department of Entomology at Oxford. Until quite recently most attention was directed at identifying model-mimic associations and describing these in detail. Opponents of the theory of mimicry (and to some extent of natural selection) tried to argue that mimicry would be ineffective because birds are not important predators of butterflies. But many butterflies were collected with recognizable beak marks on their wings and this, it was argued, indicated that birds regularly eat butterflies and that unpalatable species and their mimics were successfully attacked less frequently than non-mimetic species.

Eltringham (1910) made one of the first attempts to sort out mimetic associations in tropical African butterflies. His book is beautifully illustrated in colour with many examples of mimicry from African species, but understandably the problem is examined only in qualitative terms. Eltringham, like others writing at the time, was concerned mainly with drawing attention to the existence of mimetic assemblages and in classifying and defining which species are palatable and which unpalatable. Punnett (1915), in an illustrated book, adopted a somewhat similar approach, but included a discussion of the genetics of the polymorphic forms of the Asiatic *Papilio polytes* (Papilionidae) and a numerical analysis of the frequency of polymorphic forms of *Pseudacraea eurytus* (Nymphalidae), based largely on collections obtained by Carpenter in Uganda and on the islands of Lake Victoria.

Mimicry in butterflies is best developed in the tropics. In Africa two kinds of colour patterns predominate in most mimetic assemblages: black and white, and black and orange. Mimetic resemblance frequently involves polymorphism and thus far it is the polymorphic species that have yielded the most useful information on both the genetics and the ecology of mimicry.

Experimental evidence for mimicry

Until recently there was little direct experimental evidence that mimicry is effective in affording some degree of protection to palatable species. There had been numerous reports of predators, particularly birds, rejecting unpalatable butterflies, but such observations were not quantitative and could in most cases only be regarded as providing suggestive evidence.

L. P. Brower and J. V. Z. Brower were the first to plan and conduct experiments designed to test the efficacy of mimicry. They worked initially with North American mimetic butterflies and their models and with Diptera that are mimics of bees, using birds and toads as predators (Brower 1958a, b, c; Brower, Brower, and Westcott 1960; Brower and Brower 1962). They divided wild-caught predators (toads or birds) into two groups. The predators in one group were given quantities of palatable insects and some unpalatable models. The predators soon learned to discriminate between the two and rejected the models on sight. The same predators were then offered mimics of the models and these were also rejected. The predators in the second group were given palatable insects and mimics, almost all of which were eaten without hesitation. A statistical comparison was made of the total number of mimics eaten and not eaten by the two groups of predators and it was shown that the group that had been exposed to unpalatable models ate significantly fewer of the corresponding mimics. These results demonstrate that mimicry is effective. What is remarkable is that such results were obtained at all, for although there are a priori reasons for expecting the obtained result, it might at the same time have been expected that the difference between the two groups would have been so small as not to be detectable in the rather small samples used.

Mimicry, then, is effective provided predators can learn to discriminate on the basis of previous experience. There is now increasing evidence that predators such as birds build up specific search images of their prey such that the kind of food items taken repeatedly depends on previous experience with similar food items. Similar in this context implies similarity in colour and pattern which in turn indicates palatability. Birds have good colour vision and their ability to perceive items in their environment depends largely on the recognition of colours and patterns with which they have already had experience. They will tend to avoid prey that from previous experience has been found to be unpalatable and in so doing they will also tend to avoid palatable mimics that resemble unpalatable models.

The causes of unpalatability

The idea that some butterflies are distasteful to predators is an essential part of the theory of mimicry. Unpalatability is a relative concept; some species may be poisonous to some predators but not to others, while other species may simply be unpleasant as food without being distinctly poisonous.

Several groups of butterflies have for long been considered unpalatable. These include the Aristolochiaceae-feeding swallowtails of the tribe Troidini (the only African representative being *Atroplaneura antenor* of Madagascar), the Heliconiinae (Nymphalidae) of South and Central America, the Ithomiinae (Nymphalidae), also of South America, the Acraeidae, chiefly African with a few species in the Asian tropics, and the Danaidae, which occur throughout the world, but especially in the tropics. Brower and Brower (1964) offered examples of all of these groups, except the Acraeidae, to captive blue jays and obtained evidence that supports the notion that they are more or less unpalatable (Plate 29). Indeed Parsons (1965) has shown that a single *Danaus plexippus* (Danaidae) contains enough toxin to cause vomiting in a starling.

Almost all the species regarded as unpalatable feed as larvae on plants that contain in their tissues chemical compounds that play no part in the normal physiology of the plant but which appear to function as deterrents to herbivorous animals. For example the larvae of Danaidae feed almost exclusively on Asclepiadaceae (milkweeds) and their relatives, a group of plants that contain toxic cardiac glycosides. Chemical analysis has shown that *Danaus plexippus* butterflies contain at least three of the same cardiac glycosides, calactin, calotropin, and calotoxin, that are found in *Asclepias curassavica* upon which the larvae have been fed (Brower 1969). When *Danaus plexippus* larvae are fed on cabbage the resulting butterflies are readily eaten by birds, in marked contrast to those that have been reared on *Asclepias curassavica* which are rejected. Brower (1969) found that some species of milkweeds lack cardiac glycosides and that butterflies reared on these species were acceptable to birds.

These and similar experiments, which involve chemical analyses of the butterflies and their larval food-plants, and observations on the behaviour of predators faced with palatable and unpalatable butterflies, lend strong support to the idea, first put forward in the latter part of the nineteenth century, that many unpalatable butterflies acquire their toxic properties while feeding as larvae on plants that contain poisonous compounds. The problem of how the insects themselves are not poisoned has not been fully solved. It is known that some compounds toxic to vertebrates are not toxic to insects, indeed among vertebrates themselves there is wide variation among species in responses to toxic compounds.

Detoxification can occur chemically by adding to the molecule rather than by breaking it down; the compound is then rendered harmless, but upon being eaten by a predator the compound breaks down and becomes toxic. Insects and plants appear to have similar methods of detoxification in that they both form glycosides; vertebrates on the other hand form glucuronic acids and glucuronides.

Most of the American Heliconiinae and some of the African Acraeidae (both regarded as unpalatable groups of butterflies) feed as larvae on the Passifloraceae, a family of tropical plants that contain species bearing fruits edible to man, but also, at least in some species, a variety of toxic compounds. Thus *Adenia lobata*, a common West African member of the Passifloraceae, and the food-plant of several species of *Acraea*, is used as a means of manufacturing an arrow poison (Irvine 1961). Butterflies of the family Acraeidae produce copious quantities of yellowish, often foamy, fluid when handled, and I have recently found that in *Acraea encedon* this fluid gives off hydrogen cyanide upon decomposition. But *Acraea encedon* does not feed on Passifloraceae but on *Commelina*, a common weed that is a monocotyledon and therefore unlikely to contain toxic compounds.

It is therefore possible that at least some of the toxic compounds found in butterflies are produced metabolically and are not obtained directly from the food-plant. There is some evidence for this in other insects, including moths, and it is clear that much further chemical and biological research is necessary to determine the relative importance of *de novo* synthesis or direct acquisition of toxic compounds from plants. The present evidence is suggestive (but no more) that most unpalatable butterflies, especially those that serve as models to mimetic species, acquire their unpalatability from the larval food-plants (Brower and Brower 1964).

Mimetic associations in a West African forest

For several years I have been attempting to sort out the mimetic associations in a small area of secondary forest near Freetown, Sierra Leone. Some of the associations, especially those involving a single polymorphic mimic with a series of forms each a mimic of a different species of model, are obvious, but many are much less evident. All gradations of mimetic resemblance seem to exist and I find it impossible in many cases to decide if many of the apparent similarities between species are mimetic or if they are due to some (unknown) feature of the environment. Many older works on mimicry are quite remarkable for their positive diagnosis as to which species are models and which are mimics; I find this approach somewhat unsatisfactory as it rests solely on judgement. For instance, in the area of

secondary forest near Freetown there are three species of pale bluish butterflies with conspicuous black markings. Each bears a strong resemblance to
Danaus limniace (Danaidae), undoubtedly an unpalatable species and frequently cited as a model in older works. But *Danaus limniace* does not occur
in Sierra Leone. These three species, *Graphium leonidas* (Papilionidae)
(Plate 10), *Euxanthe eurinome* (Nymphalidae) (Plate 20), and *Pseudoneptis
coenobita* (Nymphalidae) are remarkably similar in colour and pattern
although they differ somewhat in size, and in Sierra Leone they could be
either Müllerian mimics of each other, or their similarity could be due to
some unknown factor in the environment.

In this area of forest the most obvious model species belong to the
genera *Amauris* (Danaidae) and *Bematistes* (Acraeidae). *Amauris niavius* is
the only common member of its genus, but three other species, *Amauris
egialea, Amauris hecate,* and *Amauris tartarea,* also occur. *Amauris niavius*
is a model for a wide variety of other species. These include the females of
Papilio dardanus (Papilionidae), all specimens of which in this area are
black and white. Elsewhere in Africa, as will be discussed later in this
chapter, the females of *Papilio dardanus* occur in a variety of sympatric
colour forms each of which is usually a mimic of different species of
Danaidae and Acraeidae. The females of *Papilio cynorta* are also remarkably
like *Amauris niavius,* and so is one of the colour forms of *Hypolimnas
dubius* (Nymphalidae) (Plate 20); the other colour form bears a strong
resemblance to the remaining three species of *Amauris,* which are extremely
similar to each other and cannot be easily distinguished in the field. The
females of three of the five species of *Bematistes* (Plate 1) in this area are
also similar in appearance to *Amauris niavius,* and possibly all should be
regarded as Müllerian mimics of each other. Other species of Nymphalidae
bear a resemblance to species of *Amauris,* and *Pseudaletis leonis* (Plate 21),
an extremely rare member of the Lycaenidae, looks very like a diminutive
Amauris niavius.

As mentioned above, five species of *Bematistes* occur in this forest. In
all of them the males are dark brown with orange markings and in three
species, *Bematistes epaea, Bematistes alcinoe,* and *Bematistes macaria,* the
females are black and white. The females of the remaining two species,
Bematistes vestalis and *Bematistes umbra,* are like the males. Both male and
female *Bematistes* are closely mimicked by the polymorphic colour forms
of *Pseudacraea eurytus* (Nymphalidae) (Plate 1), and by a variety of non-
polymorphic Nymphalidae, including *Najas edwardsi,* and some Lycaenidae, especially *Mimacraea neurata,* a large species both sexes of which are
very similar to the males of *Bematistes epaea. Elymnias bammakoo* (Satyridae) occurs in two colour forms (Plate 20), the common black and white
one being a mimic of the females of *Bematistes epaea* and the brown and
orange one a mimic of the males.

Forest members of the genus *Acraea* (Acraeidae) do not in general act as models for other forest butterflies in this area, but other species of *Acraea* more characteristic of clearings and forest edge are fairly often found in the forest having wandered in from outside. One of these is *Acraea egina* (Plate 13), a sexually dimorphic species, the two sexes being closely mimicked by the two sexes of *Pseudacraea boisduvali* (Nymphalidae). Other species of *Acraea* resemble closely species of *Bematistes*, especially the females of *Acraea jodutta* which are remarkably similar to the females of *Bematistes epaea*; here again the mimicry is probably Müllerian.

A variety of species of day-flying moths are also black and white or black and orange. It is possible that several Lycaenidae and Nymphalidae are mimics of these.

I have in this brief description of mimicry in a small area of West African forest mentioned only the more obvious associations. But even so it is clear that the models have to some extent a Müllerian association with each other while the Batesian mimics are in some species polymorphic, and in some the mimetic resemblance is restricted to the females. An appreciation of the complexity of the mimetic associations in an area of forest such as this provides a necessary background to the next section of this chapter in which an attempt is made to examine mimicry quantitatively.

The frequency of models and their mimics

As pointed out earlier in this chapter, for mimicry to be effective the mimic must be less frequent in the population than its corresponding model. A considerable amount of field sampling of adult butterflies suggests that this is often the case, but one important difficulty that has thus far not been adequately considered is that different species of butterflies are not equally easy to catch. In general unpalatable models such as Danaidae and Acraeidae fly rather slowly while their mimics, particularly Nymphalidae, fly more quickly and are therefore more often missed during field sampling.

The most extensive field samples of models and mimics thus far obtained in Africa are of *Pseudacraea eurytus* (Nymphalidae), a species that throughout tropical Africa is a polymorphic mimic of various species of *Bematistes* (Acraeidae). The largest samples obtained are from Uganda and the islands in Lake Victoria (Carpenter 1949); for comparison I have recently obtained similar samples in Sierra Leone. *Pseudacraea eurytus* is probably the most polymorphic and geographically variable butterfly in the world. It occurs in forested areas from Senegal in the west to Tanzania in the east, and south to Mozambique and Rhodesia. Throughout its range it occurs in an amazing variety of colour forms, many of them sympatric, some of which are confined to males, some to females, while others occur in both sexes. The genetics of the colour forms awaits investigation. Each of the colour forms is usually (but not always) a close mimic of a *Bematistes*, indeed so close is the resemblance that it is often impossible to say whether one has caught a model or a mimic until it has been removed from the net and closely examined. Different species of *Bematistes* replace each other in different areas of tropical Africa; moreover many *Bematistes* exhibit marked geographical variation, including the extent to which sexual dimorphism is developed. Specimens of the same species of *Bematistes* from opposite sides of Africa may look totally different. These variations are beautifully matched in the polymorphic forms of *Pseudacraea eurytus*. Carpenter published numerous papers on polymorphism and mimicry in *Pseudacraea eurytus* which are conveniently summarized in his last beautifully illustrated paper of 1949. Carpenter's earlier papers differ slightly in the sizes of samples reported and the degree to which the forms are separated, and I have used his last paper in the discussion that follows.

His most important finding is summarized in Table 9.1. On the mainland of Uganda in the vicinity of Entebbe the models are abundant and *Pseudacraea eurytus* represents only 18 per cent of the mimetic association. This figure is probably somewhat inaccurate as it stands because the models are easier to catch than the mimics, but comparison with the island samples is valid. On the islands of Lake Victoria the models are rather rare and the mimics relatively more abundant; in some samples, as shown in Table 9.1, mimics are more frequent than models. Carpenter found that

TABLE 9.1

Percentage of Pseudacraea eurytus *in samples of models and mimics obtained at Entebbe, Uganda, and from the islands of Lake Victoria, and percentage of variant* Pseudacraea eurytus *in these samples*†

Locality	P. eurytus as percentage of total mimetic association	Number of P. eurytus examined	Percentage variant P. eurytus‡
Entebbe (mainland)	18·0	357	4·2
Damba Island	62·3	43	34·9
Bugalea Island	73·4	356	56·2
Kome Island, 1914	22·9	80	50·8
Kome Island, 1918–19	68·5	54	53·7
Buvuma Island	42·7	109	28·0

† Adapted from Carpenter (1949).
‡ Variants are specimens that do not match the local *Bematistes* closely.

on the mainland almost all the *Pseudacraea eurytus* examined were good mimics and that only 15 (4·2 per cent) were transitional between two polymorphic forms and hence not good mimics. Using the same criteria he found that the percentage of transitional or 'variant' forms was much higher on the islands than on the mainland, as shown in Table 9.1. On two of the islands over half the mimics were transitional or variant. Thus where models are scarce mimicry tends to break down and a substantial proportion of the *Pseudacraea eurytus* population are not good mimics of *Bematistes*. Carpenter thought that the islands of Lake Victoria are not good habitats for *Bematistes*, a view with which I agree as I have also visited these islands. Lake Victoria appears to have originated in the middle or late Pleistocene, but it attained its present configuration in quite recent times (Kendall 1969). The islands have been and still are sufficiently isolated for the difference between the mainland and the island populations of *Pseudacraea eurytus* to have evolved.

In 1968–70 I obtained a sample of 878 *Bematistes* and 190 *Pseudacraea eurytus* from the area of secondary forest in Sierra Leone described earlier in this chapter. This gives 17·8 per cent of the butterflies in the association as *Pseudacraea eurytus*, a figure that is remarkably close to the 18·0 per cent obtained by Carpenter (1949) at Entebbe. Two of the *Pseudacraea eurytus* are variants (both resemble *Bematistes poggei* which does not occur in Sierra Leone) and so only 1·1 per cent are not good mimics of the local *Bematistes*, a figure which is similar to the 4·2 per cent obtained by Carpenter at Entebbe, but, of course, much smaller than the values from the islands in Lake Victoria (Table 9.1).

Next it is necessary to try and establish a correlation between the frequency of the models and the frequency of the corresponding mimics. Carpenter (1949) assembled the model *Bematistes* and the mimetic forms of *Pseudacraea eurytus* into five mimicry groups. A mimicry group is composed of species or of forms that look alike. It is important to stress at this point that the sexes of a species of *Bematistes* may fall into two different mimicry groups. This is because some (but not all) *Bematistes* are in parts of their range sexually dimorphic to such an extent that they look quite different. These dimorphisms usually consist of a brown male marked with orange and a black and white female. In addition several species (of the same or of different sexes) may fall into the same mimicry group. Thus at Entebbe the females of *Bematistes macarista*, *Bematistes alcinoe*, and *Bematistes aganice* are all similarly black and white and so fall into the same mimicry group, while the males of *Bematistes macarista* and both sexes of *Bematistes poggei* are all in another mimicry group.

I have reproduced Carpenter's figures for Entebbe in Table 9.2 and have also calculated the percentage of mimics in each group (Group 2 can be ignored as it contains only one individual model). As shown in Table 9.2 the mimics are considerably less frequent than the models, but the percentage varies between 6·5 and 30·4. In Table 9.3 I have assembled a similar sample from Sierra Leone, and here too there are five mimicry groups, numbers 1, 3, and 4 containing butterflies of similar appearance (although often of different species) to those in the corresponding groups from

TABLE 9.2

Frequency of models and mimics in samples from mimicry groups involving Bematistes *and* Pseudacraea eurytus *at Entebbe, Uganda*†

Mimicry group based on	Number of models	Number of mimics	Percentage of mimics in group
1. *B. macarista* (♂) *B. poggei* (♂♀)	569	102	15·2
2. *B. aganice* (♂)	1	5	83·3

3. *B. macarista* (♀)
   B. alcinoe (♀)
   B. aganice (♀)
	335	164	30·4

4. *B. tellus* (♂♀)	670	83	11·0
5. *B. epaea* (♂♀)	43	3	6·5

† Adapted from Carpenter (1949), who excluded the males of *Bematistes alcinoe* from these mimicry groups.

Entebbe. Again the mimics are considerably less frequent than the models, but there is much variation, and group 5 is anomalous in that the mimics actually outnumber the models.

TABLE 9.3

Frequency of models and mimics in samples from mimicry groups involving Bematistes *and* Pseudacraea eurytus *at Freetown, Sierra Leone*†

Mimicry group based on	Number of models	Number of mimics	Percentage of mimics in group
1. *B. macaria* (♂)	324	43	11·7
2. *B. alcinoe* (♂)	162	5	3·0

3. *B. epaea* (♀)
   B. macaria (♀)
   B. alcinoe (♀)
	111	68	38·0

4. *B. epaea* (♂)	268	40	13·0
5. *B. vestalis* (♂♀) *B. umbra* (♂♀)	13	32	71·1

† There is much geographical variation within species of *Bematistes*. This explains why, for instance, the males and females of *B. epaea* fall into different groups in Sierra Leone where the sexual dimorphism is striking but are placed together in Uganda (Table 9.2) where the sexual dimorphism is less obvious.

The figures in Tables 9.2 and 9.3 suggest the absence of a rigid association between the abundance of the models and their corresponding mimics.† This is not astonishing as several additional factors may be affect-

† 2 × 5 contingency tests on Tables 9.2 and 9.3 give highly significant values of χ^2. Sheppard (1959) using Carpenter's Uganda samples attempted to establish a rigid association between the abundance of the models and their mimics by calculating a correlation coefficient, but this seems inappropriate because each mimicry group was counted several times.

ing the relative abundance of both the models and their polymorphic mimics. These can be listed and discussed, but it is not in general possible to estimate their relative importance.

First, mimicry groups are often associated by sex, as indicated in Tables 9.2 and 9.3. Some groups contain females only, some males only, and some both males and females. In Sierra Leone samples of *Bematistes* collected in forest always contain a large and significant excess of males, indeed the females are sometimes quite rare in random samples. The sex ratio in reared broods of *Bematistes* does not depart significantly from the expected 1:1, and so the explanation of the excess of wild-caught males must be sought in terms of their increased probability of capture. This in fact seems to be the case in forest areas where the females may fly higher and so be out of reach much of the time, but in gardens where the vegetation is generally not so high I have found that samples of two species of *Bematistes* give the expected 1:1 ratio of males to females. In contrast the females of *Pseudacraea eurytus* appear at least as frequently as males in random samples, indeed in Sierra Leone the sample contains a significant excess of females. These considerations become important in Tables 9.2 and 9.3. Thus both the Sierra Leone and the Uganda group 3 comprise only female models, which are under-represented in field samples, and only female mimics which are if anything over-represented. This possibly explains why the mimics in group 3 represent a higher percentage of the total butterflies than, for example, in groups 1 and 4.

Secondly, the *Bematistes–Pseudacraea eurytus* mimetic assemblage is by no means discrete and isolated. The models are also mimicked by other species of Nymphalidae, Satyridae, and Lycaenidae, and there are additional models (particularly Danaidae) that are similar in appearance to some of the *Bematistes*. All this will tend to give a less precise numerical relationship when only part of the assemblage is considered.

Thirdly, all forest butterflies undergo seasonal fluctuations in numbers and a species of model may be relatively rare or abundant at different times of the year. Thus it might be that when samples are taken a model and its mimic are slightly out of seasonal phase and this would tend to introduce an additional bias.

Fourthly, not all models are necessarily equally unpalatable. A very unpalatable model may support rather more mimics than a somewhat less unpalatable model. On the basis of previous experience predators are probably able to discern species with different degrees of palatability and whether or not an individual is attacked by a predator will depend on the predator's previous experience or indeed how hungry the predator happens to be.

Lastly, the accuracy of mimetic resemblance varies. Sheppard (1959) expressed doubt about Carpenter's decisions as to what constitutes a variant or transitional form in *Pseudacraea eurytus*. My own experience suggests that Carpenter is correct in splitting the mimics into many categories. Thus in Sierra Leone the females of *Bematistes epaea*, *Bematistes macaria*, and *Bematistes alcinoe* look alike and I have placed them in the same mimicry group in Table 9.3. But *Bematistes epaea* is marked a little differently from the other two species and there is a corresponding form of *Pseudacraea eurytus* that matches exactly the female of *Bematistes epaea* and less exactly the other two *Bematistes* (Plate 1). This suggests that predators can, for instance, distinguish between the females of *Bematistes epaea* and the other two species, otherwise it is difficult to see how the corresponding mimic in *Pseudacraea eurytus* could have evolved.

To end this discussion of *Pseudacraea eurytus* and its models it is appropriate to compare directly the situation at Entebbe and Freetown. The advantage of this approach is that some of the uncontrollable variables mentioned above are reduced as one is now looking at samples with similar sources of bias. As already mentioned the mimetic resemblance in *Pseudacraea eurytus* at Entebbe and Freetown is almost complete, only a few individuals being non-mimetic, or at least not perfect mimics. In both localities there are five mimicry groups, numbers 1, 3, and 4 being effectively the same even though they involve different species. In each of these three groups the percentage of mimics in the two localities is not significantly† different and moreover the percentages vary in the same way: the higher percentage of mimics in group 3 in both localities is particularly striking and is partly explained by behavioural differences that arise because this group contains only females. It appears that both Carpenter and I encountered the same difficulties in attempting to obtain random samples of models and their mimics. I do not at the present see any way of overcoming these difficulties in collecting samples of *Pseudacraea eurytus* and its models.

Hypolimnas misippus (Nymphalidae) is another tropical African butterfly with mimetic, or apparently mimetic, polymorphism. In this species it is the females that are mimetic and polymorphic, the males being uniformly black and white. The females are mainly orange with black and white markings. There are four main female colour forms, but intermediates are frequent in all populations sampled. The females resemble both sexes of *Danaus chrysippus* (Danaidae), which is itself polymorphic in many parts of Africa. In *Danaus chrysippus* intermediates between the forms are rare or absent. The four colour forms of *Danaus chrysippus* and the corresponding forms of *Hypolimnas misippus* are shown in Fig. 9.1. Both *Danaus chrysippus* and *Hypolimnas misippus* occur in open country and do not enter into the mimetic assemblages of the forest.

† 2 × 2 contingency tests give χ^2 values that are not significant when groups 1, 3, and 4 are compared from Entebbe and Freetown.

FIG. 9.1. The four colour forms of *Danaus chrysippus* (left) and the corresponding forms of female *Hypolimnas misippus*. The male of *Hypolimnas misippus* is black and white and quite different from any of the female forms. The black and white areas in the figure are black and white as shown and the shaded area is orange.

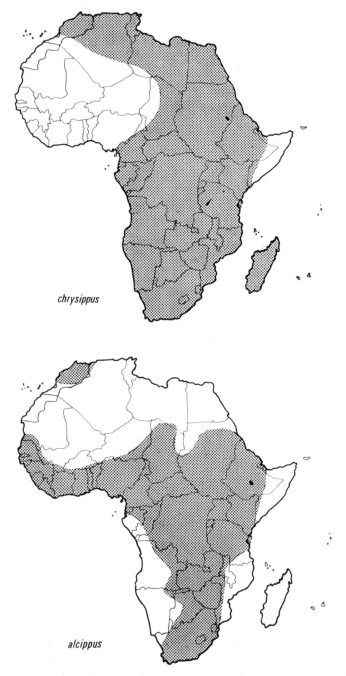

chrysippus

alcippus

FIG. 9.2. The distribution of the four colour forms of *Danaus chrysippus* in Africa.

dorippus

albinus

FIG. 9.2 (*cont.*)

Fig. 9.2 shows the distribution in Africa of the four colour forms of *Danaus chrysippus*. These maps have been prepared after examination of the large collections in the British Museum and in the Hope Department of Entomology at Oxford. The areas shown in Fig. 9.2 as being occupied by each form are necessarily generalizations, but the main trends are clear: *dorippus* occurs chiefly in the east and *albinus* only with *dorippus*; *chrysippus* occurs in most areas except West Africa, and *alcippus* has a central and western distribution, being the only form present in many parts of coastal West Africa. It is not possible from museum specimens to plot the frequency of the forms because butterfly collectors are apt to collect relatively more specimens of the rarer forms in their particular area. It is however apparent from museum specimens and from personal observations that *dorippus* is by far the most frequent form east of central Kenya and that *alcippus* is the only form in most parts of West Africa, including Sierra Leone and Ghana where large samples have been examined. There is some evidence of changes in the frequency of the forms in the Kampala–Entebbe area of Uganda; in particular *alcippus* has increased and *chrysippus* decreased in frequency between 1909–12 and 1964–6 (Owen and Chanter 1968).

Hypolimnas misippus occurs throughout the range of *Danaus chrysippus*, but in this species all the forms occur everywhere in its range; thus on Madagascar where only the *chrysippus* form of *Danaus chrysippus* occurs all forms of *Hypolimnas misippus* have been reported. In Ghana and in Sierra Leone where only the *alcippus* form of *Danaus chrysippus* occurs all forms of *Hypolimnas misippus* are known, together with many intermediates.

Two large samples of *Hypolimnas misippus* have been examined from widely separated localities in West Africa. In both localities *Danaus chrysippus* is not polymorphic, all butterflies belonging to the *alcippus* form with well developed white hindwings. Edmunds (1969a) found that 22·9 per cent of 387 females examined at Legon, Ghana, in 1965 and 1966 had some white in the hindwing, while in my garden at Freetown, Sierra Leone, I found that in 1968 and 1969 22·8 per cent of 193 females had some white in the hindwing. These two percentages are almost identical and suggest stability in the frequency of white in the hindwing over a large area. Evidently in West Africa less than a quarter of the female *Hypolimnas misippus* have white in the hindwing like the model, but even among those that have white only three or four per cent are of the true *alcippoides* form, with extensive white hindwings and a near perfect mimic of *alcippus*. The colours and markings of the forewing of *Hypolimnas misippus* are as variable as those of the hindwing. Edmunds (1969a) using the same sample found that 24·3 per cent were *inaria* or transitional *inaria-misippus*, while 20·7 per cent of the Freetown sample were classifiable in this way. Thus it is apparent that most of the *Hypolimnas misippus* at Legon and Freetown are not close mimics of *Danaus chrysippus*. The rarity of the true *alcippoides* form with much white in the hindwing cannot at present be explained, especially as the model is so abundant.

In view of the above considerations it could be argued that *Hypolimnas misippus* is not a mimic of *Danaus chrysippus*. However, in 1965 by taking random samples of models and mimics, Edmunds (1966) obtained evidence that was suggestive of a mimetic association, as shown in the first part of Table 9.4. During the period of sampling the percentage of models in the

TABLE 9.4

Numbers of Danaus chrysippus *and female* Hypolimnas misippus *and per cent* Hypolimnas misippus *with white in the hindwing captured at Legon Ghana*†

	D. chrysippus	H. misippus	Percentage of H. misippus with white in hindwing
1965			
14–27 May	34	77	44·4
28 May–10 June	9	61	24·6
11–24 June	4	62	17·8
25 June–7 July	0	56	12·5
1966			
18 Apr.–1 May	46	43 ⎱	38·9
2–15 May	65	8 ⎰	
16–29 May	56	26 ⎱	20·9
30 May–12 June	23	10 ⎰	
13–26 June	25	27	19·4
27 June–10 July	11	19	23·0
11–22 July	5	14	19·0

† From Edmunds (1969a).

sample fell from 30·6 to zero. At the same time the percentage of female *Hypolimnas misippus* with white in the hindwing decreased from 44·4 to 12·5, which is statistically highly significant. This immediately suggested that while the model is abundant *Hypolimnas misippus* with white in the hindwing are at a selective advantage over those without white, but as the model becomes rare this advantage becomes less.

These observations were repeated in 1966 (Edmunds 1969a) and although there was some fall in the frequency of *Hypolimnas misippus* with white in the hindwing this did not appear to be correlated with changes in the abundance of the model, as shown in the second part of Table 9.4.

Stride (1956, 1957) has shown that male *Hypolimnas misippus* court the females with orange hindwings more actively than those with white in the hindwings. This suggests that individuals with white hindwings are at a disadvantage during courtship and mating. However, Stride's analysis was made by using artificial test insects, and Edmunds (1969*b*) repeating the experiments with live, free-living butterflies found no evidence of sexual selection. Thus although there are *a priori* reasons for supposing that male *Hypolimnas misippus* might tend to avoid females with white hindwings because of possible confusion with *Danaus chrysippus*, the evidence for this is conflicting. Both Stride and Edmunds performed their experiments in the same area of Ghana.

Pseudacraea eurytus and *Hypolimnas misippus* are the two species of tropical butterflies that have been most extensively studied in attempts to relate the frequency of mimics to that of the models, and, as shown, both present difficulties and uncertainties. Many smaller samples of other polymorphic mimics from widely separated parts of Africa and elsewhere in the tropics suggest a general association in frequency, but I would be inclined to suggest that if these situations were studied in detail similar difficulties would be encountered. I do not find this astonishing or disappointing. Investigators necessarily have to restrict the scope of their investigations while at the same time it is evident that it is impossible to isolate a discrete mimetic association from the whole mimetic assemblage.

Polymorphic Müllerian mimics

Müllerian mimicry should in theory generate uniformity in colour and pattern and not polymorphism, and this is usually the case. There are however a few cases of polymorphic Müllerian mimicry, the best known of which is between *Danaus chrysippus* (Danaidae) and *Acraea encedon* (Acraeidae). The distribution and frequency of the polymorphic forms of *Danaus chrysippus* has just been discussed; those of *Acraea encedon* are considered in another context in Chapter 8.

Four of the many colour forms of *Acraea encedon* match the four forms of *Danaus chrysippus*. These forms, *encedon*, *alcippina*, *daira*, and *alcippina-daira* (Fig. 8.6) match, respectively, forms *chrysippus*, *alcippus*, *dorippus*, and *albinus* (Fig. 9.1). In *Danaus chrysippus* the frequency of the colour forms is stabilized over large areas of hundreds of square kilometres, but there are broad geographical trends, as shown in Fig. 9.2. In marked contrast the mimetic and other colour forms of *Acraea encedon* vary in frequency from population to population. A partial explanation of this is that *Danaus chrysippus* is a wide-ranging butterfly that does not form discrete populations, whereas *Acraea encedon* populations tend to be restricted to small areas (Chapter 8).

Table 9.5 shows the frequency of colour forms in *Acraea encedon* in nine populations in the Kampala–Entebbe area of Uganda. All of these populations are close together and some are separated by no more than 2·5 kilometres (Fig. 8.4). Yet each population is characterized by the relative frequency of its colour forms. Throughout the Kampala–Entebbe area the

relative frequency of the colour forms of *Danaus chrysippus* is stable: in
1964–6 the frequencies were 49·6 per cent *chrysippus*, 37·4 per cent *alcippus*,
9·4 per cent *dorippus* and 3·6 per cent *albinus*. As shown in Table 9.5,

TABLE 9.5

Relative frequency of mimetic and non-mimetic forms of Acraea encedon *in
populations in Uganda*†

| Population | N | Percentage mimetic | | | | Percentage non-mimetic |
		encedon	alcippina	daira	alcippina-daira	
1. Kawanda	1739	67·1	22·3	4·8	0·9	4·9
2. Kololo	1647	69·0	25·1	1·3	1·3	3·3
3. Makerere	1239	64·1	25·9	4·0	1·9	4·1
4. Lubya	8627	65·7	15·3	10·3	1·8	6·9
5. Budo	2491	65·5	14·8	8·1	1·6	10·0
6. Kazi	1119	51·6	1·5	14·3	2·7	29·9
7. Nalugala	367	47·1	0·8	18·3	1·9	31·9
8. Kagolomolo	63	34·9	—	28·6	4·8	31·7
9. Entebbe	73	43·8	—	15·1	2·7	38·4

† Many of the differences in relative frequency between populations are statistically
significant (Owen and Chanter 1969).

Acraea encedon populations 1–5, all located on the tops of small hills, contain butterflies that are nearly all Müllerian mimics of the forms of *Danaus
chrysippus*, while in populations 6–9, located on level ground near the
shore of Lake Victoria, about a third of the butterflies belong to forms that
are not mimetic. In particular the lake-shore populations contain very few
or no *alcippina* and a high frequency of *lycia*, a form with no orange ground
colour. The relative frequency of the four corresponding forms of *Danaus
chrysippus* and *Acraea encedon* on the hill-top populations may be similarly
ranked, the probability of such ranking arising by chance being 1/24, that
is, it is significant at the five per cent level. Hence the association of most
of the forms of *Acraea encedon* in these populations with all the forms of
Danaus chrysippus seems established, but breaks down to some extent in
the lake-shore populations, where the frequency of the forms of *Danaus
chrysippus* remains stable, but that of *Acraea encedon* differs. At Newton in
Sierra Leone, all the *Danaus chrysippus* are form *alcippus* (more than a
thousand have been examined), while three forms of *Acraea endecon* occur.
Two of these forms are non-mimetic and the other, *alcippina*, is an extremely good mimic of *alcippus*. In a sample of 2517 *Acraea encedon* examined at Newton in 1967–70, only one *alcippina* was found, which means
that 99·96 per cent were non-mimetic. There is evidence from other
populations of *Acraea encedon* in West Africa which suggests that although
alcippina occurs it is usually rare and that most of the butterflies are of
colour forms that are very different in appearance from *alcippus*. The

recently discovered population at Gegbwema in Sierra Leone where all the *Acraea encedon* thus far found have been *alcippina* is an exception and further study and sampling of this population is necessary.

As discussed earlier in this chapter, *Danaus* butterflies obtain their toxic properties while feeding as larvae on milkweeds. Not all milkweeds contain toxic compounds and *Danaus* fed as larvae on some species are acceptable to birds. The possibility now arises of geographical and local variation in the extent to which *Danaus* larvae feed on toxic milkweeds. It is known that in different parts of Africa different species of food-plants are utilized. If in some areas the main food-plants utilized do not contain the required compounds the resulting butterflies will be palatable. This could explain the breakdown of Müllerian mimicry in some areas but not in others. Indeed it could also explain why there are so few Batesian mimics of *Danaus chrysippus* in some areas, notably West Africa.

Polymorphism is also reported among Müllerian mimics of the genus *Heliconius* (Nymphalidae) of South and Central America. These butterflies are congeneric and therefore presumably closely related, and it is possible that the polymorphism evolved before the species, quite unlike the situation in *Danaus chrysippus* and *Acraea encedon* which belong to different families. It is also possible that some of the species of *Heliconius* have recently hybridized and given rise to polymorphic forms in this way. In two species, *Heliconius melpomene* and *Heliconius erato*, there are parallel forms, and in a small random sample collected at a single locality in Surinam in 1962 one of the forms predominated in both species (Sheppard 1963).

The selective advantage of polymorphism in Müllerian mimics is obscure. One possible explanation is that a model may be exposed to danger if it has too many palatable mimics. Hence the generation of polymorphism can be envisaged as a means of breaking down, to some extent, the resemblance of mimics to models. This might be the situation in *Danaus chrysippus* which, at least in East Africa, has a number of Batesian mimics, but does not satisfactorily explain the parallel polymorphism in this species and in *Acraea encedon*. The possibility of the effects of apostatic selection and heterozygous advantage (Chapter 8) must be entertained, but there is as yet no evidence of these operating in the species here discussed.

Mimetic swallowtails and the evolution of dominance

Almost all the examples of polymorphic mimicry that have thus far been investigated suggest that the genetic control of the forms is by a series of multiple alleles at a single locus. In some species the expression of the mimetic resemblance is sex-limited to the females.

By far the most extensive studies of the genetics of polymorphic mimicry are those of Clarke and Sheppard (1959, 1960*a*, *b*, *c*, 1962*b*, 1963, and other papers), summarized by Ford (1964), on the genetics of the African

swallowtail, *Papilio dardanus*. In this species only the females are polymorphic and mimetic. The males are yellow with black markings and are
tailed; there is considerable geographical variation in the development of
the black markings and in details of the structure of the male genitalia
(Turner 1963). Throughout much of tropical Africa the females of *Papilio
dardanus* are excellent mimics of various species of Danaidae and to a lesser
extent of *Bematistes* (Acraeidae). On Madagascar the females are like the
males in colour and pattern and are neither mimetic nor polymorphic. In
Abyssinia most females are male-like, but there is a small proportion of
mimics, which, however, have tails, unlike the females elsewhere on the
African mainland. Mimetic females of *Papilio dardanus* are quite unlike
typical swallowtails. Those that mimic *Amauris niavius* (Danaidae) are
very easily confused even by an experienced collector.

The occurrence and relative frequency of the female colour forms varies
enormously in different parts of Africa. Thus in Sierra Leone all the females
are black and white and are excellent mimics of *Amauris niavius*, while in
Uganda there are forms each of which mimics different species of Danaidae
and *Bematistes*. If the model for a particular form varies geographically the
form itself shows a similar geographical trend. Thus in western and central
Africa *Amauris niavius* has a rather dark hindwing with a white basal area
while in South Africa the hindwing is mainly white. This geographical
pattern is faithfully copied by the corresponding mimetic form of *Papilio
dardanus*.

Where the models or potential models are abundant, as in the lowland
forest areas of tropical Africa, most of the females of *Papilio dardanus* are
good mimics, but where the models are rare non-mimetic and highly
variable forms occur. Thus at Entebbe in Uganda where the models are
abundant, only four per cent of a sample of 111 females were imperfect
mimics while at Nairobi in Kenya where the models are less common, 32
per cent of 133 were imperfect mimics (Ford 1964).

The genetics of polymorphic mimicry in *Papilio dardanus* was first investigated by Ford (1936). Investigations were much extended by Clark
and Sheppard who arranged for live butterflies to be shipped from different
parts of Africa to their laboratory at Liverpool University. Here they suc-
ceeded in hand-mating selected males and females and were able to perform a remarkable number of crosses both between individuals from the
same area and individuals from widely separated parts of Africa. They
found that both mimetic and non-mimetic forms are determined by a
series of multiple alleles at a single autosomal locus (the possibility of very
close linkage cannot of course be entirely excluded) and that the expression
of the phenotypes is sex-limited to the females. Crosses made between
butterflies from the same area (or same population) gave clear-cut phenotypes with dominance, the offspring resembling closely the forms normally

found in that particular area. But crosses between widely allopatric populations much more rarely show complete dominance and intermediate phenotypes are frequent. These results suggest that dominance is evolved, through the action of modifiers, within populations in response to local ecological conditions in the form of the availability of suitable models, but breaks down when allopatric forms are crossed. Incomplete dominance is particularly clear in crosses between Madagascar butterflies and those from the African mainland. Heterozygotes obtained by crossing Madagascan and African homozygotes are variable (Plate 30) and Clarke and Sheppard (1960c) suggest that in the resultant unadjusted gene complex of the hybrids dominance is effectively absent. The selective advantage of complete dominance within populations is that the production of intermediate and variable phenotypes which would in general be poor mimics is reduced or eliminated altogether.

Throughout tropical Africa the females of *Papilio dardanus*, unlike the males, are tailless, but females from Madagascar and Abyssinia always have tails. The absence of tails (which contributes to the mimetic resemblance) is controlled by variation at a single locus which is independent of that controlling the main colour forms. When Madagascan and Abyssinian butterflies are crossed with butterflies from other areas female offspring appear with tails intermediate in length. This also suggests a breakdown of dominance when allopatric populations are crossed.

A similar series of experiments has been performed on *Papilio memnon*, a south-east Asian swallowtail in which the females are also polymorphic and mimetic (Clarke, Sheppard, and Thornton 1968). In this species dominance between sympatric forms is complete but is effectively absent when allopatric forms are crossed.

These results from breeding *Papilio dardanus* and *Papilio memnon* provide considerable support for the view of Fisher and Ford that mimicry has evolved slowly by gradual selective adjustment in which forms that most closely mimic the local models are persistently favoured. The evidence supports the theory first put forward by Fisher (1928) that dominance is not a fixed attribute of a particular pair of alleles, but is evolved slowly by natural selection. As pointed out by Clarke and Sheppard (1960c), it is of course impossible to show that dominance was absent when mimetic resemblance first arose as this took place in the distant past, but the evidence from allopatric crosses in which dominance breaks down strongly supports the notion that dominance is evolved by natural selection. The genetics of polymorphic and mimetic swallowtails appears to provide evidence that mimetic resemblance does not evolve suddenly from the unlikely chance of a single mutation that converts a non-mimetic to a mimetic form immediately, but slowly and in adjustment with the local ecological conditions. This experimental work has cleared up one of the controversies of the turn of the century, as at that time many could not see how mimetic resemblance could ever appear in the first place by direct mutation.

Some unsolved problems of mimicry and polymorphism

From what has been said in this chapter it is clear that the combination of field and laboratory studies has in recent years solved some of the major problems that hindered the acceptance of the theory of mimicry. There remain however some unsolved problems. These include the persistence of polymorphism in unpalatable models and the occurrence of parallel polymorphism in Müllerian mimics, a situation which at present cannot be satisfactorily explained, and the widespread occurrence of apparently mimetic forms in the absence of the model, as in *Hypolimnas misippus* (Nymphalidae). In addition it would be extremely useful to obtain reliable estimates of the selective value of mimicry, particularly of polymorphic mimicry, in field situations, using perhaps the technique of capture, marking, release, and recapture which has been successfully applied to industrial melanic moths in temperate areas. Such experiments would be best performed in the tropics where mimicry is so widespread in butterflies and it is to be hoped that research workers and students at tropical universities will initiate such investigations. From the point of view of genetic analysis, *Pseudacraea eurytus* (Nymphalidae), with its sex-limited forms, should reveal information of considerable interest if only someon could find a way of rearing and breeding it on a large scale.

Lastly, it is a puzzle to me (and others have been similarly puzzled) as to why so many mimics are so rare. *Pseudacraea eurytus* is much less common than the non-mimetic species of *Pseudacraea*, and some of the rarest Lycaenidae in Africa, including most of the species of *Pseudaletis*, are mimetic.

10

EVOLUTION

BUTTERFLIES are fragile animals and it is not remarkable that the fossil record provides little information as to their origin and major evolutionary trends. Many insects are known from fossils in the Carboniferous period (270 or more million years ago) but there are no butterflies in these deposits, nor indeed any other insects that are normally regarded as pollinators of flowering plants. The main radiation of the flowering plants occurred in the Cretaceous and by the beginning of the Tertiary (about 60 million years ago) the major groups of flowering plants that now occur on earth had appeared. It can be assumed that butterflies also evolved during the Cretaceous, but there is little positive evidence. The head capsule of a Lepidoptera larva of uncertain affinities has recently been discovered in Cretaceous amber in Canada; the deposit is estimated as being at least 72 million years old, and the specimen is the first piece of direct evidence for the existence of Lepidoptera in the Cretaceous (MacKay 1970). The first extensive evidence for the existence of Lepidoptera is from the Baltic amber of the Eocene and Oligocene (40 or so million years ago), but even in these deposits there are few butterflies. Some well preserved insect fossils of the Miocene (about 25 million years ago) have been found on islands in Lake Victoria (Pinhey 1968), but the specimens have evidently not yet been properly studied. Further collecting in the area may yield valuable information on the past distribution of some insects and perhaps some information on Miocene butterflies in Africa.

The intimate association between butterflies and flowering plants suggests that the two groups have evolved together. Butterflies, unlike the primitive insects of the Carboniferous, have evolved a complete metamorphosis with a well-defined larval, pupal, and adult stage. The larvae are in most cases primary consumers of green vegetation while the adults feed on liquid foods, especially the nectar of flowers. It is probable that the carnivorous lycaenid larvae represent a secondary adaptation from larvae that originally fed on green plants in close proximity to the insects upon which they now feed.

Speciation and incipient speciation

About thirteen thousand species of butterflies are known and each one is probably the result of an evolutionary process that is understood in theory but for which there is only indirect evidence. The species concept in sexually reproducing animals involves the definition that a species is a group of organisms that do not naturally interbreed with other similar organisms. That is, the species is defined in terms of reproductive isolation. This definition is useful when species are partly or completely sympatric, but is more difficult when species, or what are thought to be species, are completely allopatric. In the case of similar allopatric species the taxonomist is faced with making an intelligent guess as to whether or not two kinds of animal are distinct species. In butterflies differences in morphology, particularly in the details of the structure of the genitalia, are used in arriving at a decision. Species change by the process of evolution and two groups of animals separated in time by, say, a hundred thousand breeding generations may or may not belong to the same species if the definition given above is accepted. In butterflies the time factor cannot be considered as there is no record of the past history of populations other than museum specimens that have been accumulated over the past two hundred or so years. All butterflies reproduce by a sexual process and we are therefore not concerned with the special problems presented by asexually reproducing animals, and we can in general and with caution adopt the definition given above, but at the same time acknowledging that allopatric species may present difficulty.

The process of speciation in butterflies in all probability does not differ from that thought to occur in other sexually reproducing organisms. There appear to be several pathways towards speciation, but one in particular has received almost universal acceptance among biologists. This is speciation through geographical isolation in which a population becomes split into two or more parts that are geographically isolated from each other. Once isolated the populations can become adapted through natural selection to the environments to which they are restricted. Since these environments are geographically separated they will tend to differ in certain respects and over an unspecified number of breeding generations the two populations may become genetically distinct. If later on the two populations meet because the geographical barrier separating them has ceased to exist several possibilities arise. First, they may upon renewing contact interbreed and in so doing become a single population again. If this occurs nothing is left for the contemporary observer except a single interbreeding population and he will have no evidence as to what has happened in the past. Secondly, they may be unable to interbreed because they have evolved reproductive isolation so that when they come together they remain as distinct species. In such situations a contemporary observer may see two similar species occupying much the same habitat and range. An ecological problem is likely to arise under these circumstances as the two species are likely to be ecologically similar and the possibility of interspecific competition arises. Competition could theoretically result in the extinction of one or even both of the species. If this occurs there is again nothing left for the contemporary observer. It appears however that many species are able to evolve ecological differences that reduce the intensity of interspecific competition. In butterflies such differences involve the utilization of different species of larval food-plant and the exploitation of different habitats, to name only two.

In butterflies (and most other animals) evidence for speciation through geographical isolation is circumstantial and can only be deduced from an examination of the contemporary scene. Thus one repeatedly finds similar yet distinct species with similar ecological requirements occupying approximately the same range and it is assumed that these species evolved their special characteristics in isolation and later on became sympatric. The best examples of speciation through isolation may be seen among the butterflies of islands.

Throughout tropical Africa there is one common species of yellow and black tailless swallowtail that is characteristic of open habitats; this is *Papilio demodocus*. There is a similar species, *Papilio demoleus*, considered by some to be conspecific with *Papilio demodocus*, in the Asian tropics. On the island of Madagascar four species of the *Papilio demodocus* group occur: *Papilio erithonioides*, *Papilio morondavana*, *Papilio grosesmithi*, and *Papilio demodocus* itself, the latter probably having been introduced by man in recent times. These four species are shown in Fig. 10.1. They are extremely similar in overall appearance, all being yellow with black markings, but in each species the markings differ in details. The differences between the four species are most easily seen by comparison of the shapes and positions of the outer ring of yellow spots in the hindwing and of the extent of development of tails.

The existence on Madagascar of four similar swallowtails in the *Papilio demodocus* group is indicative of successive invasions of Madagascar by butterflies from the mainland of Africa and subsequent evolution in isolation. Provided that a considerable number of breeding generations elapse between the successive invasions the possibilities for evolution and speciation in isolation are considerable. It is not possible to place a time scale on the invasions nor is it possible to estimate the sequence of arrival and speciation, except that since *Papilio demodocus* was introduced into Madagascar by man it was the last to arrive. As already mentioned, *Papilio demodocus* occurs throughout tropical Africa and shows no geographical variation either in the form of a cline or as isolated subspecies. This is presumably because populations throughout Africa are continuous and there has been no opportunity for evolution in isolation and no opportunity for speciation or subspeciation. The existence of four species on Madagascar demonstrates most effectively the origin of species in isolation. Unfortunately, with the exception of *Papilio demodocus*, the Madagascar

Fig. 10.1. Four closely similar and presumably closely related species of *Papilio* from Madagascar. (1) *Papilio demodocus*, (2) *Papilio erithonioides*, (3) *Papilio morondavana*, (4) *Papilio grosesmithi*. These four species are extremely similar in overall appearance, being pale yellow with black markings, but almost all the markings differ in each of the species. All have two weakly developed eye spots in the hindwing, one lower and one upper. The upper eye spot has a black outer ring and is pale blue inside overlaid with a mixture of orange and black scales, leaving a blue ring next to the black ring. In the lower eye spot the lower area is red and the upper blue speckled with black and a few orange scales. In *Papilio morondavana*, but not in the other three species, the shaded area distal to the upper eye spot is orange. The differences between the four species can most easily be seen by comparison of the position of the outer ring of yellow spots in the hindwing and by looking at the development of tails. *Papilio demodocus* is the widespread and common species on the African mainland; it does not have tails.

species are rare and nothing is known of their life history or ecology. It could be predicted that there are ecological differences between them but these await investigation. The most likely differences would be in choice of habitat.

Similar processes have undoubtedly occurred on the mainland of Africa. During the Tertiary period the extent of the forest has repeatedly changed and the climate has been both drier and more humid than now. Populations of butterflies have presumably become isolated and have evolved differences, and later have met as new species. In West Africa there are three very similar species of swallowtail in the *Papilio nireus* group: *Papilio bromius*, *Papilio sosia*, and *Papilio nireus* itself (Plate 33). All three are quite common, but *Papilio nireus* is the most abundant in almost all areas. All are essentially forest species, the larvae feeding on wild species of Rutaceae, but all have moved out into the open to some extent and the larvae are frequently found on introduced *Citrus*. All three are black with an iridescent blue band, the width of which varies with the species. Because of their extreme similarity it can be assumed that the three have evolved from a common ancestor, and it is likely that each has evolved in isolation. They have now become almost completely sympatric but maintain their distinctiveness and do not hybridize. Again little is known of the ecological differences between them, but it can be predicted that with a thorough investigation differences will be found.

Many similar examples could be cited, and it would appear that speciation in butterflies within Africa has progressed mainly through geographical isolation resulting from climatic and vegetational changes and the subsequent coming together of previously isolated populations. Nothing is known of the rate of speciation, which in any case must be reckoned in terms of the number of breeding generations rather than the number of years, but there is no reason why, given sufficient isolation, speciation should not occur in as short a time as a hundred years which in many species is equivalent to about a thousand breeding generations.

Evidence for incipient speciation through geographical isolation can be seen in geographical variation in species that occupy a large range. Many butterflies have a range that covers most of tropical Africa. Many of them show geographical variation in pattern and colour in the form of a cline. A common tendency is for a gradual darkening in colour from east to west, the darkest specimens inhabiting West Africa and the palest East Africa. Fig. 10.2 shows clinal variation in *Acraea natalica* (Acraeidae) (Plate 13), a common butterfly of open country. As shown, specimens from West Africa are much darker than those from the East and South. This species has a continuous distribution and does not form isolated populations. But if for instance the West African populations were isolated by a geographical barrier from the East African populations the possibility would arise of

FIG. 10.2. Clinal variation in *Acraea natalica*. The butterfly is reddish-orange variously suffused and marked with black. There is a north-west/south-east cline, specimens from Sierra Leone being the darkest and specimens from East and South Africa the palest. In addition the dark margin of the hindwing is more developed in southern Africa than elsewhere. The specimens shown are from the following localities: (1) Sierra Leone, (2) Ghana, (3) Fernando Poo, (4) southern Nigeria, (5) Angola, (6) Congo Kinshasa, (7) Abyssinia, (8) Uganda, (9) Tanzania, (10) Zambia, (11) South Africa.

further adaptive changes once gene flow had been halted. It is indeed possible that the West African butterflies would become darker and the East African paler. Other genetic changes could also occur in isolation and speciation could result. In this example the existence of a marked cline in variation provides the necessary arena for further differentiation; all that is needed is for the present continuous distribution to be broken by a geographical barrier and for sufficient time to elapse for evolution in isolation.

East and West African subspecies of *Papilio dardanus* (Papilionidae) differ in the structure of the male genitalia as well as in colour and in the occurrence and frequency of polymorphic female colour forms. The valves of the male genitalia of East and West African subspecies are shown in Fig. 10.3. The most striking difference is the presence of a long spine in the

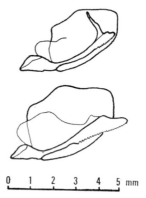

FIG. 10.3. The upper drawing shows a valve of the male genitalia of the eastern subspecies of *Papilio dardanus*; the lower drawing that of a male of the western subspecies. From Turner *et al.* (1961).

eastern males which is absent in the western males. Turner, Clarke, and Sheppard (1961) have shown that when eastern and western *Papilio dardanus* are crossed the resulting offspring indicate that the presence of a spine is dominant to its absence. The necessary crosses were performed in the laboratory by hand-mating, and it is likely that wild matings between the two types would be restricted or even impossible. Whether or not this is so cannot be ascertained, but in this example the difference between widely separated subspecies involves the structure of the genital armature and this in itself suggests that if the present continuous distribution of the species were broken by a geographical barrier the possibility of reproductive isolation and speciation would be considerable.

Even on the islands of Lake Victoria there is evidence of incipient speciation. Stempffer and Jackson (1962) found that on Bugala Island three species of Lycaenidae, *Deudorix lorisona* (=*bimaculata*), *Anthene sylvanus*, and *Thermoniphas togara* have formed distinct subspecies. Bugala is only eight kilometres from the Uganda mainland at its nearest point; such a narrow stretch of water would not be a great barrier to most species of butterflies and it is likely that Bugala and other islands in the Lake are continually receiving immigrants from the mainland. Nevertheless Stempffer and Jackson (1962) estimate the time of formation of these three subspecies of Lycaenidae as 300 000 years ago, on the basis that at that time Lake Victoria was effectively dry and Bugala would have been joined to the mainland. Relying on faulty geological information (Bugala has prob-

ably been joined to the mainland much more recently), they do not enter-
tain the possibility of colonization of Bugala from the mainland in more
recent times. When one considers that the butterfly fauna of Madagascar
must have been derived from butterflies reaching the island from continental Africa there is no reason why the short stretch of water between
Bugala and the mainland should present a major barrier. It is possible
therefore that these three subspecies are of much more recent origin and
that Bugala was colonized by their ancestors much more recently than
300 000 years ago. What is important is that gene flow between Bugala
and the mainland is now restricted otherwise the butterflies would have
had no opportunity to become distinct.

The discussion of variation in *Acraea encedon* (Acraeidae) in Chapters 8
and 9 can now be reviewed in the context of evolution in isolation. It will
be recalled that populations of this butterfly can be characterized by the
distribution and frequency of spots on the hindwing and by the occurrence
and frequency of polymorphic colour forms. The evolution of these differences would not have been possible if the populations were not more or less
isolated. There is as yet no evidence of *Acraea encedon* undergoing speciation, but the possibility certainly exists in this and other butterflies that
tend to form discrete populations. Indeed we have recently experienced
considerable difficulty in getting butterflies from two widely separated
populations in Sierra Leone to mate successfully.

The possibility of sympatric speciation without geographical isolation
cannot be entirely ruled out. Sympatric speciation has been postulated for
a number of groups of organisms, but on the whole the evidence is against
it. The most likely mechanism of sympatric speciation is through a system
of assortative mating, especially where there are sympatric colour forms.
If there is a statistical tendency for like forms to mate the population
will become more homozygous for the alleles in question and its genetic
variance will be increased. Complete or nearly complete assortative
mating could result in the virtual elimination of the heterozygotes and the
population will become divided into two genetically distinct components.
Once divided, additional differences (possibly affecting different alleles)
can develop and, given time, reproductive isolation could occur, and the
population would have split itself into two species. The widespread occurrence of colour polymorphism in tropical butterflies provides possibilities
for assortative mating, but thus far no evidence for or against it has been
found, mainly because few people have looked. Hence at the moment the
possibility can simply be entertained and no more.

Sexual dimorphism

In many species of butterflies the two sexes are quite different in colour
and marking while in others the sexes are alike. In some species, as dis-

cussed in Chapter 9, the females are mimetic but the males are not; this is presumably because the females are more vulnerable to predators.

There are 26 species of *Charaxes* (Nymphalidae) in the Freetown area. In 13 of these the females are quite different in appearance from the males while in another five there is some sexual dimorphism in colour and pattern. In the remaining eight the sexes are alike. Some examples of sexual dimorphism in *Charaxes* are shown in Plate 32. Sexual dimorphism in *Charaxes* and other butterflies (Plate 31) is presumably evolved as a means of recognition of one sex by the other. In species lacking sexual dimorphism it is likely that one or both sexes produces a distinctive pheromone that enables an individual to recognize the other sex of its species. A parallel situation seems to exist in birds: some species show considerable sexual dimorphism while others do not, but in many of those that lack sexual dimorphism the male sings distinctively in the breeding season which presumably facilitates recognition by the female.

Concluding remarks on evolution

The diversity of butterflies in the world is in all probability the result of the same kinds of evolutionary processes that have occurred and are occurring in other sexually reproducing organisms. The importance of isolation in the origin of species seems reasonably well established. Tropical butterflies with short breeding generations have considerable evolutionary potential for animals of their size and with the drastic alteration of the environment that is now taking place as a result of rising human numbers we can expect further evolutionary adjustments. No one knows how long it takes to evolve two species from one; but I would suggest that the time scale may be in hundreds rather than the more generally accepted figure of hundreds of thousands of years.

Summarizing past evolutionary trends in butterflies in the light of what exists at present is necessarily a highly speculative business. But compared with temperate species tropical butterflies appear to have produced more unpalatable groups thus opening up opportunities for mimicry and mimetic polymorphism. Environmentally determined seasonal forms also seem more frequent in tropical than in temperate species. In the recent past the forest fauna was probably quite distinct from the savanna fauna, but with the alteration of the landscape by man there has been a considerable merging of these two components. There is little doubt that in the future the major environmental factor that will affect the evolution of butterflies is man.

II

THE BEHAVIOUR OF
ADULT BUTTERFLIES

THE sequence of behaviour of an adult butterfly is determined by the environmental stimuli it receives, including stimuli from other butterflies of the same or different species. In consequence it is impossible to consider behaviour as an isolated phenomenon; rather it should be considered in relation to ecology and genetics because the behaviour of an individual will in large measure determine its chances of survival and reproduction. In describing butterfly behaviour I am accepting the proposition that all behaviour is adaptive and is directed towards survival and reproduction. The adaptive significance of some behaviour is obscure, but this does not mean that such behaviour has no adaptive significance. Crane (1957) has described what she calls 'irrelevant behaviour' in *Heliconius* (Nymphalidae) butterflies. Such behaviour tends to occur during courtship when a male is thwarted by the unresponsiveness of the female, but it could be doubted if this behaviour is really irrelevant in the sense that the word is usually understood; it is more likely that the behaviour is adaptive, but that the nature of the adaptation is unclear.

The behaviour of adult butterflies is in many ways paralleled by the behaviour of two other groups of diurnal animals, birds and lizards. In all three groups courtship before mating is conspicuous and bright colours in one or both sexes often play a part in interactions between the sexes. There is increasing evidence that scent in the form of pheromones plays an important part in the pre-mating behaviour of butterflies which sets them apart from birds and lizards which do not in general elaborate pheromones. Territorial and aggressive behaviour is well developed in all three groups. Predators are evaded by either keeping still or moving quickly away from the source of danger and there are many behavioural responses to changes in the weather that are common to all three groups of animals.

In attempting to describe adult behaviour in butterflies it must be emphasized that although it is necessary to break down behaviour into components an individual butterfly may be faced with a variety of situations and receive a variety of stimuli even within the space of a few minutes. Thus a male butterfly courting a female may be attacked by a predator; after the attack the female may be no longer available and the male (if it escapes) may feed or seek out a resting place. These very different events may take place very quickly, the butterfly changing its responses as the external stimuli change. In the account that follows I have broken behaviour down into a sequence that approximates to the life history of an adult butterfly.

Courtship and mating

Soon after emergence from the pupa a butterfly takes its first flight. In many species mating is possible on the day of emergence, but in some, particularly butterflies that are migratory, mating and mating behaviour may be delayed for days or even weeks. Some species, such as *Precis octavia* (Nymphalidae), in which individuals may emerge at the beginning of the dry season, show no sign of mating behaviour, and after feeding for a few days at flowers, go into aestivation and remain in a state of partial dormancy for months. Similar behaviour occurs in some European butterflies, such as *Aglais urticae* and *Nymphalis io* (Nymphalidae), which emerge in late summer and hibernate through the winter.

But whether mating occurs soon after emergence or whether it is delayed, there is in almost all species a period of courtship. The extent to which courtship behaviour occurs appears to depend on the age of the female. In tropical American *Heliconius* (Nymphalidae), full courtship behaviour occurs only two or three days after a female has emerged from the pupa. Mating may take place much earlier than this, sometimes only a few hours after emergence, but in such circumstances the females elicit very little courtship behaviour from the males (Crane 1957). Male *Heliconius* show no signs of courtship behaviour until at least 24 hours old.

There have been relatively few attempts to describe courtship and mating behaviour in butterflies and we are not yet in a position to analyse courtship on a comparative basis as has been possible in birds. The classic work of Tinbergen, Meeuse, Boerema, and Varossieau (1942) on the European grayling butterfly, *Eumenis semele* (Satyridae), paved the way for further studies, including the analysis of some tropical species. In recent years studies of courtship and mating have become integrated with studies of the fine structure of butterfly sense organs, particularly the antennae, and with the chemistry of pheromones that are used by some species during courtship. The combination of descriptive behaviour, micro-anatomy, and chemistry is beginning to produce some valuable results, some of which are summarized below.

The most detailed research has been on the tropical American *Danaus gilippus* (Danaidae) whose range extends into the southern United States. The account of courtship behaviour that follows is based on Brower, Brower, and Cranston (1965), Brower and Jones (1965), Myers and Brower (1969), Meinwald, Meinwald, and Mazzocchi (1969), and Pliske and Eisner (1969). The males of *Danaus gilippus*, like the males of other Danaidae, are equipped with a pair of bundles of hair pencils which during certain phases of courtship are everted from the tip of the abdomen (Plates 34 and 35). In addition there is a gland on the upper surface of each hindwing which varies in structure considerably in different genera of Danaidae, but in *Danaus* forms a pocket into which the hair pencils may be inserted. In *Danaus gilippus* the hair pencils contain in the form of particles a pheromone which has been identified as a crystalline ketone, and also a viscous terpenoid alcohol. The chemical structures of both compounds are known (Meinwald *et al.* 1969), and the crystalline ketone has also been identified in another tropical American danaid, *Lycorea ceres* (Meinwald, Meinwald, Wheeler, Eisner, and Brower 1966). The crystalline ketone is transferred in the form of dust particles to the antennae of the female (Plate 35) while the other compound appears to function as a means of sticking the dust to the female's antennae. During courtship the male pursues the female and induces her to alight by lightly brushing her antennae with his hair pencils. The production of the pheromone appears to prevent the female from escaping and to make her quiescent. Before alighting beside the female the male hovers over her displaying his hair pencils, but eventually alights beside her and copulates. Once joined the pair can move off, the male carrying the pair in flight. Males deprived of hair pencils are capable of courtship, but females do not respond to them. For some unknown reason males reared in captivity produce subnormal amounts of the ketone and these too are less capable of successful mating, but their competence can be restored by the addition of synthetic ketone. The function of the wing glands is not fully understood, but on the basis of their histology they seem to be secretory. The males push their hair pencils into the wing glands when they are by themselves and not involved in courtship and it is possible that hair pencil and wing gland secretions combine to form the functional pheromone.

The entire sequence of events in the courtship of *Danaus gilippus* is shown diagrammatically in Fig. 11.1. It appears that both the hair pencilling behaviour and the deposition of the pheromone on the antennae of the female are essential for successful copulation. There is no doubt that the pheromone is deposited on the antennae of the female as its presence has been detected on the surface and on the sensory pegs of antennae of females that have just mated, but it is absent from the antennae of virgin females. Two of the three types of sensilla on the antennae of female *Danaus gilippus* do not appear to be receptive to the pheromone as when they are completely blocked out normal courtship is still possible. This leaves the short, thin-walled sensilla as the receptors of the male pheromone (Myers and Brower 1969). It is estimated that between 1000 and 1500 (about five per cent of the total) of these widely distributed antennal receptors (Plate 36) are necessary for normal courtship to occur.

An essentially similar sequence of events appears to occur in the African

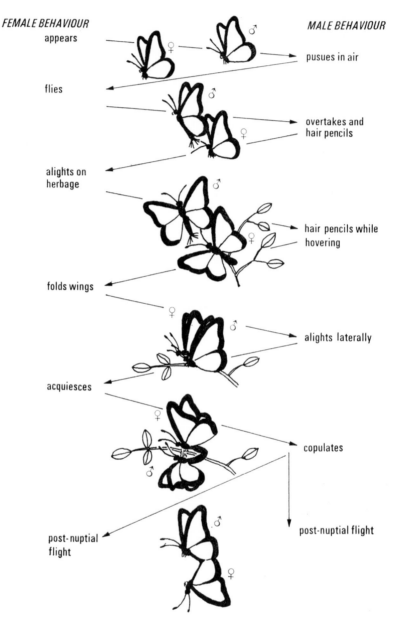

FIG. 11.1. The sequence of courtship behaviour in *Danaus gilippus*. From Brower *et al.* (1965).

Danaus chrysippus, but the behaviour of this species has not been properly studied. The hair pencil secretions of *Danaus chrysippus* are currently undergoing analysis and Dr. T. Eisner (personal communication) has confirmed the presence of the ketone.

Brower *et al.* (1965) speculate that different species of Danaidae are likely to have somewhat different pheromones that function as an arrestant to the female's flight. If this is so males would only be able to arrest the flight of females of their own species, which perhaps is an important consideration in butterflies that act as models for many mimetic species and where interspecific confusion can result if colour and pattern alone are utilized as a means of sex recognition.

Much is now known about the chemistry of the hair pencil secretion, and the courtship behaviour of some Danaidae has been analysed experimentally and quantitatively. It is therefore not without interest to record that the general significance of hair pencils and the wing glands in Danaidae was appreciated over fifty years ago by Lamborn, who was also responsible for elucidating the life histories of African Lycaenidae that enter into close associations with ants (see Chapter 3).

Hypolimnas misippus (Nymphalidae) is the only African butterfly whose courtship and mating have been studied in detail (Stride 1956, 1957, 1958). Stride's approach was quite different from that described for *Danaus gilippus*, in that he used various artificial test insects to investigate the male's visual abilities at recognizing and courting females. He did not investigate the possible role of pheromones in courtship, but acknowledged that these could play a part. The male of *Hypolimnas misippus* is black with bold white spots and the females are orange with variable black and white markings (Fig. 9.1). As in *Heliconius* (Nymphalidae), the females are able to mate the day they emerge from the pupa, but courtship is best observed in females at least two days old. Stride's work was carried out in Ghana.

The males of *Hypolimnas misippus*, like the males of most other butterflies, are more active than the females and are therefore more frequently seen. They tend to select a particular patch of ground where they are able to rest and sun themselves (the significance of sunning is discussed later in this chapter), and from this spot they dart off and investigate other insects that fly past, returning to the same spot when the investigation has been completed. Stride (1956) reports that they will even investigate weaver birds flying to and from a nesting colony. The males show more interest in butterflies of approximately the same size as themselves than in smaller or larger insects, and they show particular interest in butterflies of the same general coloration as female *Hypolimnas misippus*. It would therefore seem that this investigating behaviour is not aggressive and that the sorties are undertaken in order to find mates. When a male encounters a female it interrupts her flight and commences a quivering movement of the wings.

The female also quivers her wings and the two pass slowly over the herbage, the male flying a little below the female. If the female is ready to mate she comes to rest and holds her wings open which seems to stimulate the male to further activity, but a female that is not ready to mate comes to rest with wings closed. Mating takes place among the herbage and the two remained joined for some hours. A conspicuous feature of the courtship behaviour in *Hypolimnas misippus* is the ascending flight in which the female rises slowly to ten or more metres with wings quivering. The male follows, but the female only stops the ascending flight when the male has broken off and returned to base. Virgin females do not perform the ascending flight and it appears that this behaviour is directed towards the avoidance of mating by an already fertilized female.

By using test insects in which the colours of both males and females were altered Stride established the importance of visual stimuli in the early stages of courtship in *Hypolimnas misippus*. For instance he painted black the white spots on the wings of males and produced all-black test insects, and also removed the scales from the wings of males to produce colourless test insects. These males were far less successful in courtship than normal males. He also prepared test females from the wings of freshly killed butter-flies, including females with male forewings and female hindwings and vice versa. He claimed that the presence of white on the hindwing of a female exerts a strong inhibitory effect on the courtship of the male. Females with white hindwings are the best mimics of *Danaus chrysippus* (Danaidae) (Chapter 9). Edmunds (1969b) using field observations of court-ship rather than test insects claims that there is no significant difference in females with and without white hindwings in the frequency of courtship behaviour. Stride's analysis would suggest that in West Africa *Hypolimnas misippus* females with white hindwings may be at a selective advantage be-cause of their close resemblance to *Danaus chrysippus*, but at a disadvantage in that the males tend to avoid them, but in view of Edmund's findings no conclusions can be reached on this point.

Although there are no proper studies it is likely that courtship behaviour reaches a considerable level of complexity among the mimetic assemblages of forest butterflies. Thus it is possible to catch several similar looking butterflies that are chasing each other around in apparent courtship and upon close examination they will often turn out to be members of different species or even of different families. Evidently there is very often initial confusion between individuals of *Pseudacraea eurytus* (Nymphalidae), a polymorphic mimic, and various species of *Bematistes* (Acraeidae), the models. I have on many occasions seen the beginnings of courtship between a male *Pseudacraea eurytus* and a female *Bematistes*, or vice versa. In these butterflies visual stimuli are likely to be of little importance once the encounters develop, and I would predict that pheromones play an im-

34. Fully expanded bundle of hair pencils of *Danaus gilippus* (Danaidae). The diameter of the expanded bundle is about 1 cm. (*Photo by T. Eisner*)

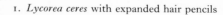

1. *Lycorea ceres* with expanded hair pencils

2–4. Consecutive stages in the extrusion of hair pencils from the tip of the abdomen of male *Lycorea ceres*. The sheath containing the hair pencils can be seen in (2). The diameter of the fully expanded bundle is about 1 cm

1

2

3

5. Particles of hair-pencil pheromone on the surface of hair pencils of *Danaus gilippus*. The length of hair shown in the photograph is approximately 300 μm

6. Particle of hair-pencil pheromone on sensory peg of antenna of freshly courted virgin female *Danaus gilippus*. The length of peg shown is about 20 μm

35. Hair pencils of *Lycorea ceres* and pheromone particles of *Danaus gilippus* (Danaidae). (*Photos by T. Eisner*)

portant part in courtship once the butterflies have established their identities with each other.

Egg-laying

No detailed analysis has been made of egg-laying in any species of tropical butterfly, but some generalizations are possible, upon which, it is to be hoped, more detailed studies will be based. Many female butterflies are able to commence egg-laying within a day of mating. One major behavioural problem is how a female intent on laying eggs can avoid the attentions of males that want to mate with her. In *Hypolimnas misippus*, as already described, the ascending flight of a fertilized female acts as a signal to males that she is not ready to mate. In all probability there are similar behavioural patterns in other species, perhaps not so obvious to the human observer, but functional in the sense that the male eventually gives up his attempts and the female proceeds with laying her eggs. In Sierra Leone I once watched female *Pseudopontia paradoxa* (Pieridae) laying eggs on the leaves of Acanthaceae growing on the floor of primary forest. This species flies very weakly and the females flapped slowly from plant to plant occasionally depositing an egg on the underside of a leaf. In each case a male flapped slowly about ten centimetres above the female, but there was no obvious interaction between the two sexes. It is possible that although the males may have been attempting courtship the females were providing signals (behavioural or chemical) which eventually put the males off, or at least prevented them from establishing physical contact with the female. The possibility of a specific egg-laying pheromone that deters the male can be entertained, but as yet there is no evidence for its existence.

Another problem is in finding the correct larval food-plant. Most species of butterflies are restricted to a small range of plants, often members of a single plant genus or family, and, particularly in forest where the diversity of plants is high, finding the right larval food-plant for egg-laying may present problems. I have watched females of *Pseudacraea eurytus* (Nymphalidae) moving slowly through secondary forest frequently pausing for a moment and touching the leaves of a shrub before moving on to the next. In this way a female may examine shrubs of a variety of species, quickly rejecting each until the correct plant is found; almost certainly the smell of the plant elicits the appropriate response. Most plants contain in their tissues chemical compounds that have presumably been evolved as a means of deterring herbivorous animals. Animals such as butterflies have in turn become adapted to respond to a small range of these compounds as a means of finding the correct food-plant when egg-laying. Thus the females of *Papilio demodocus* (Papilionidae) seek out plants of the family Rutaceae which even to man have a most distinctive smell (the crushed leaves of *Citrus* are highly aromatic). If *Citrus* leaves are crushed on the hand it is possible to induce a caged female *Papilio demodocus* to inspect and even lay an egg on the hand, which provides reasonable evidence that the butterfly is responding to smell rather than to a visual stimulus.

But although butterflies may be remarkably good chemists in detecting the correct food-plant for egg-laying, they seem to be quite unable to judge quantity. I have repeatedly found butterflies of a variety of species laying their eggs on tiny plants which would be quite unable to support the resulting larvae.

Territory and feeding

A territory is defined as a defended area. The concept was first used in connection with studies of bird behaviour, and has been extended to other groups, including insects. The defence of an area is usually thought of in terms of keeping other members (especially males) of the same species out of the specified area. In birds territories are developed mainly in the breeding season and function as a means of securing a mate and providing an area in which food can be obtained for the young.

Many butterflies exhibit what appears to be territorial behaviour. An individual will remain in one place and constantly drive off other individuals of the same or of different species entering the vicinity. In most cases it is not apparent why other individuals are driven off. Butterfly territories differ from bird territories in that the space defended can change from day to day or even within a few minutes. The term *individual distance* has been used to describe parallel behaviour in birds, and in butterflies this is perhaps more appropriate than territory.

Individual distance in butterflies is best observed when several are feeding from a patch of flowers. A feeding butterfly will defend its flower from others that attempt to alight, but occasionally will be driven off by the intruder. The defence is usually in the form of jerking the wings and pointing the head at the intruder. Occasionally a butterfly will strike another with its wings, but usually, as in birds, threatening behaviour suffices to drive off the intruder. Whether in butterflies there is any form of behavioural dominance as in some birds and mammals is not known, but it would appear that butterflies often recognize a more powerful individual and move away without a fight.

Flowers are generally well dispersed, but other sources of food favoured by some species are often extremely localized. As described in Chapter 3, many species feed on rotten fruit which tends to occur in quantity only in restricted places. In such places Nymphalidae of a variety of species will congregate and it is possible to observe aggressive behaviour between individuals. In tropical Africa rotten bananas placed in a suitable site will often attract numbers of *Charaxes*. These butterflies have powerful wings and the leading edge is thickened and serrated. If, when a *Charaxes* is feeding, another approaches, the wings are jerked rapidly and the intruder may be hit. Frequently a larger *Charaxes* will displace a smaller individual and take its place at the food source. The behaviour of *Charaxes* at rotten fruit is reminiscent of birds at a feeding table in winter; individual distances are maintained by aggressive postures and the butterflies may displace one another from the source of food. Indeed it is possible to construct a feeding table for Nymphalidae along the same lines as a bird table (Plate 38) and, as described in Chapter 15, it is possible to convert the feeding table into a trap similar to those used by bird ringers for catching small birds.

Weather and behaviour

Butterflies, unlike birds and mammals but like reptiles, are heliotherms deriving their heat from the sun. Heat from the sun is received through the wings (in which blood circulates) and the efficiency of the wings as heat receptors is improved by modifications in their shape, colour, and pattern, but particularly by the behaviour of the butterfly under varying temperatures. Heat is gained by basking in the sun and by contact with the ground if the ground has a higher temperature than the butterfly. Heat may be lost by seeking shelter from the sun. Behavioural aspects of temperature regulation in butterflies are reviewed by Clench (1966) who draws attention to the many similarities between butterflies and reptiles, and points out that moths differ from both groups as they derive heat from muscular energy.

In the tropics air temperatures are moderately high most of the time, with greater daily than seasonal fluctuations. But the temperature may fall suddenly in the evening and especially after a heavy downpour of rain. Many tropical butterflies sun themselves with wings spread, especially in the early morning and after heavy rain, while in very hot weather they will seek shade. Forest species are more apt to move out of the forest into the open in the wet season, possibly seeking sunshine, while savanna species move into forest during the dry season presumably in search of shade.

The veins of a butterfly's wings are able to transfer heat received from the sun to other parts of the body; relatively little heat can be transferred from the wing membrane. In many butterflies the veins are conspicuous because they are pigmented with black and this presumably facilitates heat absorption as matt black surfaces absorb and radiate heat more quickly than smooth pale surfaces. Thus advantage may be taken of short spells of sunshine when heat will be gained relatively rapidly through the exposed veins. The colour of a butterfly's wing functions in a variety of ways, but it is likely that in almost all species there are components of the colour that are adapted to heat absorption.

Clench (1966) has listed the behavioural devices by which butterflies may gain or lose heat and correctly notes that it is harder to identify devices by which butterflies lose heat than devices for gaining heat. As regards heat gain, dorsal basking, in which the wings are spread and the butterfly orients to the sun so that the upperside of the wings receives the maximum amount of heat, is most common. This is the commonly observed 'sunning' behaviour. In many Hesperiidae only the hindwings are fully expanded, the forewings being held half open; the significance of this is obscure, but it may be nothing to do with temperature regulation. The extent to which the wings are expanded and the angle of orientation can be controlled by the individual butterfly and heat gain can thus be regulated. Lateral basking is when the wings are closed and the butterfly orients itself so that the sun's rays are normal to the wing surface. This occurs especially in Satyridae, but also in some Nymphalidae, Pieridae, and Lycaenidae. Heat may be gained from the ground by the butterfly pressing its body onto the ground (often to rock or bare earth) that is at a higher temperature than itself. Heat is also gained during flight as a result of metabolic processes, and in some Hesperiidae (as in many moths) heat may be gained by shivering. Many butterflies that sun themselves avoid strong wind. Apart from the danger of being blown about, cooling occurs more rapidly in a moving air current. On windy days Nymphalidae such as *Precis pelarga* seek out sheltered glades for sunning themselves.

Heat loss is probably mainly achieved by seeking shade, but heat will tend to be lost whenever the temperature of the butterfly is above that of its surroundings. Clench (1966) considers that evaporative cooling is a major heat losing device in butterflies, but this has been disputed by Watt (1968) on the basis of experiments on North American *Colias* (Pieridae). It is unlikely that a butterfly often needs to lose heat; the adaptations are mainly directed towards avoiding excessive heat gain, either by seeking shade or by resting with wings closed and oriented in line with the sun's rays.

The foregoing observations on behavioural temperature regulation in butterflies have not in general been backed by experimental investigation. Thus although there are *a priori* reasons for supposing that some of the behaviour of butterflies is associated with temperature regulation, it is now necessary to back up these observations with direct measurements of the temperature of living butterflies in relation to their behaviour and coloration, and to the ambient temperature.

Such experiments have been conducted on various species of North American *Colias* (Pieridae) by Watt (1968), and although this work is outside the scope of this book, brief mention is worth while. Watt was able to implant minute thermistor probes into the thoracic muscles of the butterflies and to relate the temperatures recorded to the butterflies' behaviour under different temperatures. He was also able to establish that dark *Colias* heat up and attain a higher steady-state body temperature more quickly than paler butterflies and was able to rule out evaporative cooling as a means of losing heat. These results are extremely valuable as they establish for the first time a relationship between body temperature, behaviour, and coloration.

In the butterflies of humid tropical regions keeping dry is probably as important as maintaining a steady body temperature, although the two are not of course unrelated. Rain in the humid tropics is considerably heavier than elsewhere in the world and is often heaviest at the time of year that is otherwise most favourable to butterflies. In Sierra Leone the delicate Lycaenidae occur most abundantly as adults in the dry season and are relatively rare at the peak of the rains. This in itself may be an adaptation to high rainfall, as in Uganda, where there is less rainfall, Lycaenidae occur commonly in all months of the year.

Butterflies avoid heavy rain by sheltering under leaves and branches. Many species hang upside down with the wings slightly open so that rain-drops run off. Presumably if the wings were tightly pressed together in the normal resting position there would be a danger of their sticking thus disabling the butterfly.

12

MIGRATIONS AND MOVEMENTS

SOON after a butterfly has emerged from its pupa and its wings are fully dried and hardened it takes its first flight. This flight may cover a very short distance and often the butterfly will seek a source of food such as a flower. Most newly emerged butterflies spend the first day or so feeding, but the females of many species mate before flying any great distance. On sunny mornings males of *Papilio demodocus* (Papilionidae) fly in and out of vegetation searching for females; in this species mating normally takes place before the first flight of the female, indeed her first flight may occur while she is still joined to the male.

Males are in general more active fliers than females and travel greater distances, often in search of mates. This is why most collections contain an excess of males over females. A male may have to fly a considerable distance before locating a receptive female, and both sexes may cover large distances in search of food. *Charaxes* (Nymphalidae) that feed chiefly at rotten fruit and decaying animal matter often congregate in large numbers at a good source of food, and presumably many have travelled considerable distances to locate such a source. But there is evidently much variation in the distances covered. Small, weak-flying Lycaenidae that are associated with a particular food-plant may move no more than a few metres during their entire life. Large species of Papilionidae possibly travel great distances even within the course of a single day. Other species capable of long distance flights tend to remain in restricted areas.

Observers in the tropics have frequently reported mass flights of particular species, sometimes involving hundreds of thousands or even millions of individuals. Such flights may be regular in the sense that they tend to occur at certain times of the year, or they may be irregular. Frequently the butterflies seen are moving in a fixed direction and the movement may continue for several days. Williams (1930) has documented many such flights in detail and has suggested that many tropical species undertake long distance migrations. By migration I mean a regular relatively long-distance flight to and from a breeding area. Breeding may occur during the migration, but very often the individuals participating show no signs of mating or egg-laying. In the north temperate region, especially in Europe and North America, there is now evidence that butterflies and other insects undertake seasonal movements comparable to the well-known migrations of birds. In particular, some butterflies move northwards in the spring and southwards in the late summer or autumn. Breeding takes place in the northern summer, but populations so established cannot survive the winter and therefore the adults (or some of them) move southwards. These migrations differ from those of birds in two important respects. Firstly, the southward flight is undertaken by the offspring of those that came north in the spring and hence it is the population that is migratory, not the individual. There is however evidence obtained by marking, releasing, and recapturing, as well as by careful observation, that in North America *Danaus plexippus* (Danaidae) flies south from the northern United States and Canada to Mexico and Central America in autumn and that some of the same individuals make the return flight next spring (Urquhart 1960). The possibility that individual *Vanessa cardui* (Nymphalidae) undertake a similar migration to southern Europe and North Africa and back again to northern Europe in the spring must also be entertained; in addition it is possible that individuals of this species make a double journey between various parts of tropical Africa. Secondly, the migrations of butterflies are less predictable than those of birds. Thus although it is possible that in every year some *Colias croceus* (Pieridae) move north from southern Europe and North Africa, the numbers doing so fluctuate enormously from year to year; in England *Colias croceus* may be extremely abundant and widespread in some years, as it was in 1947, but rare or absent altogether in other years. There is some evidence of similar variation in the numbers of individuals involved in migratory flights in tropical Africa, but so far there have been few attempts to study the migration of African butterflies on a long term basis.

It would appear that butterfly migrations are much more directly stimulated by ecological events at the point of origin than bird migrations. A likely cause of mass migration would be the local scarcity of a particular food-plant which in turn could be determined by weather, especially drought.

As with many ecological problems, there are two sorts of questions to be asked about butterfly migration. Firstly, what are the proximate factors stimulating migration and how do the butterflies 'know' the direction in which to fly, and how do they find their way or navigate? Secondly, what are the ultimate factors, or what is the ecological or evolutionary significance of the migration?

No positive answer can be provided for either of these questions. At high latitudes migration may be proximately stimulated by changes in day length and temperature, or, more directly, by the local failure of a particular resource. In the tropics the alternation of wet and dry seasons may stimulate migration at particular times of the year, and in this regard it may be noted that most of the tropical butterflies known to be migratory are savanna species; the savanna is seasonally more varied than the forest, and many savanna areas go through a long dry season during which ecological conditions may be very unfavourable for insects.

Migrating butterflies undoubtedly use guide lines, such as the sea coast or a belt of trees, but such guide lines are of limited value for an individual travelling great distances. Butterflies have also been seen migrating at a constant angle to the wind, and spectacular movements have been recorded through mountain passes in Venezuela and the Pyrenees (Williams 1958). But although butterfly (and other insect) migrations and movements have been extensively observed and well documented, the places of origin, the means of navigation, and the selective advantage of the migrations and movements have been scarcely considered. It is known that under certain unknown conditions migrant individuals, sometimes in enormous numbers, suddenly appear in an otherwise resident population, or invade a previously unoccupied area. These individuals often move on, sometimes in a constant direction, rarely pausing to feed or to lay eggs, and are often joined by other individuals of the same or of different species. Eventually the migration stops and breeding occurs in a region at a considerable distance from the place of origin. This may be followed by a return flight of the offspring of the original parents. The return flight is essential if the migratory habit is to be maintained for more than a few generations.

A theory of butterfly migration

A theory has recently been proposed to explain the migratory behaviour of butterflies (Baker 1968), the essentials of which are as follows:

The larvae of many butterflies feed on plants that are well distributed in a particular area, the distribution of such plants being subject to a certain amount of change. Particularly in seasonally dry areas plants may appear and disappear over quite short periods of time; this is especially obvious in cultivated areas where the food-plants may be crops or weeds. Selection would then be expected to produce butterflies that fly from one source of potential larval food-plant to another. Selection would also favour individual butterflies that spend the minimum time in areas unsuitable for their larval food-plants, and since plants are immobile, the most efficient flight path for a searching butterfly is one that does not take the butterfly over the same area more than once. Random movements are clearly disadvantageous. Some possible paths, all equally efficient, are shown in Fig. 12.1. It is quite possible to see these and other similar kinds of flight path if one stands for a time in an area where butterflies are common. The various alternatives shown in Fig. 12.1, with the exception of the spiral flight, lead the butterfly more or less in a straight line. It is however essential that the approximate straight line of flight be continued over a period of days otherwise the butterfly would tend to double back on itself. There are presumably distractions for a butterfly flying in an approximately straight line for a considerable time; these would include flowers and other butterflies. It is unlikely that butterflies have sufficient memory to continue on one day an activity started the previous day, and so one must look for some other factor to which an individual could respond. As already mentioned, there are observations of butterflies flying at a constant angle to the wind; but a few metres from the ground, where most flight takes place, there are

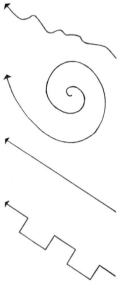

Fig. 12.1. Equally efficient flight paths for a butterfly seeking dispersed immobile plants. From Baker (1968).

small hills, trees, and other obstacles which set up local air currents such that a butterfly flying at a constant angle to the wind would often fly in a circle. Moreover the wind frequently changes direction overnight and a butterfly would often find itself going over territory covered the previous day. Many butterflies fly only when the sun is shining and rest whenever the sun is obscured by cloud. Indeed insects in general are very responsive to the sun, and such a response would certainly enable a butterfly to fly in an approximately straight line. The sun changes its position during the day, but the rate of change is slow and Baker proposes that an approximately straight line can be maintained if the butterfly flies at a constant angle to the sun. He further suggests that in butterflies whose larval food-plant is well dispersed, the habit of flying at a constant angle to the sun will result in finding new sources of potential food more rapidly than those whose movements are random. There are probably two ways in which the angle to the sun could be fixed by an individual butterfly. There could be some form of imprinting in which the angle subtended on the eye is the one adopted during the rest of the individual's lifetime, or there could be a genetic bias towards a certain angle; the second possibility seems the more likely because the first would tend to be ineffective on overcast days.

Thus far Baker's proposal does not allow any particular angle of the sun to be favoured and yet observations of butterfly migrations and movements suggest that certain flight directions are favoured. However certain angles would be more likely to lead to a favourable ecological situation at certain times of the year than at others and selection could be expected to operate on butterflies such that particular flight directions are evolved at specific times of the year. If there is some feature in the local environment that exists in the form of a gradient the appropriate angle to the sun could be selected by a response (negative or positive) to that gradient. Baker suggests several possible gradients: (1) in the abundance of a predator or a parasite, (2) in the abundance of a food-plant, (3) in day length, and (4) in climate, especially temperature and humidity. Not all of these gradients will be equally important and there may be variation between species and between geographical areas. Temperature is likely to be the most important gradient, especially in temperate regions. Indeed the theory outlined presents some difficulties when applied to tropical species that occur in areas where temperature is rather constant, but in general it provides a logical interpretation of butterfly movements and the evolution of the migratory habit.

Migrant butterflies in tropical Africa

As already mentioned, observations in the north temperate region indicate a predominantly northerly flight in spring and early summer, and a southerly return flight in late summer or autumn. Observations in the tropics have failed to demonstrate a similar regular flight pattern (Williams 1930), and in particular there is little evidence of return flights. Evidence for migration and movement among tropical butterflies comes from three different sorts of observation: (1) a flight of butterflies moving in a fixed direction over a period of time, (2) the sudden appearance of very large numbers of a particular species in an area where there is little or no sign of extensive local breeding, and (3) the occurrence of individuals of species known to be migratory elsewhere in areas where they are not normally resident.

In Africa the following species have been repeatedly recorded as migrants or as moving in or out of certain areas: *Belenois creona, Belenois aurota, Catopsilia florella* (Pieridae), *Danaus chrysippus* (Danaidae), *Vanessa cardui, Hypolimnas misippus*, and several species of *Asterope* (Nymphalidae), *Libythea labdaca* (Libytheidae), and *Andronymus neander* (Hesperiidae). All of these species are characteristic of open country and cultivated land, and the following is a summary of the more important migrations and movements that have been recorded.

Belenois creona and *Belenois aurota.* Large flights of these two and possibly other species of *Belenois* have been repeatedly recorded in East and South Africa. In East Africa most of the observed flights have been towards the south or south-east, but there are records of flight in almost all directions. There is considerable evidence that *Belenois aurota* populations build up to almost plague proportions in some savanna areas and that there is widespread defoliation of the larval food-plant, *Capparis*, a common savanna bush. Pitman (1928) gives a graphic account of a breeding ground of *Belenois aurota* in West Nile, Uganda, in March 1928. He wote: 'One can only describe as amazing the vast breeding-grounds encountered. I have never seen before such countless myriads of butterflies, and as far as the eye could see there was a shimmer of white just above the surface of the ground. The majority of the food shrubs (*Maerua oblongifolia*, Capparidaceae) seemed practically leafless—larvae and chrysalises were everywhere, as also countless thousands *in cop.*' Williams (1930) is inclined to the view that many of the observed East African flights of this species originate in the Nile provinces of Uganda, where the larval food-plant is abundant. After a large movement of *Belenois aurota* through Nairobi, Kenya, in January and February 1926, an isolated bush of *Capparis* about a metre high and probably the only bush of its kind in the area, was estimated to hold 57 thousand eggs and young larvae (Williams 1958). At least four other species of *Belenois* have been recorded moving in large flights and there are numerous records of movements of unidentified species of *Belenois*.

Catopsilia florella. The genus *Catopsilia* includes some of the best known migrant butterflies in the tropics of Central and South America, Africa, Asia, and Australia. The larvae feed on various species of *Cassia*, which are mainly savanna trees and bushes, but which include species planted in gardens for ornamental purposes. Most of the mass flights recorded in *Catopsilia florella* (Williams 1930) refer to East and South Africa, but the species is everywhere abundant in Africa, except in forest. Williams (1958) describes a movement at Amani, Tanzania, that started on about 25 December 1928 and continued until 2 April 1929, a total period of over fifteen weeks. Almost all the butterflies were flying against the wind to the north or north-east. Records covering 24 years collected by G. F. Cockbill at Salisbury, Rhodesia, show that nearly every year there was a south or south-west flight in December and early January followed about six weeks later in March by a movement, much smaller in size, to the north or north-east. This suggests a return flight by the same individuals or their immediate offspring (in tropical Africa the generation time is about a month, but it is presumably rather longer in Rhodesia where it is cooler). In Egypt the species is an irregular visitor, presumably from the south, but larvae have been recorded from time to time.

Danaus chrysippus. Most reports of movements of this species refer to the East African colour form *dorippus*, the central and western populations apparently not undertaking migrations. On 22 February 1966, at Vipingo, just north of Mombasa, Kenya, I observed many *Danaus chrysippus* (form *dorippus*) flying steadily north at a rate of two or three a minute. Their flight was definite and sustained and many thousands must have been involved (Owen and Chanter 1968). A similar flight was observed in June 1928 at Amani, Tanzania (Williams 1930). The butterflies passed east and south-east and at a rate of less than one a minute over a period of 19 days. *Danaus chrysippus* is also reported as being migratory in Australia (Williams 1930).

Vanessa cardui. The Painted Lady (Plate 11) occurs throughout the world with the possible exception of South America and is one of the best known of all migrant butterflies. It is particularly fond of the tops of small hills and at times it is a common garden butterfly. In coastal West Africa it appears every year in September and October and is apparently rare or absent in this area at other times of the year. It possibly does not breed in the forested part of West Africa, but is reported as breeding in almost plague proportions in Northern Nigeria (Boorman and Roche 1959). In 1968–70 I kept records (by marking and releasing) of *Vanessa cardui* in my garden at Freetown, Sierra Leone. These records are shown in Table 12.1.

TABLE 12.1

Records of Vanessa cardui *in a garden at Freetown, Sierra Leone, during 24 consecutive months*

Month	Number recorded	Month	Number recorded
Sept. 1968	'Common'	Sept. 1969	143
Oct.	3	Oct.	130
Nov.	—	Nov.	5
Dec.	1	Dec.	1
Jan. 1969	—	Jan. 1970	—
Feb.	—	Feb.	—
Mar.	6	Mar.	—
Apr.	—	Apr.	—
May	—	May	—
June	—	June	—
July	—	July	—
Aug.	—	Aug.	—

When records began in September 1968 the butterfly was common but the number present was not ascertained. It disappeared in early October 1968 and apart from one in December and six in March 1969, it was absent until the following September when on the 15th of the month it arrived in the Freetown area in large numbers. The butterflies were all rather worn and were extremely active, although showing no signs of breeding. During September and October *Vanessa cardui* became one of the commonest species locally and fresh waves of immigrants arrived periodically, especially on 2 October when 57 different individuals were caught and marked in an hour. Recaptures were few and mostly on the following day, but one individual is known to have remained for six days. They disappeared in early November, but one apparently freshly emerged specimen was found in the garden on 9 November and another was recorded in December. But nevertheless it is quite clear that in general *Vanessa cardui* is a migrant through the Freetown area and does not breed extensively. It seems certain that the butterflies breed in the savanna to the north and that they migrate south with the onset of the dry season in September and October. The March 1969 records possibly suggest a return flight, but if this is so numbers are much reduced; and none appeared in March 1970.

Elsewhere in Africa there are numerous scattered records of *Vanessa cardui* suddenly appearing and disappearing. In Europe the species flies north in the spring from North Africa and south across the Mediterranean in autumn. The possibility exists that Painted Ladies cross the Sahara from north to tropical Africa (or vice versa), and it would be interesting to obtain evidence of such a long distance migration. Painted Ladies were exceptionally abundant in Britain in 1969, the year when numbers were higher than usual in West Africa.

Hypolimnas misippus. This is another widespread and common butterfly in many parts of the Old World. It has recently been established in the Americas, possibly having been introduced from Africa by man. On the other hand the butterfly may have colonized the Americas by transatlantic flights as it has several times been taken at sea in the Atlantic Ocean and on the Canary Islands. It is a species that has undoubtedly increased in numbers in Africa as a result of agriculture and this increase may have led to the colonization of the New World, rather in the way the cattle egret has apparently colonized the Americas from Africa. Evidence for migratory movements in Africa is scanty, but the butterfly sometimes appears in unprecedented numbers. Its ability to colonize quickly areas of cleared forest suggests that it is highly mobile and capable of considerable powers of long distance flight.

Asterope. In Sierra Leone the two species are hardly ever seen except in traps baited with bananas. They appear only in May and June at the onset of the rains and are absent for the rest of the year; this suggests migration from elsewhere, but it is possible that local populations undergo prolonged aestivation. There are however reports from South Africa and East Africa of immense swarms of *Asterope natalensis* and *Asterope boisduvali* moving in fixed directions. One report of *Asterope boisduvali* describes 'millions like a snowstorm' at Wagiri, Tanzania (Williams 1930).

Libythea labdaca. This butterfly occurs throughout tropical Africa and is conspicuously erratic in its time of appearance. In Uganda I have on several occasions seen immense swarms on forest roads such that the entire surface appeared to be covered with small dead leaves. My experience of this butterfly in East and West Africa is that it constantly appears in numbers in unexpected places at unexpected times. Similarly I have found *Libythea bachmanni* to be erratic in the United States and several references in the literature confirm this. It is now well established that in West Africa there is a large southward flight of *Libythea labdaca* in April and May and a smaller northward flight in October and November (Williams 1951). Some published records of the southward flight refer to 'millions' of butterflies.

Andronymus neander. This skipper has been observed moving in large numbers in East Africa (Williams 1930, 1958) and there is at least one record of large-scale movement in the Cameroons (Fox *et al.* 1965). At Amani in Tanzania a flight of these butterflies took place on every fine day for seven weeks from March to May 1928, reaching a peak of 500 a minute on a 20 metre front on 1 April. The butterflies were moving south-south-westerly. Similar flights were recorded at the same locality in 1906 (flying to the south-east) and in March 1930 (to the south-south-west) but none was seen in 1929 despite a close watch for them (Williams 1930).

Many other African butterflies have occasionally been reported moving or appearing in unusual numbers. There is plenty of evidence to suggest that many species are migratory, but the main patterns of migration within Africa remain obscure. An observer stationed in one area for a year or more could contribute valuable information by recording suspected migrants, preferably by marking and releasing. In this way it might be possible eventually to work out the general trend of migration in Africa.

13

BUTTERFLIES AND AGRICULTURE

THERE are three ways in which butterflies can interact with agriculture. Firstly, many adult butterflies visit flowers for nectar and in so doing undoubtedly aid in the pollination of plants. Secondly, since most butterfly larvae are herbivorous at least some species are likely to feed on crops. And thirdly, some butterfly larvae feed on agricultural weeds or are predators of plant bugs and are thus potentially beneficial.

Compared with the temperate regions many fewer species of tropical plants are wind pollinated, the vast majority being pollinated by animals, including birds and bats as well as insects. Little is known of the importance of butterflies as pollinators, but since butterflies are common and are frequent flower visitors it can be assumed that they play an important role.

In Africa the larvae of butterflies are not in general a serious threat to agriculture. There are no species that cause damage on the scale of the European *Pieris brassicae* and *Pieris rapae* (Pieridae) whose larvae are often serious pests of cabbages, or of the North American *Colias* (Pieridae) whose larvae are capable of devastating lucerne crops. No species of butterfly that is damaging to crops has been introduced into Africa from another part of the world and there are no major programmes of pest control directed against any species of African butterfly. There are however species that feed on crops and these could become pests as subsistence agriculture is replaced by monocultures of cash crops. Several species of moth larvae are important pests of crops. Among them are several genera of Noctuidae whose larvae bore into the stems of cereal crops such as maize, rice, and sorghum, and the larvae of the so-called 'army worm', *Spodoptera*, a moth of world-wide distribution which in parts of Africa occasionally reaches plague proportions and causes extensive damage to many kinds of crop.

Butterfly pests in Africa

Citrus (oranges, lemons, grapefuit, limes, etc.), like many crops, has been introduced into Africa. It is not known exactly when *Citrus* was first introduced but its widespread occurrence in the forest region of tropical Africa is undoubtedly a recent phenomenon probably dating back no more than two hundred years. *Citrus* is grown as a cash crop in South Africa and attempts are made there to control its insect pests by spraying with insecticide, but in tropical Africa the trees are usually left to the attacks of insects. There are few tropical crops that are as susceptible to insect damage as *Citrus*. In West Africa *Citrus* trees are usually infested with a wide variety of insects, particularly Homoptera that suck the juices from leaves and young stems. Several species of *Papilio* (Papilionidae) have evidently moved from wild species of Rutaceae (to which *Citrus* belongs) to cultivated *Citrus*, and the larvae of one species, *Papilio demodocus*, are now found mainly on *Citrus*. The females of *Papilio demodocus* lay their eggs on the new leaves, especially those of seedling trees, and the young larvae feed exclusively on the new leaves, refusing to eat if offered only the older and tougher leaves. The actual amount of leaf destroyed by *Papilio demodocus* larvae is quite small but because of the preference for new leaves at the growing points of young trees they inhibit the growth of the tree, and small trees may often die. In South Africa the larvae are regarded as a minor pest and they are destroyed by picking them off by hand. Several other species of *Papilio*, among them *Papilio dardanus* and *Papilio nireus*, have also moved onto *Citrus* and there is evidence of additional species changing from wild Rutaceae to *Citrus*: in Sierra Leone I have recently found a larva of *Papilio menestheus*, a forest species, on *Citrus*, and this appears to be the first record of the occurrence of this species on anything but wild Rutaceae. All species of *Papilio* known from *Citrus* still occur on wild Rutaceae. In Sierra Leone *Papilio demodocus* occurs as larvae and adults in all months of the year. Its wild food-plant, *Fagara*, is deciduous in the dry season, while *Citrus* is not, and hence it would seem that before the introduction of *Citrus* the butterfly must have had a much more seasonal pattern of occurrence in this area as for a considerable part of the dry season there is no wild larval food-plant available. It is also likely that the butterfly has become more common in recent years and has spread into habitats where *Citrus* is grown but where *Fagara* does not occur. *Papilio* larvae, then, can be regarded as minor pests with the potential of causing considerable damage. It is unlikely that in the underdeveloped countries of tropical Africa anything will be done to reduce their numbers as the crop is of little commercial importance and the tendency is to grow many trees with a poor yield rather than limited plantations of high yielding trees. In addition most of the people that grow *Citrus* have no capital to initiate programmes of pest control.

The larvae of many species of Satyridae are grass feeders and are thus potential pests of pasture grasses and cereal crops, but the extent to which these butterflies are of economic importance is not known. The larvae of *Melanitis leda* have occasionally been reported as causing damage to rice both in Africa and elsewhere in the tropics. In West Africa the larvae of *Appias epaphia* (Pieridae) (Fig. 13.1) sometimes cause damage to brassicas and in East Africa the larvae of *Colias electo* (Pieridae) feed on lucerne and castor oil, two strikingly dissimilar crops. *Catopsilia florella* (Pieridae) larvae defoliate ornamental *Cassia* trees and they have been reported as a pest of senna in the Sudan (Schmutterer 1969), but this crop is no longer

1. Part of the surface of an antenna of *Danaus gilippus*. The pegs sensitive to the male pheromone are shown in the lower half of the picture; they scarcely project beyond the general surface of the antenna. In the picture 13 mm = 10 μm

2. Part of the area shown above enlarged to show four of the pegs receptive to the male pheromone. In the upper part of the picture the larger curved pegs that are known by experiment not to be receptive to the male pheromone are shown

36. Sensory pegs on the antennae of *Danaus gilippus* (Danaidae). (*Stereoscan electron micrographs by H. E. Hinton*)

1. Malaise trap of the type described by Townes (1962) in operation in a garden at Kampala, Uganda

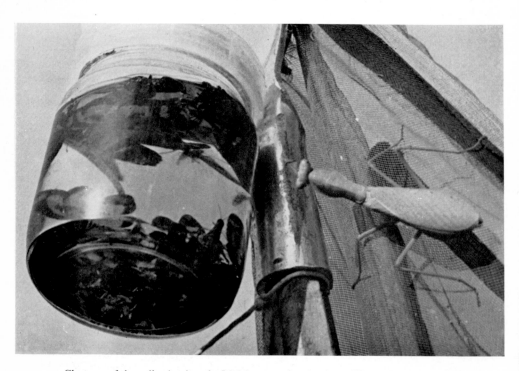

2. Close-up of the collecting jar of a Malaise trap showing butterflies and other insects in alcohol. A praying mantis is inspecting the jar. These, together with spiders and lizards, frequently station themselves near the plastic collecting jar to which the killing jar is attached

37. Malaise traps

1. General view of the table with rotten banana as bait. *Charaxes boueti* and *Euriphene plautilla* are feeding

2. *Euriphene plautilla* feeding at rotten banana

38. Nymphalidae at a feeding table. (*Photos by D. O. Chanter*)

1. *Charaxes boueti* feeding

2. *Charaxes brutus* that has been feeding at banana bait. The abdomen is much distended. There is an ink mark on the white band of the hindwing

39. Nymphalidae at a feeding table. (*Photos by D. O. Chanter and Jennifer Owen*)

of great agricultural importance. The larvae of the Acraeidae are gregarious and often cause local defoliation of the food-plant. In East Africa the larvae of *Acraea acerata* are sometimes important pests of sweet potato, the gregarious larvae defoliating the leaves and spinning a protective web that inhibits the growth of the plant. *Acraea terpsichore*, a savanna species that has invaded agricultural areas, is reported as a pest of jute in southern Nigeria and is reported on tobacco and edible *Hibiscus* in East Africa (Le Pelley 1959).

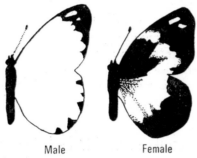

Male   Female

FIG. 13.1. *Appias epaphia*, male and female.

The larvae of many species of Lycaenidae feed on the flowers and in the seed pods of legumes, including edible beans and peas. *Lampides boeticus* is one of the most abundant and widespread butterflies in the world and was considered a pest of sufficient importance in America to be included in quarantine regulations in 1949 concerning fruit and vegetables exported from Hawaii. Many African lycaenids feed as larvae within the seed pods of edible legumes and it would be interesting to know the extent to which they reduce the yield. My impression in Sierra Leone is that considerable damage is caused to edible legumes by lycaenid larvae and since legumes are important sources of protein food in areas where protein is scarce I suspect that it would be worth-while to investigate lycaenid damage with a view to limiting it as much as possible. The larvae of *Deudorix lorisona* (=*bimaculata*) attack coffee berries and this species has been recorded as a minor pest in Ghana and in the Sudan.

The extent to which butterfly larvae damage economically important trees is not known. Many larvae feed selectively on the younger growing leaves and so may retard growth or alter the normal growth form of the tree.

Beneficial butterflies

Agricultural development in Africa has resulted in a spectacular spread of weeds and crops. Some of the commonest African butterflies feed as larvae on weeds, but unfortunately there has been insufficient study of the importance of weeds in African agriculture; thus, although it is known that butterfly larvae feed on weeds it is impossible to assess their importance in the biological control of weeds. One increasingly important weed, *Lantana camara* (Verbenaceae), originally introduced from Central America, is now recognized as being worthy of control and herbivorous bugs that feed on it have been introduced into East Africa in the hope that they will check its spread. No butterfly larvae are known to feed on *Lantana*; indeed butterflies are very much attracted to its flowers and are probably important in its pollination.

The larvae of carnivorous Lycaenidae are primarily predators of plant bugs which extract juices near the growing point of the plant. It would therefore appear that these larvae are potentially beneficial. In 1937 *Spalgis epius* was introduced into Kenya from Java to feed on the plant bug, *Planococcus kenyae*, a pest of a wide variety of plants of agricultural and horticultural interest, but it does not appear to be known whether the experiment was successful.

The impact of agriculture on butterflies

As pointed out in Chapter 1, the vegetation maps of Africa are misleading. The natural vegetation of the whole continent has been drastically altered by rising human numbers and human needs. Subsistence agriculture has created vast areas of secondary bush and this in turn is being replaced by plantation agriculture in which the bush is being eliminated. The spread of crops and their weeds in comparatively recent times has resulted in changes in the distribution and abundance of many species of insects, including butterflies. The most important single event likely to affect butterflies is the destruction of the rain forest. Forest butterflies are likely to have evolved in forests and have become adapted to the forest ecosystem. As trees are cut down and replaced by crops many of the butterflies are likely to disappear if they are unable to adapt to the rapidly changing environment. In the next chapter prospects for the conservation of butterflies are considered and I shall make some attempt to predict future changes in the light of what is happening now.

14

CONSERVATION

THE tropical regions of the world are undergoing an explosion in human numbers that is unprecedented in the history of the world. In many tropical countries the human population is increasing at a rate of about three per cent per year which means that the total population doubles itself every twenty or thirty years. In Africa this spectacular rise in human numbers has been caused by the introduction of preventive measures against and cures for lethal diseases, such as malaria, and by the introduction of easily grown carbohydrate staple foods from elsewhere in the tropics. The very high infant mortality which until recently was universal in tropical Africa has now been drastically reduced, but there has been no corresponding reduction in the birth rate. Most tropical countries are backward and underdeveloped (the term 'developing countries' much used in polite circles is a misnomer), and although a visitor may obtain a superficial impression of affluence in the big cities, the vast majority of people living in the tropics are extremely poor and uneducated. In Sierra Leone and other African countries ninety per cent of the people are totally illiterate. Even among the educated there is very little interest in natural history; butterfly collecting and similar hobbies do not form part of a child's educational development, and even wealthy parents do not encourage in their children the sort of interests that in Europe are commonplace.

It is against this background that we have to consider the prospects for conservation of animal and plant life. In Africa thus far it is only in national parks (which bring in badly needed foreign capital from tourists) that there is a serious attempt at conservation. National parks are mainly in savanna areas where large mammals can be seen easily. There is no area of rain forest that has been designated as a national park, although there are considerable patches of forest in some of the East African parks, notably in Queen Elizabeth National Park in Uganda.

Butterflies are attractive animals and, in marked contrast to most other groups of insects, tourists sometimes notice and admire them. Many species seem to be rare and it is obvious that because in most cases nothing is known about their life history it is impossible to consider conservation programmes for individual species as has been attempted in Britain for several of the rarer species, notably *Lycaena dispar* (Lycaenidae) and *Papilio machaon* (Papilionidae). It follows therefore that it is only by the conservation of habitats that rare species will survive, unless of course they can adapt to agricultural land and secondary bush which is rapidly becoming the most important habitat in tropical Africa.

Although there is no detailed information my impression is that savanna butterflies are better able to adapt to agriculture than forest species. Savanna species tend to have a wider range of larval food-plants and many have been able to exploit agricultural weeds which often come from savanna rather than from forest. If my impression is correct it is the forest species that are in greatest danger of extinction.

Prospects for the conservation of the forest ecosystem in Africa are not good. Forest growing on precipitous slopes is likely to survive longer than forest on level ground because the trees cannot easily be removed and in high rainfall areas the cultivation of steep slopes is difficult because of soil erosion. There is a considerable amount of forest left on the Freetown peninsula in Sierra Leone mainly because the peninsula is hilly and difficult to cultivate. Inland in Sierra Leone where it is less hilly the forest has almost disappeared and what remains is rapidly being cut down. But throughout West Africa one frequently encounters small patches of apparently undisturbed forest, sometimes no more than a few square kilometres in extent, and often near human settlement. These small patches of forest are fetish woods preserved because of religious fears and beliefs and likely to remain preserved unless missionaries are able to convert the people to Christianity or some other imported doctrine and persuade them to abandon their traditional taboos. I am grateful to Mr. Dennis Leston of the University of Ghana for drawing attention to the importance of fetish woods in the conservation of the forest ecosystem in West Africa.

In this book I have repeatedly drawn upon data obtained by collecting and observing butterflies in tropical gardens. Gardens well planted with flowers and with patches of shade can support a wide range of species of butterflies. Unfortunately the intense fear of snakes among even the most educated Africans does not encourage them to develop gardens of the sort that would be attractive to butterflies. Most gardens owned by Africans are kept well trimmed; level grass is preferred to a luxuriant growth of flowers and shrubs.

In Britain it is now recognized that over-collecting has been responsible for the decline or extinction of some of the rarer species of butterflies. Attempts are now being made to encourage observation by photography rather than collecting. In Africa big game hunting has been largely replaced by photographic expeditions in which tourists are encouraged to shoot big game with a camera. Unfortunately there is a considerable trade in tropical butterflies, especially in some of the rarer, larger, and brightly coloured species. I recently drew attention to this trade in a letter in the *New Scientist* (Owen 1969b). My letter was followed by another (Sitwell 1969) in which attention was drawn to the large trade in showy insects that has developed in south-east Asia. Evidently Taiwan earns about 30 million dollars a year from the sale of exotic butterflies, which, as Sitwell suggests, sounds impossibly high, but which was praised by a British cabinet minister as being a good example of a successful cottage industry. Exotic butterflies are in demand not only for collections but also as a means of decorating trays and similar articles. Dealers and private collectors continually send requests to people in the tropics asking them to collect and sell exotic butterflies and other insects. Some pretend to have a scientific interest in the specimens they require but one cannot help noting that the requests are invariably for the large and showy species and never for small dull-coloured species. One firm in Britain offers 25s. for male and £5 for female *Papilio antimachus* (Papilionidae), the largest butterfly in Africa, now probably rare because of the widespread destruction of its forest habitat. The same firm re-sells the males for £7 each. Offers of 1s. 6d. to 7s. 6d. each are made for African *Charaxes* (Nymphalidae) which can be trapped in hundreds throughout much of tropical Africa. Appeals for specimens are made to people in all walks of life, some even suggesting that by selling butterflies children and students can pay their way through school or college. Here is an extract from a circular letter I received recently in Sierra Leone: 'We are trying to reach missionaries in your section who might be able to supply us with butterflies and beetles. I am sure you know someone who might be interested in earning money in his spare time, as we pay from ten cents to ten dollars and more per specimen.' Yes, indeed, I know many people in Sierra Leone who would like to earn money, but fortunately for the butterflies and beetles these people are not skilled enough to collect specimens properly and moreover they do not have the capital for the initial expenditure on postage. It is my view that the time has come for some restrictions to be placed on the trade in large and showy insects. If this is not done some of the rarest tropical butterflies will suffer the same fate as many of the birds and mammals in the tropics and some of the butterflies in Europe.

Scientific journals and popular magazines concerned with conservation concentrate on large mammals and birds. There is however an increasing awareness that habitats, not species, should be conserved, and it is to be hoped that some progress will be made in the future in the conservation of tropical habitats, above all areas of forest which once destroyed are likely to be lost for ever. Little has been said by conservationists about the conservation of butterflies and other insects, which is remarkable because butterflies are beautiful animals and worthy of protection. Indeed the most sucessful attempt at drawing attention to the need for the conservation of butterflies has been through picture cards of butterflies given free in packets of Brooke Bond tea and coffee. These cards, which can be stuck into an album supplied by the firm containing captions and accurate life history information, depict a variety of species of butterflies, many of them tropical, and urge conservation rather than wanton collecting. These cards undoubtedly fall into the hands of many people who know nothing of conservation journals and magazines and it is likely that they have done a considerable amount of good.

It must be admitted however that prospects for the conservation of butterflies in the tropics are not good. It is no use passing legislation in an attempt to conserve habitats and species in countries where most of the people have just enough food to keep them going, where they never have access to newspapers or other media and in any case cannot read, when the rich and developed nations are exploiting or destroying the natural world for profit or for political ideals. The chemical defoliation of the forests of south-east Asia in the interests of democratic ideals that are alien or incomprehensible to the people that live there is perhaps the most significant single anti-conservation event the world has ever experienced. Human numbers, especially in the tropics, continue to rise alarmingly, the rich get richer and the poor get poorer. Some butterflies are adapting to the rapidly changing world, but many will be lost. Indeed some will be lost before we know anything about them except that they exist as pinned specimens in museums.

15

HOW TO STUDY
TROPICAL BUTTERFLIES

SOME years ago there was a strong feeling that the biology syllabuses for secondary schools in English-speaking tropical Africa should delete all reference to European animals and plants and instead use African examples. One candidate for deletion was the European cabbage white butterfly whose life history thousands of African school children had learnt from books with no possibility of studying the living animals. An African butterfly had to be found to replace the cabbage white and the obvious choice was the citrus swallowtail, *Papilio demodocus* (Papilionidae). This butterfly is common throughout tropical Africa; it is easily reared and the larvae are easy to find on cultivated *Citrus* which is grown almost everywhere. Several text books written for the new syllabuses described the life history of the citrus swallowtail; UNESCO even made a short film about it which was sent to many biology teachers. The pupils now learnt about an African butterfly and so all was well: the colonialist cabbage white had finally been disposed of and everyone was happy.

But although there were now opportunities to study live material the pupils and their teachers continued to rely upon the text books. Very few if any teachers bothered to go out and collect larvae from *Citrus* growing in their gardens, and very few attempted to match the illustrations in the books with the large yellow and black butterfly that flew around everywhere. I found that students starting the zoology course at the University of Sierra Leone had memorized the life history of the citrus swallowtail while at school, and were happy that at last the cabbage white had been disposed of, but on questioning they admitted they had never seen a citrus swallowtail, alive or dead, in any stages of its life cycle. What then had the educators who had 'Africanized' the syllabus achieved? Some satisfaction no doubt at having got rid of the cabbage white, but they had certainly not changed the syllabus sufficiently to persuade pupils and their teachers to go out and find living material.

In Africa in general and in West Africa in particular biology educators have in recent years felt that the school syllabus should adopt what has been termed the ecological approach to biology. It is argued, with some justification, that ecology is more relevant in underdeveloped countries than cell biology, physiology, and related topics. Moreover ecology is less costly to teach as expensive equipment is not required. But many teachers appear to be somewhat frightened by the new approach. They say that they were never taught ecology and that they have little idea where to find animals and plants in nature. Also, they argue, there are few reliable keys to the identification of the African fauna and flora, and if they cannot identify organisms how can they possibly be expected to teach ecology? The difficulty, I suggest, is that for some reason ecology has become confused with making lists of animals and plants in specified habitats. Some examination questions demanding this kind of knowledge still appear. But since there is usually a choice of questions on the examination papers, teachers and pupils alike tend to avoid tackling what they consider to be difficult topics.

Part of my aim in this final chapter is to make some suggestions as to how butterflies can be studied in tropical schools and universities as part of the curriculum in ecology. Butterflies are conspicuous and compared with most groups of tropical animals are not difficult to identify, not that exact identification is essential for their study. I shall not provide detailed instructions on how to make a butterfly collection; this information is contained in almost every book that has been published on butterflies, including the new field guide to the African species (Williams 1969) and a book on insect study in Africa (Pinhey 1968). I shall however mention briefly some of the special problems encountered in assembling a collection in the tropics. I also want to encourage amateur naturalists in the tropics to do a little more than simply amass a collection. Many of the unsolved problems in butterfly biology mentioned in this book can be solved by people with no formal training in biology provided they are opportunist and are able to take advantage of the local situation. One does not need to go on expeditions to the primary forest to contribute to the general fund of information; in the tropics one can start in one's own garden, indeed the garden can become so absorbing that there may be no need to look elsewhere.

How to identify African butterflies

The standard work on African butterflies is Aurivillius in Seitz (1925). The two volumes, one of text and one of coloured plates, are exceedingly expensive, virtually unobtainable, and out of date. Copies exist in the libraries of several African universities, including the University of Ghana and the University of Sierra Leone. Access to the coloured plates can provide useful preliminary information about the identification of a species, but the Latin names should be checked in a museum collection or in the African check list of species (Peters 1952). The main difficulty with Aurivillius (apart from the difficulty of access) is that in 1925 the species concept was poorly understood and that many of his 'species' are now known to be polymorphic forms, geographical subspecies or even male and female of the same species.

For the beginner the recently published field guide to the butterflies of Africa south of the Sahara, excluding Madagascar (Williams 1969), provides an excellent introduction to the more common and colourful species. The book contains many coloured plates and each of the 436 species chosen is illustrated in black and white. There are of course many more than 436 species of butterflies in Africa, but as an introduction this book is valuable. Unfortunately relatively few Lycaenidae and Hesperiidae are mentioned, and the beginner is unlikely to receive much assistance in the identification of butterflies in these two groups.

Useful illustrated guides and keys to the identification of the Papilionidae, Acraeidae, and Danaidae of East Africa have been published by Carcasson (1960, 1961, 1963); the first two being obtainable as separately printed supplements to the *Journal of the East Africa Natural History Society*. Many of the species figured and described also occur in West Africa. In 1957, Boorman (sometimes in collaboration with Roche) started producing a photographic atlas of Nigerian butterflies with brief notes on identification. So far the following volumes have appeared: Papilionidae (Boorman and Roche 1957); Nymphalidae: *Pseudacraea, Neptis, Kallima, Hypolimnas, Precis*, and related genera (Boorman and Roche 1959); Nymphalidae: *Euxanthe, Charaxes, Palla*, and *Cymothoe* (Boorman 1965); and Acraeidae (Boorman 1961). Additional volumes are promised, but the publishers seem uncertain as to when they are likely to appear. These guides are useful for observers in West Africa, but must be used with caution. The volume on the Acraeidae contains several serious errors and the volume that includes *Charaxes* is incomplete, even omitting *Charaxes pollux*, a common Nigerian species.

Stempffer (1957) has produced a partly illustrated guide to West African Lycaenidae, from which many African species may be identified, and Villiers (1957) has produced a similar guide to the Papilionidae, which includes notes on life histories. The coloured illustrations in Evans (1937) are helpful in identifying African Hesperiidae, and Eltringham (1912) may be used as a guide to the genus *Acraea*. The monograph of the butterflies of Liberia (Fox *et al.* 1965) is the best source of information as to what species may be expected in West Africa west of Ghana, but the book does not pretend to be a ready guide to identification, although keys are provided to species in the more difficult genera.

As regards southern Africa, the field guide to the butterflies of Malawi (Gifford 1965) is of some value, but the illustrations are disappointing. A similar guide has been published for South African species (Pinhey 1965), but the book contains numerous irritating details about the derivation of Latin names and anecdotes which appear out of place in this kind of publication. Van Son (1949, 1955, 1963) has monographed the South African Papilionidae, Pieridae (first volume), Danaidae and Satyridae (second volume), and Acraeidae (third volume); much detailed information on life histories is given in these three volumes. Murray (*n.d.*) has provided a detailed monograph of the South African Lycaenidae, with illustrations and life history information for many of the species.

For Madagascar, the Hesperiidae have been monographed by Viette (1956), the Danaidae, Nymphalidae, and Acraeidae by Paulian (1956), and the Papilionidae by Paulian and Viette (1968). These three volumes are essential for anyone interested in Madagascan butterflies.

From time to time the British Museum of Natural History and other museums produce revisional treatments of selected groups of butterflies, often including descriptions of newly discovered species and subspecies. Such publications are somewhat specialist and will not in general be of much value to the average observer. At the time of writing, five volumes of revisional notes on African *Charaxes* (Nymphalidae) have been published (van Someren 1963–69), but these are unnecessarily detailed even for the specialist as quite small variations within species are formally named.

An enormous amount of information on the systematics of African butterflies exists in specialist journals that are unlikely to be available to most people. Perhaps some day someone will undertake the mammoth task of assembling this information to produce a complete guide to the African species.

In the foregoing account I have indicated what I consider to be the most helpful publications on the identification of African butterflies. It remains to be said that if a collection is formed a visit to a large museum can be most rewarding. In Africa itself the National Museum at Nairobi, Kenya, has an extensive collection of tropical species, while many of the South African museums have good collections of South African material. In Britain the extensive collections at the British Museum of Natural History in London and at Tring contain vast numbers of African butterflies, including many type specimens. Many of the national continental museums, especially Paris, have large African collections. There is a fine collection of African butterflies, especially of mimetic species, at the Hope Department of Entomology at the University of Oxford, and anyone contemplating investigations into mimicry or polymorphism should examine this collection. In the United States, the Carnegie Museum at Pittsburgh has a large collection of African butterflies, particularly from Liberia and elsewhere in West Africa. Curators of museums are usually most helpful in allowing access to the collections in their charge, and with the help of these collections and the publications mentioned earlier it should be possible to identify all specimens obtained. The possibility of securing specimens of undescribed species is considerable in tropical areas, and collectors should be aware of this in their attempts at identifying their specimens.

Collecting in the tropics

The information contained in this section is supplementary to that contained in other books that provide instructions on how to collect and preserve butterflies.

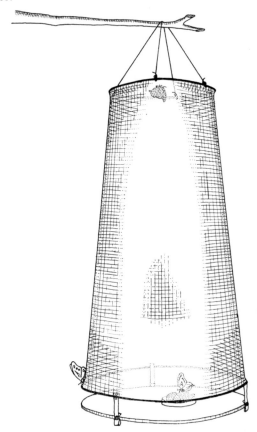

FIG. 15.1. A baited trap hanging from a branch. The mesh cylinder is attached to the wooden base by tapes sewn to the mesh and pinned to the base. The trap is about 1 m high, and the space where the butterflies enter is about 5 cm. The rotten fruit is placed in a shallow tray.

A remarkable number of tropical butterflies can be attracted to baits of various kinds. Many species visit patches of mammal urine, rotten fruit, dead animals, dung, etc., and the collector, especially in forest areas, is advised to exploit this behaviour. A dead rat, cut open to expose the viscera and placed in the sun, will often attract large numbers of Papilionidae,

Pieridae, and Lycaenidae; I normally carry a dead rat or two whenever I go collecting in the forest. Rotten fruit is especially attractive to Nymphalidae; the best way to discover what species of *Charaxes* occur in an area is to place rotten fruit in strategic locations in order to attract them. Fig. 15.1 shows the design of a simple trap which is extremely effective in catching Satyridae and Nymphalidae, especially *Charaxes*. The butterflies enter the trap at the space shown and feed at the fruit. When they have finished feeding or when they are disturbed they fly upwards and can then be removed. Such a trap operated continuously in a garden not only provides specimens and records but also information on seasonal changes in numbers and in species composition. Plates 20 and 21 show some of the species of Nymphalidae trapped in my garden in Sierra Leone.

Tropical gardens can be made attractive to butterflies by planting flowers and flowering shrubs; I have found in particular that *Cosmos* daisies planted in a garden will attract large numbers of butterflies. Other flowering plants that are attractive include most species of Compositae, including the weed species, and *Lantana*, which in many areas will flower all the year round. If it is intended to rear butterflies from eggs or larvae, and especially if genetic experiments are planned, it is advisable to grow the larval food-plants in pots. The growing plants can then be moved into breeding cages when desired, and in addition a growing plant is far more satisfactory as food for young larvae than cut leaves.

In the humid tropics the storage of specimens often presents a considerable problem. If available, an air-conditioned room is strongly recommended as specimens tend to develop mould at high humidities. Ants and other insects are more of a problem to the butterfly collector in the tropics than in temperate regions and insect-proof airtight boxes are essential. Two or three drops of beechwood creosote should be introduced into the storage box about once every two months, as a deterrent to pests. Each specimen should bear the usual label giving locality and date of capture and the collector's name. Many African place names are spelt in a variety of ways, which is to be expected as these names have only been written down in relatively recent times, and it is thus important to include the name of the province or district as well as the exact locality.

It is not my intention to advocate large scale collecting of tropical butterflies. On the contrary I feel that collecting should be kept to a minimum as there are far more interesting things that can be done. But at least a small reference collection is necessary, and if kept to reasonable proportions, it will provide a basis for some of the field and laboratory work suggested in the next section. If, however, field and laboratory observations are not contemplated, I would suggest one or both of the following possibilities: (1) a comprehensive collection of butterflies from a small area, such as a garden or a patch of agricultural land; (2) a representative collection of the less well known families, such as Lycaenidae, Satyridae, and Hesperiidae. The large and colourful tropical species are in general known and additions to knowledge are far more likely if the collecting is restricted to the less known groups.

Life histories and breeding

The life histories of most species of tropical butterflies are not known. A record should therefore be kept of larval food-plants discovered and, where possible, descriptions (including photographs) of eggs, larvae, and pupae. The developmental time from the laying of the egg to the emergence of the adult is not known for most species and since this is apparently much shorter and geographically more variable than in the temperate regions, local information is desirable. In this regard simple measurements of temperature and humidity are useful as these appear to have important effects on the rate of development of the early stages of many butterflies. Parasitoids, such as ichneumonids and tachinids, reared from larvae should be pinned and labelled with the name of the host as well as the usual details of date and locality. If lycaenid larvae are found in association with ants or if they are feeding on Homoptera, specimens of the ants and the Homoptera should be kept. Close observation is necessary to establish the precise relationships between lycaenids and other insects and care must be exercised as superficial impressions may be wrong; thus it is not known whether ants always obtain secretions from the lycaenid larvae or whether in some cases the ants are feeding on the sap of the leaves chewed by the larvae.

A female butterfly collected in the wild is likely to have already mated and when caged with larval food-plant will often lay eggs. For genetic crosses (about which more will be said later) it is necessary to control the matings so that the phenotypes of both parents are known and one can be sure that the resulting offspring are the result of a single mating. Getting butterflies to mate in captivity is by no means easy and usually requires a large outdoor cage with a plentiful supply of flowers. Some species will mate in small cages, but in general matings are difficult to obtain in cages less than eight cubic metres in volume.

Once eggs have been obtained they may be transferred still attached to the larval food-plant to a glass jar. It is advisable to isolate the jar so that ants cannot enter; this is best done by standing it on a brick or stone placed in a tray containing water. When the eggs hatch there should be available fresh larval food-plant, preferably new and tender leaves as many species are unable to eat the older leaves. As the larvae grow the inside of the jar is liable to become damp with condensation; when this occurs the lid of the jar should be replaced by a piece of filter or blotting paper which will absorb surplus moisture, but the food-plant must not be allowed to desiccate. The larvae of small species can be left in the jar until ready for pupation, and even the larvae of large species such as *Papilio demodocus* (Papilionidae) can be left in a jar, provided there are no more than two or three together. Large batches of larvae should be transferred to mesh cages (Fig. 15.2) and the food-plant placed in a jar of water within the cage.

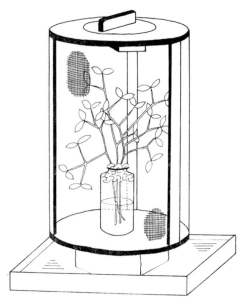

FIG. 15.2. A rearing cage for larvae. The cage is about 50 cm high and is placed on a brick or stone in a tray of water. The larval food-plant is placed in a jar containing water and the neck of the jar stuffed with cotton wool to prevent larvae falling into the water.

In the tropics an outbreak of a virus disease among larvae is often associated with high humidity within the breeding cage. Such outbreaks can be prevented by keeping the cage clean and well aired, and by carefully cleaning infected containers with a disinfectant. The pupae are usually formed attached to the breeding cage or to the larval food-plant; they should not be moved as this often results in damaged and deformed butterflies.

Life histories in themselves are of somewhat limited interest and in the next section I suggest some simple ecological and genetic investigations which should yield more information and which, if sufficiently detailed, may be published in scientific journals.

Studying living butterflies

A great deal of biological information may be obtained by capturing, marking, and releasing butterflies. In this way one can establish the frequency of polymorphic (including mimetic) colour forms within a population, the frequency of seasonal forms at different times of the year, the sex ratio (which must be confirmed by breeding as in nearly all species males are more frequently encountered than females), and the diversity and abundance of species in an area. Large butterflies are best marked with felt pens. These can be obtained in a variety of colours, but reds, blacks, greens, and blues are best, while some colours, such as yellow, are to be avoided as they do not show up well on the wing. One or more spots can be placed on the wings, the hindwings being easier to mark than the forewings (Plate 25).

The advantage of marking and releasing is that an individual can be subsequently recognized and will not be scored more than once, and also that information can be obtained on survival and movement. Many of the results discussed in earlier chapters of this book were obtained by marking and releasing. The technique also has the advantage that the butterflies are not killed. Thus in our work on sex ratios and polymorphism in *Acraea encedon* (Acraeidae), D. O. Chanter and I have marked and released more than 20 000 individuals in many parts of Africa. Had it not been possible to mark them most of these butterflies would have been killed as it was essential that individuals were not counted more than once.

For small butterflies and for dark-coloured species marking with a felt pen is unsatisfactory. The scales of small and delicate species become detached onto the tip of the pen and coloured spots do not show up well on the wings of dark species. Such butterflies are best marked with a small dab of nail varnish, pink being the most readily available colour. Nail varnish is not absorbed by the wing membrane but is attached on top of the scales and dries extremely quickly. I have found that the paler wet season form of *Precis octavia* (Nymphalidae) can be marked satisfactorily with a felt pen, but similar marks on the darker dry season form do not show well and they therefore have to be marked with nail varnish.

Relative frequencies of genetically and environmentally determined forms can be estimated by unbiased hand-netting of the butterflies, but seasonal fluctuations in numbers are best determined by some form of trapping. The simplest design for a trap is shown in Fig. 15.1. Butterflies entering the trap can be removed, marked, and released, and provided a fresh supply of bait is added from time to time, the weekly or monthly totals will give an estimate of seasonal changes in overall numbers and in species composition. The operation of such a trap (which also attracts other insects such as beetles and moths) is the kind of practical work that is suitable for school biology classes, especially if the results are correlated with weather records. Many butterflies can be attracted to a feeding table supplied with rotten fruit (Plates 38–40). It is then possible to observe interactions between species and individuals and there are good possibilities for photography of live butterflies. Baited traps and feeding tables attract only butterflies of

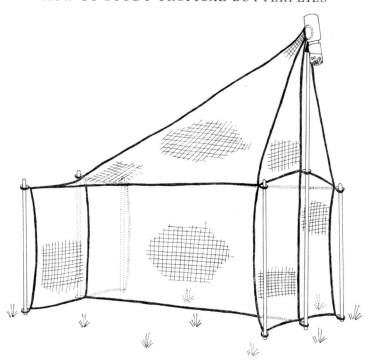

FIG. 15.3. A Malaise trap. The collecting jar is attached to a plastic bottle and is about 2 m from the ground. A full description of the construction of a slightly different design of Malaise trap (Plate 37) is given by Townes (1962).

certain families, but there is another kind of trap that collects butterflies without bias.

The Malaise trap (so named after its inventor) is essentially a tent-like structure of fine mesh supported by a wooden frame. One design is shown in Fig. 15.3 and another in Plate 37. Insects wander into the net and upon encountering the mesh tend to fly upwards to escape. If a jar containing alcohol or some other poison is attached to the highest point many insects will be collected. Its disadvantage is that everything collected is necessarily killed, but its advantage is that since its action does not depend upon bait, a representative sample of insects is obtained. Some results from Malaise trapping are discussed in Chapter 5. Its full potential has not yet been explored in the tropics, but preliminary results suggest that Malaise traps can provide numerical data on seasonal fluctuations in numbers and on the diversity of species present in a limited area. In addition it might be added that Malaise traps have provided my only records of several species of Lycaenidae in Sierra Leone.

If genetic work is contemplated I would suggest that at least initially polymorphic forms are more likely to repay investigation than other types of variation of greater complexity. These forms are usually controlled by multiple alleles with dominance. Hence like $\times$ like matings that produce some offspring unlike the parents indicate that the parents were heterozygotes with the dominant phenotype. The frequencies of different types of offspring in a brood should be tested against the expected frequencies by using a χ^2 test, the use of which is outlined in most elementary statistics books. In many tropical butterflies polymorphism is limited to the female. This is often incorrectly referred to as sex-linkage. In fact the genes controlling the polymorphism are present in both sexes (as can be established by breeding) but express themselves only in one sex. Linkage and sex-linkage are apparently unusual in butterflies, possibly because butterflies have a high chromosome number which reduces the probability of linkage.

Little or nothing is known of the genetics of polymorphism in the following common African species: *Danaus chrysippus* (Danaidae), *Nepheronia argia*, *Nepheronia thalassina*, *Catopsilia florella* (Pieridae), *Aterica galene*, *Pseudacraea eurytus*, *Hypolimnas dubius*, *Lachnoptera iole* (Nymphalidae), *Papilio phorcas* (Papilionidae), and *Elymnias bammakoo* (Satyridae). Investigations into the mode of inheritance of the polymorphic forms of these species would therefore be well worth while.

Concluding remarks

Because butterflies are well known and conspicuous they provide ideal material for biological investigations in schools and universities. At the elementary level the life history of a butterfly illustrates well the phenomenon of metamorphosis, while at a more advanced level they may be used to introduce the quantitative approach to biology which, until recently, has been sadly neglected in school and university courses. In this chapter, indeed throughout this book, I have tried to show that valuable information can be obtained from the study of butterflies by using techniques that are extremely simple. But reading a book has its limitations; why not start some practical or field work and try to solve one of the many problems in the biology of butterflies?

GLOSSARY

The terms in this glossary are defined in the way they are used in the book; some terms have other meanings in a different context.

aestivation, reduced activity of an animal associated with metabolic adjustments to hot or dry weather.

allele, an alternative form of a gene at a given locus on a chromosome.

allopatric, occurring in different localities.

apostatic selection, natural selection for alleles producing a phenotype that contrasts with the normal.

assortative mating, selective mating of like phenotypes in a population.

autosome, a chromosome other than a sex chromosome.

Batesian mimicry, the resemblance of a palatable mimic to an unpalatable model.

chromosome, a thread-like structure containing genes located in the cell of an organism.

cline, a continuous trend of geographical variation in a species.

competition, an interaction of individuals or species resulting from utilization of essential resources that are in short supply.

congeneric, belonging to the same genus.

conspecific, belonging to the same species.

consumer, an organism that feeds on living organisms.

cryptic colours and patterns, colours and patterns that tend to conceal an animal by matching it to the background against which it lives.

decomposer, an organism that obtains its nutrients from dead organic matter.

density-dependent events or factors, ecological events or factors whose effect varies with the density of the population.

density-independent events or factors, ecological events or factors whose effect does not vary with the density of the population.

dimorphism, the existence of two forms, e.g. two sexes.

diversity of species, the number of species present in an area in relation to their abundance; also simply the number of species present.

dominant, an alternative allele that produces the same phenotype when present in the homozygous or heterozygous state.

ecology, the study of relationships between organisms and their environment.

ecosystem, the interrelated organisms in an environment. The concept of the ecosystem incorporates the sum total of interactions between organisms and their interactions with the non-living part of the environment.

endemic, confined to a particular geographical area.

evolution, a cumulative inheritable change in a population.

fitness, the relative ability of an organism to transmit its genes to the next generation.

founder effect or principle, the concept that when a population is established or re-established its genetic structure differs from the parent population because of sampling errors (q.v.).

gene, a hereditary unit which through transcription has a specific effect on the phenotype, and which can mutate to various allelic forms.

gene flow, the movement of genes between populations of the same species.

gene frequency, in a given population, the number of loci at which a given allele is found divided by the total number of loci at which it could occur.

genetic drift, random fluctuations in gene frequency due to sampling errors; often abbreviated to *drift*.

genetics, the study of heredity.

genotype, the genetic constitution of an organism.

gynandromorph, an individual made up of a mosaic of male and female characters.

hair pencils, brush-like structures at the tip of the abdomen of male Danaidae.

Hardy–Weinberg ratio, a law stating that genotype frequencies will remain constant from generation to generation in an infinitely large, interbreeding population in which mating is random and there is no selection, migration, or mutation. If with one pair of alleles (B and b) the frequencies of B and b are defined as p and q respectively, then at equilibrium the genotype frequencies are p^2 (BB), $2pq$ (Bb), and q^2 (bb).

heterogeneity, the property of being made up of different kinds.

heterozygote, an individual with two dissimilar alleles at a given locus.

homozygote, an individual with two identical alleles at a given locus.

individual distance, an area around an individual from which other individuals are excluded.

instar, the stage between successive moults in an insect larva.

linkage, the tendency of genes to be inherited together because they are on the same chromosome.

locus, the position a gene occupies in a chromosome.

logarithmic series, a mathematical description of the occurrence of rare and abundant species.

mean, a calculated average.

migration, a regular movement by individuals or populations to and from a breeding area.

mimic, an organism that superficially resembles another of a different species so that one or both benefit.

model, an unpalatable organism resembled by a mimic.

modifier, a gene that modifies the effect of another gene.

monoculture, a pure stand of a crop.

monotypic, of a taxonomic category, containing only one species, genus, etc.

Müllerian mimicry, the resemblance of several, often unrelated, unpalatable species.

mutation, a sudden and haphazard change in a gene.

N, the number of individuals in a sample.

natural selection, the non-random elimination of individuals (and therefore of genes) from a population; often abbreviated to *selection*.

niche, the particular environment in which an organism lives and the way in which it utilizes this environment.

osmeterium, an extrusible gland in a *Papilio* larva.

parasitoid, a parasite that eventually kills the host.

parthenogenesis, the production of offspring without fertilization.

phenotype, the physical characteristics of an organism; the product of its genotype and the environment.

pheromone, a chemical substance released by an animal in interactions with another animal of the same species.

phylogeny, the evolutionary relationships between organisms.

pluviation, reduced activity of an animal during wet weather. (Used for the first time in this book.)

polygenic, of a mode of inheritance, determined by several or many genes.

polymorphism, the occurrence together in a population of two or more distinct forms in such proportions that the rarest of them cannot be maintained by recurrent mutation alone.

polyphyletic, of taxonomic categories, having separate evolutionary origins.

population, a group of organisms of the same species living together.

primary forest, forest that has not been altered by human activities.

producer, a green plant that obtains its energy by the process of photosynthesis.

proximate factors, environmental factors that stimulate periodic events in organisms; 'biological triggers'.

recessive, an allele whose effect is expressed in the phenotype only when present in the homozygous state.

relative frequency, the number of observed occurrences of an event divided by the total number of occasions on which it might have been observed.

sampling error, variability due to limited numbers of individuals present in or starting a population.

S, the number of species in a sample.

savanna, open grassy country with scattered trees or clumps of bushes.

secondary forest, forest that has been altered by human activity and subsequently allowed to regenerate.

sex-limited, of a gene that may be present in both sexes but expresses itself in the phenotype of one sex only.

sex-linked, of a gene that occurs on the sex (X or Y) chromosomes.

sex ratio, the relative proportion of males and females of a specified age group in a population, usually expressed as the percentage of males.

40. *Charaxes castor* (left) and *Charaxes boueti* (Nymphalidae) at banana on feeding table. The *Charaxes castor* is a marked individual. (*Photo by D. O. Chanter*)

speciation, an evolutionary process leading to the formation of species.

species, a population of interbreeding organisms reproductively isolated from other organisms.

specific search image, a predator's pictorial memory of the appearance of prey.

spermatophore, a sac containing sperms.

standard error, an estimate of the reliability of a calculated figure; figures with small standard errors are more reliable than those with large ones.

statistical significance, of a result that is unlikely to have been arrived at by chance; often abbreviated to *significance*.

subspecies, named geographical variants of a species.

sympatric, occurring in the same place.

taxonomy, the study of naming and classifying organisms.

territory, an area defended by an individual against members of the same species.

ultimate factors, environmental factors that determine why an organism evolves the habit of breeding, migrating, etc., at a particular time.

χ^2 *test*, a statistical test applied to ascertain whether data fit a given hypothesis.

BIBLIOGRAPHY

ALEXANDER, A. J. (1961) A study of the biology and behavior of the caterpillars, pupae and emerging butterflies of the subfamily Heliconiinae in Trinidad, West Indies. Part 1. Some aspects of larval behavior. *Zoologica, N.Y.* **46**, 1–24.

AURIVILLIUS, C. (1925) *The African Rhopalocera.* In SEITZ, A. *The Macrolepidoptera of the world*, Vol. 13. Alfred Kernen, Stuttgart.

BAKER, R. R. (1968) A possible method of evolution of the migratory habit in butterflies. *Phil. Trans. R. Soc. Lond.* B **253**, 309–41.

BERNARDI, G. (1962) Missions Ph. Bruneau de Miré au Tibesti: Lépidoptères Pieridae, Nymphalidae et Danaidae. *Bull. Inst. fr. Afr. Noire* **24**, 813–51.

BOORMAN, J. (1961) *The Nigerian butterflies*. Part 6. *Acraeidae.* Ibadan University Press.

—— (1965) *The Nigerian butterflies.* Part 3. *Nymphalidae (section 1).* Ibadan University Press.

—— and ROCHE, P. (1957) *The Nigerian butterflies.* Part 1. *Papilionidae.* Ibadan University Press.

—— —— (1959) *The Nigerian butterflies.* Part 5. *Nymphalidae (section 3).* Ibadan University Press.

BROWER, J. V. Z. (1958a) Experimental studies of mimicry in some North American butterflies. 1. *Danaus plexippus* and *Limenitis archippus archippus. Evolution, Lancaster, Pa.* **12**, 32–47.

—— (1958b) Experimental studies of mimicry in some North American butterflies. 2. *Battus philenor* and *Papilio troilus, P. polyxenes*, and *P. glaucus. Evolution, Lancaster, Pa.* **12**, 123–36.

—— (1958c) Experimental studies of mimicry in some North American butterflies. 3. *Danaus gilippus berenice* and *Limenitis archippus floridensis. Evolution, Lancaster, Pa.* **12**, 273–85.

—— and BROWER, L. P. (1962) Experimental studies of mimicry. 6. The reaction of toads (*Bufo terrestris*) to honeybees (*Apis mellifera*) and their dronefly mimics (*Eristalis vinetorum*). *Am. Nat.* **96**, 297–308.

BROWER, L. P. (1961) Experimental analyses of egg cannibalism in the monarch and queen butterflies, *Danaus plexippus* and *D. gilippus berenice. Physiol. Zoöl.* **34**, 287–96.

—— (1962) Evidence for interspecific competition in natural populations of the monarch and queen butterflies, *Danaus plexippus* and *D. gilippus berenice* in south central Florida. *Ecology* **43**, 549–52.

—— (1969) Ecological chemistry. *Scient. Am.* **220** (Feb.), 22–9.

—— and BROWER, J. V. Z. (1964) Birds, butterflies, and plant poisons: a study in ecological chemistry. *Zoologica, N.Y.* **46**, 137–59.

—— —— and CRANSTON, F. P. (1965) Courtship behavior of the queen butterfly, *Danaus gilippus berenice* (Cramer). *Zoologica, N.Y.* **50**, 1–39.

—— —— and WESTCOTT, P. W. (1960) Experimental studies of mimicry. 5. The reactions of toads (*Bufo terrestris*) to bumblebees (*Bombus americanorum*) and their robberfly mimics (*Mallophora bomboides*) with a discussion of aggressive mimicry. *Am. Nat.* **94**, 343–56.

—— and JONES, M. A. (1965) Precourtship interaction of wing and abdominal sex glands in male *Danaus* butterflies. *Proc. R. ent. Soc. Lond.* A **40**, 147–51.

BURNS, J. M. (1966) Preferential mating versus mimicry: disruptive selection and sex-limited dimorphisms in *Papilio glaucus*. *Science, N.Y.* **153**, 551–3.

CARCASSON, R. H. (1960) The swallowtail butterflies of East Africa (Lepidoptera, Papilionidae). *Jl E. Africa nat. Hist. Soc.* Suppl. no. 6.

—— (1961) The *Acraea* butterflies of East Africa (Lepidoptera, Acraeidae). *Jl E. Africa nat. Hist. Soc.* Suppl. no. 8.

—— (1963) The milkweed butterflies of East Africa (Lepidoptera, Danaidae). *Jl E. Africa nat. Hist. Soc.* **24**, 19–32.

—— (1964) A preliminary survey of the zoogeography of African butterflies. *E. Afr. Wildlife J.* **2**, 122–57.

CARPENTER, G. D. H. (1941) The relative frequency of beak-marks on butterflies of different edibility to birds. *Proc. zool. Soc. Lond.* A **111**, 223–31.

—— (1949) *Pseudacraea eurytus* (L.) (Lep. Nymphalidae): a study of a polymorphic mimic in various degrees of speciation. *Trans. R. ent. Soc. Lond.* **100**, 71–133.

CLARKE, C. A., DICKSON, C. G. C., and SHEPPARD, P. M. (1963) Larval color pattern in *Papilio demodocus*. *Evolution, Lancaster, Pa.* **17**, 130–7.

—— and SHEPPARD, P. M. (1959) The genetics of *Papilio dardanus*, Brown. 1. Race *cenea* from South Africa. *Genetics, Princeton* **44**, 1347–58.

—— —— (1960a) The genetics of *Papilio dardanus*, Brown. 2. Races *dardanus*, *polytrophus, meseres*, and *tibullus*. *Genetics, Princeton* **45**, 439–57.

—— —— (1960b) The genetics of *Papilio dardanus*, Brown. 3. Race *antinorii* from Abyssinia and race *meriones* from Madagascar. *Genetics, Princeton* **45**, 683–98.

—— —— (1960c) The evolution of dominance under disruptive selection. *Heredity, Lond.* **14**, 73–87.

—— —— (1962a) The genetics of the mimetic butterfly *Papilio glaucus*. *Ecology* **43**, 159–61.

—— —— (1962b) The genetics of *Papilio dardanus*, Brown. 4. Data on race *ochracea*, race *flavicornis*, and further information on races *polytrophus* and *dardanus*. *Genetics, Princeton* **47**, 909–20.

—— —— (1963) Interactions between major genes and polygenes in the determination of the mimetic patterns of *Papilio dardanus*. *Evolution, Lancaster, Pa.* **17**, 404–13.

—— —— and THORNTON, I. W. B. (1968) The genetics of the mimetic butterfly *Papilio memnon* L. *Phil. Trans. R. Soc. Lond.* B **254**, 37–89.

CLENCH, H. K. (1966) Behavioral thermoregulation in butterflies. *Ecology* **47**, 1021–34.

CRANE, J. (1957) Imaginal behavior in butterflies of the family Heliconiidae: changing social patterns and irrelevant actions. *Zoologica, N.Y.* **42**, 135–45.

EDMUNDS, M. (1966) Natural selection in the mimetic butterfly *Hypolimnas misippus* L. in Ghana. *Nature, Lond.* **212**, 1478.

—— (1969a) Polymorphism in the mimetic butterfly *Hypolimnas misippus* L. in Ghana. *Heredity, Lond.* **24**, 281–302.

—— (1969b) Evidence for sexual selection in the mimetic butterfly *Hypolimnas misippus* L. *Nature, Lond.* **221**, 488.

EHRLICH, P. R. and RAVEN, P. H. (1965) Butterflies and plants: a study in coevolution. *Evolution, Lancaster, Pa.* **18**, 586–608.

EISNER, T. and MEINWALD, Y. C. (1965) Defensive secretion of a caterpillar (*Papilio*). *Science, N.Y.* **150**, 1733–5.

ELTRINGHAM, H. (1910) *African mimetic butterflies.* Clarendon Press, Oxford.

—— (1912) A monograph of the African species of the genus *Acraea*, Fab., with a supplement of those of the Oriental region. *Trans. ent. Soc. Lond.* 1912, 1–374.

EVANS, W. H. (1937) *A catalogue of the African Hesperiidae in the British Museum.* British Museum, London.

FARQUHARSON, C. O. (1921) Five years' observations (1914–1918) on the bionomics of southern Nigerian insects, chiefly directed to the investigation of lycaenid life histories and to the relation of Lycaenidae, Diptera, and other insects to ants. *Trans. ent. Soc. Lond.* 1921, 325–530.

FISHER, R. A. (1928) The possible modification of response of the wild-type to recurrent mutations. *Am. Nat.* **62**, 115–26.

—— (1930) *The genetical theory of natural selection.* Clarendon Press, Oxford.

—— CORBET, A. S., and WILLIAMS, C. B. (1943) The relation between the number of species and the number of individuals in a random sample of an animal population. *J. Anim. Ecol.* **12**, 42–58.

—— and FORD, E. B. (1947) The spread of a gene in natural conditions in a colony of the moth, *Panaxia dominula* L. *Heredity, Lond.* **1**, 143–74.

FORD, E. B. (1936) The genetics of *Papilio dardanus* Brown (Lep.). *Trans. R. ent. Soc. Lond.* **85**, 435–66.

—— (1945) *Butterflies.* Collins, London.

—— (1953) The genetics of polymorphism in the Lepidoptera. *Adv. Genet.* **5**, 43–87.

—— (1964) *Ecological genetics.* Methuen, London.

FOX, R. M., LINDSEY, A. W., CLENCH, H. K., and MILLER, L. D. (1965) The butterflies of Liberia. *Mem. Am. ent. Soc.* **19**, 1–438.

GIFFORD, D. (1965) *Butterflies of Malawi.* Society of Malawi, Blantyre.

HAMILTON, W. D. (1967) Extraordinary sex ratios. *Science, N.Y.* **156**, 477–88.

HOPKINS, B. (1965) *Forest and savanna.* Heinemann, London.

HOVANITZ, W. (1948) Differences in the field activity of two female color phases of *Colias* butterflies at various times of the day. *Contr. Lab. vertebr. Biol. Univ. Mich.* **41**, 1–37.

IRVINE, F. R. (1961) *Woody plants of Ghana.* Oxford University Press, London.

JACKSON, T. H. E. (1961) Entomological studies from a high tower in Mpanga Forest, Uganda. 9. Observations on Lepidoptera (Rhopalocera). *Trans. R. ent. Soc. Lond.* **113**, 346–50.

KENDALL, R. L. (1969) An ecological history of the Lake Victoria basin. *Ecol. Monogr.* **39**, 121–76.

LAMBORN, W. A. (1913) On the relationship between certain West African insects, especially ants, Lycaenidae and Homoptera. *Trans. ent. Soc. Lond.* 1913, 436–520.

LE PELLEY, R. H. (1959) *Agricultural insects of East Africa.* East African High Commission, Nairobi.

MACKAY, M. R. (1970) Lepidoptera in Cretaceous amber. *Science, N.Y.* **167**, 379–80.

McLEOD, L. (1968) Controlled environment experiments with *Precis octavia* Cram. (Nymphalidae). *J. Res. Lepidop.* **7**, 1–18.

MEINWALD, J., MEINWALD, Y. C., and MAZZOCCHI, P. H. (1969) Sex pheromone of the queen butterfly: chemistry. *Science, N.Y.* **164**, 1174–5.

—— —— WHEELER, J. W., EISNER, T., and BROWER, L. P. (1966) Major components in the exocrine secretion of a male butterfly (*Lycorea*). *Science, N.Y.* **151**, 583–5.

MELVILLE, E. A. (1849) *A residence at Sierra Leone.* John Murray, London.

MOORE, S. (1960) A revised annotated list of the butterflies of Michigan. *Occ. Pap. Mus. Zool. Univ. Mich.* **617**, 1–39.

MOREAU, R. E. (1966) *The bird faunas of Africa and its islands.* Academic Press, London and New York.

MORTON, J. K. (1967) The Commelinaceae of West Africa: A biosystematic study. *J. Linn. Soc.* (Bot.) **60**, 167–221.

MURRAY, D. P. (*n.d.*) *South African butterflies. A monograph of the family Lycaenidae.* Staples Press, London.

MYERS, J. and BROWER, L. P. (1969) A behavioural analysis of the courtship pheromone receptors of the queen butterfly, *Danaus gilippus berenice. J. Insect Physiol.* **15**, 2117–30.

OWEN, D. F. (1959) Ecological segregation in butterflies in Britain. *Entomologist's Gaz.* **10**, 27–38.

—— (1965) Change in sex ratio in an African butterfly. *Nature, Lond.* **206**, 744.

—— (1966) Predominantly female populations of an African butterfly. *Heredity, Lond.* **21**, 443–51.

—— (1969*a*) Species diversity and seasonal abundance in tropical Sphingidae (Lepidoptera). *Proc. R. ent. Soc. Lond.* A **44**, 162–8.

—— (1969*b*) Insect trade. *New Scientist,* 21 August 1969.

—— (1970) Inheritance of sex ratio in the butterfly, *Acraea encedon. Nature, Lond.* **225**, 662–3.

—— and CHANTER, D. O. (1968) Population biology of tropical African butterflies. 2. Sex ratio and polymorphism in *Danaus chrysippus* L. *Revue Zool. Bot. afr.* **78**, 81–97.

—— —— (1969) Population biology of tropical African butterflies. Sex ratio and genetic variation in *Acraea encedon. J. Zool.* **157**, 345–74.

—— —— (1971) Polymorphism in West African populations of the butterfly, *Acraea encedon. J. Zool.* **163**, 481–488.

PARSONS, J. A. (1965) A digitalis-like toxin in the monarch butterfly, *Danaus plexippus* L. *J. Physiol., Lond.* **178**, 290–304.

PAULIAN, R. (1956) Insectes: Lépidoptères Danaidae, Nymphalidae, Acraeidae. *Faune Madagascar* **2**, 1–102.

—— and VIETTE, P. (1968) Insectes: Lépidoptères Papilionidae. *Faune Mada-gascar* **27**, 1–97.

PETERS, W. (1952) *A provisional check-list of the butterflies of the Ethiopian region*. Classey, Feltham, Middlesex.

PINHEY, E. (1965) *Butterflies of southern Africa*. Nelson, London.

—— (1968) *Introduction to insect study in Africa*. Oxford University Press, London.

PITMAN, C. R. S. (1928) The area in the West Nile provinces of Uganda from which starts the great southward migrations of *Belenois mesentina* Cram. in Uganda and Kenya. *Proc. R. ent. Soc. Lond.* **3**, 45–6.

PLISKE, T. E. and EISNER, T. (1969) Sex pheromone of the queen butterfly: biology. *Science, N.Y.* **164**, 1170–2.

POULTON, E. B. (1908) *Essays on evolution 1889–1907*. Clarendon Press, Oxford.

—— (1914) W. A. Lamborn's breeding experiments upon *Acraea encedon* (Linn.) in the Lagos district of West Africa, 1910–1912. *J. Linn. Soc.* **32**, 391–416.

PUNNETT, R. C. (1915) *Mimicry in butterflies*. Cambridge University Press.

REICHSTEIN, T., VON EUW, J., PARSONS, J. A., and ROTHSCHILD, M. (1968) Heart poisons in the monarch butterfly. *Science, N.Y.* **161**, 861–6.

RICHARDS, P. W. (1952) *The tropical rain forest: an ecological study*. Cambridge University Press.

SCHMUTTERER, H. (1969) *Pests of crops in northeast and central Africa with particular reference to the Sudan*. Gustav Fischer, Stuttgart.

SHEPPARD, P. M. (1959) The evolution of mimicry; a problem in ecology and genetics. *Cold Spring Harb. Symp. quant. Biol.* **24**, 131–40.

—— (1963) Some genetic studies of Müllerian mimics in butterflies of the genus *Heliconius*. *Zoologica, N.Y.* **48**, 145–54.

SITWELL, N. (1969) Insect trade. *New Scientist*, 11 September 1969.

STEMPFFER, H. (1957) Les lépidoptères de L'Afrique noire française. Fasc. 3. Lycaenidés. *Init. afr.* **14**, 1–228.

—— and JACKSON, T. H. E. (1962) A note on the Rhopalocera of Bugalla Island, Sesse Isles, Uganda. *Proc. R. ent. Soc. Lond.* B **31**, 33–7.

STRIDE, G. O. (1956) On the courtship behaviour of *Hypolimnas misippus* L. (Lepidoptera, Nymphalidae), with notes on the mimetic association with *Danaus chrysippus* L. (Lepidoptera, Danaidae). *Br. J. Anim. Behav.* **4**, 52–68.

—— (1957) Investigations into the courtship behaviour of the male of *Hypo-limnas misippus* L. (Lepidoptera, Nymphalidae), with special reference to the role of visual stimuli. *Br. J. Anim. Behav.* **5**, 153–67.

—— (1958) Further studies on the courtship behaviour of African mimetic butterflies. *Anim. Behav.* **6**, 224–30.

TINBERGEN, N., MEEUSE, B. J. D., BOEREMA, L. K. and VAROSSIEAU, W. W. (1942) Die Balz des Samtfalters *Eumenis* (=*Satyrus*) *semele* (L.). *Z. Tier-psychol.* **5**, 182–226.

TOWNES, H. (1962) Design for a Malaise trap. *Proc. ent. Soc. Wash.* **64**, 253–62.

—— (1969) The genera of Ichneumonidae. Part 1. *Mem. Am. ent. Inst.* **11**, 1–300.

TURNER, J. R. G. (1963) Geographical variation and evolution in the males of the butterfly *Papilio dardanus* Brown (Lepidoptera: Papilionidae). *Trans. R. ent. Soc. Lond.* **115**, 239–59.

—— CLARKE, C. A., and SHEPPARD, P. M. (1961) Genetics of a difference in the male genitalia of East and West African stocks of *Papilio dardanus* (Lep.) *Nature, Lond.* **191**, 935–6.

URQUHART, F. A. (1960) *The monarch butterfly*. University of Toronto Press.

VAN SOMEREN, V. G. L. (1963–69) Revisional notes on African *Charaxes* (Lepidoptera: Nymphalidae). Parts 1–5. *Bull. Br. Mus. nat. Hist.* (Entomol.) **13**, 197–242; **15**, 183–235; **18**, 47–101, 279–316; **23**, 77–166.

VAN SON, G. (1949) *The butterflies of southern Africa*. Part 1. *Papilionidae and Pieridae*. Transvaal Museum, Pretoria.

—— (1955) *The butterflies of southern Africa*. Part 2. *Nymphalidae: Danainae and Satyrinae*. Transvaal Museum, Pretoria.

—— (1963) *The butterflies of southern Africa*. Part 3. *Nymphalidae: Acraeinae* Transvaal Museum: Pretoria.

VIETTE, P. (1956) Insectes: Lépidoptères Hesperiidae. *Faune Madagascar* **3**, 1–85.

VILLIERS, A. (1957) Les lépidoptères de L'Afrique noire Française. Fasc. 2. Papilionidés. *Init. afr.* **14**, 1–49.

WATT, W. B. (1968) Adaptive significance of pigment polymorphisms in *Colias* butterflies. 1. Variation of melanin pigment in relation to thermoregulation. *Evolution, Lancaster, Pa.* **22**, 437–58.

WILLIAMS, C. B. (1930) *The migration of butterflies*. Oliver and Boyd, Edinburgh and London.

—— (1951) The migrations of libytheine butterflies in Africa. *Niger. Fld* **16**, 152–9.

—— (1958) *Insect migration*. Collins, London.

—— (1964) *Patterns in the balance of nature and related problems in quantitative ecology*. Academic Press, London and New York.

WILLIAMS, J. G. (1969) *A field guide to the butterflies of Africa*. Collins, London.

INDEX OF BUTTERFLIES

Butterflies are indexed under the generic name followed by the specific name. Where a generic name of a butterfly and the family name derived from that genus appear together, e.g. *Papilio* (Papilionidae), it is only indexed under the generic name, but where the roots of the names are different, e.g. *Precis* (Nymphalidae), both names are entered. References to plates are in **bold type**.

GENERAL INDEX

References to plates are in **bold type**.

DATE DUE